1

Studies in the History of Medieval Religion

VOLUME XXXIV

THE MEDIEVAL CHANTRY CHAPEL
An archaeology

Studies in the History of Medieval Religion

ISSN: 0955-2480

General Editor
Christopher Harper-Bill

Previously published titles in the series
are listed at the back of this volume

THE MEDIEVAL CHANTRY CHAPEL

An archaeology

SIMON ROFFEY

THE BOYDELL PRESS

First published 2007
The Boydell Press, Woodbridge

ISBN 978-1-84383-334-5

The Boydell Press is an imprint of Boydell & Brewer Ltd
PO Box 9, Woodbridge, Suffolk IP12 3DF, UK
and of Boydell & Brewer Inc.
668 Mt Hope Avenue, Rochester, NY 14620, USA
website: www.boydellandbrewer.com

A CIP record of this publication is available from the British Library

This publication is printed on acid-free paper

Typeset by Carnegie Book Production, Lancaster
Printed in Great Britain by
Antony Rowe Ltd, Chippenham, Wiltshire

Contents

Illustrations

Figures

To my mother and father

Acknowledgements

First and foremost I would like to thank the supervisors of the PhD from which much of this research is drawn from, Professor Michael Hicks and Dr Andrew Reynolds. Thanks also to Professor Colin Platt and Mr Gustav Milne for their invaluable help in the early stages of research. I would also like to give special thanks to Dr Clive Burgess with whom I have discussed some of the themes of this book in great length. I thank him also for his patience. For the reading and commenting on early drafts of chapters I would like to thank Dr John Blair, Dr Beat Kümin, Professor Roberta Gilchrist, Dr Pamela Graves, Professor Tom James and Professor Barbara Yorke.

I would also like to express my gratitude to others who have given me help and advice on the way: Dr John Goodall for his helpful advice on terminology, Alex Langlands for his invaluable help in getting to grips with the illustration software and my brother, Steven, for helping to me with my computer. Thanks also to Professor Caroline Barron, Dr Stefan Narkiewicz, Dr Amanda Richardson, Dr Sarah Semple, Professor Steven Shennan, Dr Nick Thorpe and the staff and students of University of Winchester, who have helped me explore some of the themes of this research in meetings, conversation, lectures and seminars. My gratitude also goes out to the churchwardens and incumbents of the parish churches visited and recorded, and especially for trusting me with the keys! Thanks are due also to the staff of the YHA youth hostel, Street, Somerset, and The Barge, Stanton St Bernard, Wiltshire, for providing pleasant and comfortable accommodation facilities. I am also indebted to the Arts and Humanities Research Board and the University of Winchester for funding much of this project.

Thank you also to Myra Wilkinson for copy-editing and compiling the index, Caroline Palmer at Boydell & Brewer and Sensei Simon Budden for providing me with a chance to remain fit whilst otherwise spending endless months sat in front of a computer! Eternal gratitude to my wife, Suna, and my parents, Brian and Janet, who, as always, have provided invaluable support throughout the period of my research. It is to them that this book is dedicated.

Symbols Used in Illustrations

Ledger tomb

Free-standing tomb

Conjectured site of altar/celebrant

Conjectured location of laity in chapel

Conjectured visual relationship between altars/celebrants/laity

Reconstructed sight-lines

Abbreviations

Antiq. Journ.	*Antiquaries Journal*
Arch. Journ.	*Archaeological Journal*
BAR	British Archaeological Reports
CBA	Council for British Archaeology
HE	*Historia Ecclesiastica*
HFCAS	*Proceedings of the Hampshire Field Club and Archaeological Society*
PRO	Public Record Office, Kew, London. Now the National Archives.
SAS	*Proceedings of the Somerset Archaeological Society*
VA	*Vernacular Architecture*
VCH	*Victoria County History*
WAM	Wiltshire Archaeology and Natural History Society Magazine

PART I

INTRODUCTION AND BACKGROUND

1

Introduction

The chantry was probably the most common, and also one of the most distinctive, of all late medieval religious foundations. Chantry foundations in the parish church contributed to both a religiously vibrant, and a socially active, community and were of great significance to the lives of ordinary people. Often, chantry endowment provided a provision for charity and the establishment of a localised system of welfare, including regular almsgiving and the establishment of schools and hospitals. Many, in the form of guilds and fraternities, were corporate ventures from the outset, making intercession more available to wider members of medieval society.

In essence, the chantry can be described as a foundation and endowment of a mass by one or more benefactors, to be celebrated at an altar, for the souls of the founders and other specified persons. The majority of them were intended to be of only a temporary duration and generated very little in the way of physical remains as they were simply celebrated at existing altars within the founder's parish church. But a number of chantries, founded usually by wealthier men and women, were intended to last in perpetuity, and the very

Figure 1   Church and chapel, Brympton d'Evercy.

rich may also have built special altars and chapels to serve and to house the celebrations from which they sought to profit. These structures, although much altered with time, are still a very noticeable feature of many late medieval parish churches (Fig. 1). As yet, they await any systematic, thorough or comparative examination as structures for what they may reveal about contemporary devotion, aspiration and planning. This book will attempt to remedy this by applying a contextual approach to the archaeological study of chantries and chapels with a particular perspective on the parish churches of Hampshire, Somerset and Wiltshire. Much of the research derives from the detailed recording and analysis of 80 examples taken from a sample of 63 parish churches which preserve significant structural evidence for former chapels (Table 1), and aims to make the most of the rich evidence which hitherto has been woefully neglected.

Table 1.   Chapels from the research area which were subject to detailed structural analysis

Hampshire chantry chapels
Champflour chapel, St Laurence, Alton
St Stephen's chapel, St Michael, Basingstoke
Paulet north chapel, St Mary, Old Basing
Paulet south chapel, St Mary, Old Basing
de la Bere chapel, Holy Cross, Binsted
Fortibus chapel, St John, Boldre
Oglander chapel, St Mary, Brading
South chapel, St Mary, Droxford
Afton chapel, All Saints, Freshwater
Leigh chapel, All Saints, Godshill
North chapel, SS Peter and Paul, King's Somborne
Cheke chapel, SS Peter and Paul, Mottistone
Brocas chapel, St Andrew, Sherborne St John
Hampton chapel, SS Mary and Michael, Stoke Charity
Tichborne chapel, St Andrew, Tichborne
Southampton chapel, St Peter, Titchfield
North chapel, St John the Baptist, Winchester
South chapel, St John the Baptist, Winchester

Wiltshire chantry chapels
Goddard chapel, St Michael, Aldbourne
St Mary's chapel, St Michael, Aldbourne
Beauchamp chapel, All Saints, All Cannings
Our Lady chapel, St Mary, Bishops Cannings
South chapel, St John the Baptist, Bishopstone
North chapel, St John the Baptist, Bishopstone
Giffard chapel, St Mary, Boyton
Horton chapel, Holy Trinity, Bradford-on-Avon
Tocotes and Beauchamp chapel, St Nicholas, Bromham
North chapel, St Mary, Castle Eaton
Tropenell chapel, St Bartholomew, Corsham

Beauchamp chapel, St John, Devizes
Lamb chapel, St John, Devizes
South chapel, All Saints, Great Chalfield
Sharrington chapel, St Cyriac, Lacock
Brydge chapel, St James, Ludgershall
Bettisthorne chapel, St Michael, Mere
North chapel, St Michael, Mere
Stafford chapel, St Nicholas, North Bradley
Darrell chapel, Holy Cross, Ramsbury
Godmanstone chapel, St Thomas, Salisbury
Swayne chapel, St Thomas, Salisbury
North chapel, Holy Cross, Sherston
Long chapel, St James, South Wraxall
South chapel, St Michael and All Angels, Urchfont
Borbach chapel, St Mary, West Dean
Dauncey chapel, All Saints, West Lavington

Somerset chantry chapels
North chapel, St Mary, Bridgwater
North chapel, St Andrew, Brympton d'Evercy
Sydenham chapel, St Andrew, Brympton d'Evercy
Dinham chapel, St Michael, Buckland Dinham
St Nectan's chapel, St Andrew, Cheddar
Trinity chapel, St Andrew, Cheddar
Huse chapel, St Andrew, Cheddar
Our Lady chapel, St Andrew, Chew Magna
North chapel, St John the Baptist, Churchill
North chapel, St Bartholomew, Crewkerne
North chapel, St Andrew, Curry Rivel
St Anne's chapel, St Leonard, Farleigh Hungerford
St Nicholas's chapel, St John the Baptist, Frome
North chapel, St Mary Major, Ilchester
Wadham chapel, St Mary, Ilminster
Gyvernay chapel, St Mary, Limington
Choke chapel, All Saints, Long Ashton
North chapel, St Michael, Minehead
North chancel chapel, St Michael, Minehead
Phelips chapel, St Catherine, Montacute
Ralegh chapel, St Mary, Nettlecombe
Trevelyan chapel, St Mary, Nettlecombe
North chapel, St Mary, Portbury
Rodney chapel, St Leonard, Rodney Stoke
Sydenham chapel, St Mary, Stogumber
North chapel, St James, Taunton
North chapel, St Mary Magdalene, Taunton
Our Lady chapel, St Mary, Wedmore
Holy Trinity chapel, St Cuthbert, Wells
St Catherine's chapel, St Cuthbert, Wells
Tanner's chapel, St Cuthbert, Wells
St Cuthbert's chapel, St Cuthbert, Wells
Bluett chapel, St Andrew, Whitestaunton

Brett chapel, St Andrew, Whitestaunton
de Wyke chapel, St Mary, Yatton
Newton chapel, St Mary, Yatton

Terms and conventions

One of the most complex terms to define is the concept of the 'chantry' itself. Technically, it is a service rather than a physical entity, and hence, not visible archaeologically. The context for some, particularly perpetual, chantry practice – the chapel itself – provides the physical evidence and the basis for this book. Often, as will be seen, relevant documents for chantry foundation may not have survived and primary historical documents relating to the parish church in general are few and far between. However, the chantry chapel as a physical entity may survive, and, through its architecture and surviving tombs and memorials, hint at former private function or foundation. Hence, the term 'chapel' is used throughout the book and applies to structures that were instigated by individuals, or group of individuals, (as opposed to chapels controlled by the clergy), and who were prominent or influential in their inception or administration. Such chapels were often seen by their founders as perpetual chantries – foundations that would, in theory at least, last forever. In a wider sense, both undocumented 'private' chapels and documented chantries may be viewed together as 'centres for facilitating salvation'.[1] Likewise, archaeologically there is often no difference between the chapels of guilds, fraternities and chantries and in essence they were 'different incarnations of the same intercessory impulse',[2] effectively 'poor men's chantries'.[3]

A major hypothesis of this book is that far from being primarily individualist or indeed 'private' monuments, chantry chapels were in fact of great relevance to the wider community. Hence throughout this book the terms 'community' and 'public' both refer to the collective parishioners of the church at all levels of society.

Background

Prior to the 1990s, many traditional archaeological studies of the medieval church generally focussed on its form, fabric and layout. Principal works on church archaeology have often emphasised a largely general and descriptive approach to the archaeological evidence, with little attention paid to the wider social and religious context of individual examples. Here, the emphasis was on the establishment of chronologies of development and the creation of

[1]   Burgess 1988: 73.
[2]   Kümin 1996: 159.
[3]   Cook 1947: 25.

'academic compartmentation' which led to 'an increasingly detailed knowledge of particular aspects of the churches, but little advance in understanding them *in toto*'.[4] More recently, the application of high-quality recording techniques and detailed structural analysis has led to the re-evaluation of many sites. Now, archaeologists over the last decade or so have begun to focus on what the construction, organisation and embellishment of churches can actually tell us about social structure and the specific nature of religious experience enacted within their spaces.[5] Coupled with this, the work of some historians and art historians, such as Burgess, Duffy and Goodall, and more recently Barnwell, Cross and Rycroft and Marks,[6] has focussed on the reassessment of surviving documents and their value to the study of church fabric and fixtures. Overall, these studies have begun to revise our understanding of the communal nature of medieval religion and have shown that pre-Reformation religious practice was an intrinsic, vital, and hugely popular aspect of medieval life.[7]

The late medieval chantry constitutes one of the most important and influential religious institutions of the later medieval period. Though there have been general, mainly historical or art-historical, studies of medieval chantries and chantry chapels, the surviving physical evidence has received comparatively little archaeological attention when compared with the study of monastic or parish churches overall. Much of the deficit lies in the fact that most endowed chantries were probably founded in larger institutions and consequently chantry chapels founded in monastic houses and cathedrals have received more attention compared with parish varieties.[8] The work of Cook, in particular, provides an excellent, though now outdated, survey of some of the more outstanding examples but is drawn largely from former monasteries and cathedrals.[9] With regard to chantry foundation in the parish church, Kathleen Wood-Legh has written the most comprehensive study to date.[10] She considers the wider social and economic, as well as religious, role of the medieval parish chantry, albeit with little emphasis on the physical evidence from surviving examples. Such historical emphasis on the parish church chantry has led to more focussed studies of localised chantry foundations, for example, Bristol, Canterbury, London and York, and regionally in Dorset, Gloucestershire, and Northamptonshire among others.[11] Some historical-based work focussing on individual parish church chantry foundations has also been undertaken.[12] However, as Hicks notes in his studies of the chantry foundations of the

4   Rodwell 1997, 8.
5   E.g. Gilchrist, 1995, 2005; Giles 2000; Graves 2000.
6   Barnwell, Cross and Rycroft 2005; Burgess 2000; Duffy 1992, 2003; Goodall 2001; Marks 2004.
7   Roffey 2006.
8   E.g. Biver and Howard 1909; Bond 1913: Cook 1947; Gee 1984; Colvin 1991; Boldrick 1996; Binski 1996.
9   Cook 1947.
10   Wood-Legh 1965.
11   Bristol (Williams 1950; Burgess 1985, 1996), Canterbury (Tatton-Brown 1981; Boldrick 1997), London (Hill 1971), Gloucestershire (Wilkinson 1895), Dorset (Fry 1905–9), Northamptonshire (Parsons 2000), and York (Gee 1984).
12   E.g. Maclean 1883; Godfrey 1954; Williams 1950; Hicks 1985.

Hungerford family, much of this historical research has been directed towards specific status groups and particular classes of record. Consequently he suggests that 'without some understanding of the institutions themselves breakdowns of benefactors and types of benefactor are little use'.[13] However, the work of Burgess, focussing more recently on the parish churches in London and Bristol, has highlighted the wide impact and effect that such foundations had, not just on memorial and private piety, but on the wider community and parish as a whole.[14] In particular he has shown the important contribution that surviving churchwardens' accounts can make to our study of late medieval piety and the role of chantries in particular. However, despite the insights that documentary and architectural study can provide with regard to the popularity of religion prior to the Reformation, archaeological examination of parish church fabric can illustrate further aspects of religious practice that may only be hinted at in historical documents. Here, the combination of relevant historical sources, such as accounts and wills, can be used in conjunction with the detailed archaeological analysis of surviving church fabric. For example, in a comparative study of Devon and Norfolk, Pamela Graves has examined how the influence of sets of documented individuals affected the fabric of the parish church and consequently her research has produced a 'narrative of the social experience of Christianity in specific historical contexts'.[15] Here, Graves produces an alternative to generalised and traditional studies of late medieval religion by combining the evidence presented by historical accounts, such as wills, with the surviving fabric of medieval churches. In this sense, she moves beyond the often standardised and limited documents themselves to investigate the actual physical imprints of the past and how testators left their presence within the fabric of their churches. However, it must be said that the survival of such documents is rare. In the case of chantry founda-tion, in many cases, there are no surviving records. Here archaeology must necessarily lead the way. Jonathan Finch, in his study of commemoration and church monuments in Norfolk, indicates how much the systematic study of the surviving church fabric can reveal about the form and function of religious belief in relation to memorial practice,[16] as has John Goodall in his study of a specific parish church institution – God's House at Ewelme, Oxfordshire.[17] Recent work on the guildhalls of York has shown how an explicitly theoretical approach, particularly that of structuralism, can be brought to the study of the standing fabric.[18] Such studies demonstrate how the investigation of parish churches and their monuments at parish level can reveal much about religious practice in medieval England and also how such practices defined both the space and fabric of the parish churches and their parishioners.

13   Hicks 1985: 123.
14   Burgess 1985, 1987a, 1987b, 1991a, 1991b, 1995, 1996, 2000.
15   Graves 2000: 166.
16   Finch 2000.
17   Goodall 2001.
18   Giles 2000.

This study aims to build on such valuable work and focus more specifically on the surviving evidence for medieval chantry chapels. Inevitably, only a few of the finest, predominantly monastic, examples have been studied in detail, and the application of archaeological approaches to the surviving fabric of parish church chantry chapels can remedy what has hitherto been a comparatively neglected field of study.[19] However, it should be borne in mind that distinct physical evidence of religious practice and devotion within the fabric of late medieval parish churches is relatively rare. Most churches have been drastically reformed, reconstructed and 'restored' in the centuries following the Reformation. Nevertheless, detailed archaeological investigation can reconstruct many aspects of chantry foundation, especially when taken collectively. Hence, it will be possible to investigate the relationship between intercessory practice and communal piety, a connection that has yet to be fully explained. Such a comprehensive approach, utilising a wide range of examples coupled with detailed recording and analysis, can help to explain these institutions in more detail and to highlight their wider social role. Here, it is not the intention to examine the social and economic history of chantry chapels, and the various forms of foundation – or to even discuss in any detail non-perpetual chantries – but to investigate the various physical forms and components of chantry chapels and how they actually 'worked' in practice.

Outline of work

This work is divided into three parts. Part I of this book provides a general background to the subject. Part II is based more specifically on the detailed structural analysis of 80 chantry chapels in the south and west of England.[20] Part III then provides a broader analysis and looks at the evidence presented in Part II in a wider national context.

More specifically, Chapter 1 provides a general introduction. Chapter 2 considers the religious context of chantry foundation, in particular the nature and development of intercession and purgatorial doctrine. Chapter 3 investigates the physical evidence for intercession in the local or 'parish' churches prior to the first documented chantries of the thirteenth century. Parts II and III then focus more specifically on the chantry chapels of the later medieval period. Here, Chapter 4 describes the range of sources and approaches to the study of medieval chantries and chapels. Chapter 5 examines the nature and extent of the archaeological evidence from the sample area. It brings together the evidence collected and recorded by the fieldwork and is divided into various fields of evidence including external and internal structure, individual features, fixtures and fittings and spatial analysis. Chapter 6 provides an interpretive discussion putting the evidence into a wider context by examining the range of parish church chantry chapels. It also examines the various types

[19]   Hicks 1985: 123.
[20]   Roffey 2004b.

of foundation as well as orientation and location within the parish church. Furthermore, this chapter will explore the polarity between individual foundations intended to 'draw in' the congregating community, and the function of the chantry chapel as a personal statement intended to make a communal contribution. It examines spatial and visual relationship between tombs, altars and other areas of parish church topography and the role of chapels and chantries in public and private piety. In particular, it looks at how sight lines were used within parish church ritual topography. Chapter 7 discusses the effects of the Reformation. It will assess physical evidence for the reuse of former chapels as a context for commemoration as well as the iconoclasm of space in the conscious reorganisation of chapel topography, in particular the placing of dominant status-driven monuments with the intention to effectively de-ritualise former liturgical space. Chapter 8 contains detailed case studies of the chantry chapels at Bridgwater, Mere and Stoke Charity. Chapter 9 provides a broad discussion and conclusion, examining chantry chapels in a wider, national, context. Finally, this chapter considers the overall value of an archaeological approach to the study of such monuments and to the parish church as a whole, suggesting directions for future research. The book concludes with a glossary of terms and select gazetteer of some of the best surviving chapels.

2

Medieval Visions of the Afterlife

Intercession and the afterlife

Before we consider the archaeology of medieval chantry chapels in more detail, we should first examine the cultural and religious context behind their foundation, in particular medieval beliefs concerning death and the afterlife. The theme of death dominated medieval society and to the medieval mind belief in the afterlife was a paramount concern. Throughout the medieval period, much of how one thought and acted was related to a strong sense that there was some form of existence after natural death. As a result, in the late medieval age the concept of purgatory dominated the religion and beliefs of the ordinary people. Purgatory was a state where the sinful soul was purged of its venal sins and therefore able to reach heaven and eventual salvation. It was a place, or a state, where one was literally purged of the stain of past misdeeds.

Throughout the Middle Ages, however, there seems to have been some confusion, or lack of agreement at least, on what the nature of purgatory actually was. To some, purgatory represented an antechamber to heaven; a place of trial, but a place in which eventual salvation was assured. To others, however, purgatory represented a very real state of ordeal and suffering which could last, almost, for an eternity. The way one acted in life informed, and had direct influence on, the amount of time one spent in purgatory. But there were mitigating factors. Such factors represented various strategies for intercession which presumed that certain positive activities or actions carried out by the living could have some influence upon the dead. In short, they provided what has been termed a 'simple, entirely calculable, rationale': aimed at the 'remission of a prison sentence'.[1] These various strategies often included works of charity and good deeds, pilgrimage, acts of patronage and the foundation of institutions, such as monasteries, colleges and, more specifically, the establishment of chantries. Furthermore, these strategies, often carried out during one's lifetime, would ensure that 'one could make a good start in life' and that the process could be 'completed (and might be wholly satisfied) in

---

[1] Binksi 1996: 25.

purgatory'.[2] The concept of purgatory has been seen as largely a phenomenon of the late twelfth century onward. But concepts of a penitential afterlife, as well as related rituals and contexts aimed at personal intercession, can be found to be much earlier.

Doctrinal developments in the twelfth and thirteenth centuries, particularly within the schools of Paris, established a formal means of dealing with penances attached to purgatory. These doctrinal developments were largely ratified at the Council of Lyon in 1274. However, beliefs surrounding the notion of purgatory as an intermediate and penitential world between heaven and hell appear prior to this. For example, precedents can be identified in the apocryphal *II Maccabees*, and the Classical teachings of the early Greek fathers Origen (third century), and Clement of Alexandria (d. c.215).[3] Moreover, these teachings bear conceptual similarities within the earlier Jewish pseudographia of Enoch and with the Vedic Hindu 'three paths of the dead' which date to at least the sixth century BCE.[4] Furthermore, notions of a 'purgatory' can perhaps also be seen in the afterlife 'journeys' of civilisations as diverse as the early Germanic peoples and ancient Egyptians.

An essential element that was to become crucial to later medieval intercession was the contribution of, often mutual, prayers for the dead. One of the earliest documented accounts of prayers for an individual soul comes from the *Confessions* of the late fourth-century theologian St Augustine of Hippo. In this account, containing prayers for his deceased mother, Augustine informs us that 'All she wanted was that we should remember her at your altar ... for she knew that at your altar we receive the holy victim ... inspire those who read this book to remember Monica, your servant, at your altar'.[5] The relevance of this excerpt is that it tells us three key things about early intercessory prayers. Firstly, Augustine's conviction that prayers could be influential. Secondly, the relevance of the 'holy victim', or eucharist, and finally that the participation of others is especially beneficial. Significantly, it is these three factors that would form the basis for later medieval chantry-based practice.

One of the more important figures in the evolution of doctrines relating to intercession for the dead was Pope Gregory the Great (c.540–604). It has been claimed that Gregory was the first to erect an altar over the tomb of St Peter in Rome, 'thereby forging a link between eucharistic worship and the veneration of relics'.[6] The link between intercession and patron deities is of particular relevance in the dedication of church altars and of those founded in later medieval chantries and chapels. Significantly, Gregory is credited with introducing the 'Trental', a series of thirty intercessory masses, which was increasingly favoured by later medieval English testators. The 'Trental' appears as part of the memorial liturgy in the *Regularis Concordia* composed

2   Burgess 2000: 49.
3   Le Goff 1984.
4   Le Goff 1984: 35.
5   Book IX, Coffin 1961: 204.
6   Cobb 1978: 474.

at Winchester by the reforming bishop Aethelwold in the mid-tenth century.[7] Its importance can also be seen throughout the medieval period. It occurs, for example, some four hundred years later, in the will of Edward Curteys of 1413, who requested 'Gregrestrental' to be celebrated after his death in the church of St Cuthbert, Wells.[8]

By the eighth century, the English monk Bede was providing a clearer geography of the afterlife. In his *Homilies* he warns that 'some are taken after death by the flames of purgatorial fire and severely punished. Either they are cleansed of their vices by a long trial in this fire, or thanks to the prayers, alms, fasting, tears and Eucharistic offerings of their faithful friends they are delivered from punishment.'[9] Again, in his *Vision of Drythelm*, Bede describes souls in purgatorial fire being helped by the offering of masses. (*HE* V: xii). Likewise in the *Life of St Cuthbert*, Bede also refers to a petition for St Cuthbert to 'remember at mass my servant … who had died yesterday.[10] Like Gregory before him, Bede provides us with further insight into the nature of intercessory practice that not only involves eucharistic celebration, but also the importance of good works through the giving of alms. These factors are highly significant. Not only were they to become central factors of later medieval chantry foundation and later practice, but they also indicate to us that intercessory practice and purgatorial ideology were important elements in Anglo-Saxon religious ideology at a comparatively early date.

By the eleventh century the so-called monastic revival had introduced a more formal and universal codification of liturgical practice. At the heart of the monastic reforms lies the *Regularis Concordia* composed at Winchester by bishop Aethelwold in the 970s. The *Concordia* introduces two extra offices to those extant, the 'Office for All Saints' and the 'Office for the Dead'.[11] Significantly, the text also refers to private prayers conducted in separate chapels and includes prayers for the royal house, indicative, perhaps, of a growing trend for private masses. Such trends were also mirrored on the continent, particularly at Cluny, a renowned 'centre for intercession' where anniversary services had become graded according to individual status,[12] suggesting a movement toward individualised intercession.

In England, evidence suggests that this is also a period that coincides with the increasing elaboration of rites associated with the consecration of cemeteries including the use of prayers, masses and lights.[13] Requests for soul masses increasingly appear in Anglo-Saxon wills from the tenth century onwards. By this time many monastic houses had a *Liber Vitae* or 'Book of Life' in which was inscribed the names of all the deceased abbots, monks and patrons.[14]

---

[7]   Symons 1951.
[8]   Weaver 1901: 65.
[9]   Le Goff 1984: 102.
[10] Chapter 34, Colgrave and Mynors 1969: 86.
[11] Symons 1953: xxxii.
[12] Colvin 2000.
[13] Gittos 2001: 59.
[14] One of the earliest is the Durham *Liber Vitae*, begun in the ninth century. It contains the names of some 3150 people (Colvin 2000: 167).

Such books were placed on the high altar and the names read out on the anniversaries of their deaths. The Winchester *Liber Vitae*, produced at Hyde Abbey around 1031, provides us with an actual illustrated geography of the afterlife. One page contains a triptych depicting St Peter at the top welcoming the just into heaven, while at the bottom, the damned are cast into the hell-mouth. However, between these two realms we see a third: that of purgatory where an angel, perhaps St Michael, can clearly be seen smiting a demon, whilst behind it the souls of the dead are carried away by angels. Not only does this depiction reveal to us this third realm between heaven and hell, but also the capacity of saints to effectively intercede on our behalf, a role that was to last throughout the medieval period until the Reformation.

Despite various notions of 'purgatory' in Anglo-Saxon eschatology, it was only by the late twelfth century that the concept of purgatory became formalised and part of the official 'language' of the western church. Indeed, it is only from this period that we begin to see the use of the noun *purgatorium* as a definitive identification. This has led some scholars, such as Le Goff, to suggest that the 'birth of purgatory' occurred in this second half of the twelfth century.[15] This, it should be noted, has been refuted by others, such as Richard Southern,[16] who are unhappy with the linguistic basis of such interpretations and place it a century earlier. Whatever the true origins of the formal definition, the later twelfth century witnessed doctrinal developments which began to offer more coherent means of dealing with the penances attached to sin, which, it may be argued, gave a more structured and legal framework for intercessory practice. Thus, in the 1150s, in his *Sentences*, Peter Lombard expressed this 'new emerging orthodoxy' and stated that the 'satisfaction' still required after the absolution of sin could be made 'after death in the purging fires of the middle places'.[17] In the thirteenth century, the reinvention of penance and the rise of purgatorial doctrine, promoted and facilitated no doubt by the monastic institutions and formally ratified by church councils, particularly that of Lyon in 1274, had percolated down to parish level. It is in this period that we begin to encounter the first documented chantry foundations,[18] the physical remains of which provide the major focus of this work.

Purgatory and burial custom

It may be wise at this stage to briefly examine another form of evidence that may shed some light on the evolution of purgatorial doctrine: the archaeological evidence presented by medieval burials. The period between the ninth

---

15   Le Goff 1984
16   Southern 1982.
17   Watkins 2002.
18   However, it should be noted that there is a paucity of surviving documents before the 1200s. David Crouch (2001) has suggested that one of the earliest chantries may be that established by Roger Rustein at Snettisham, Norfolk, sometime after 1193.

and twelfth centuries witnessed the appearance of a range of different funerary customs that may be linked to changing beliefs in the afterlife and the doctrinal development of purgatorial doctrine and related penance, as noted above. Thompson has noted that some burials of this period tend to fall into one of three categories: burials with a foreign substance, such as charcoal; burials where the body is placed in an elaborate container and burials where the grave has been constructed from materials such as stone or tile.[19] The presence of ash or charcoal in some burials of this period may be of particular interest here. Charcoal burials consist of graves that contain a spread or scatter of foreign or burnt material, found for example at Old Minster, Winchester, and in many smaller churches such as St Nicholas, Shambles, London. This may have symbolised the use of 'ash' used in traditional acts of penitence. The presence of ash itself is rarer, though recent excavations carried out by the University of Leicester's Archaeological Services at St Margaret's, Leicester, found a layer of ash in some of the coffined burials excavated inside the church.[20] Similarly, the use of 'pillow stones' supporting the head of burials, as found at St Nicholas and also at other sites including Raunds, Northamptonshire, and St Peter's, Barton-on-Humber, Lincolnshire, may also be suggestive of penitential practice linked to the afterlife. Many graves of this period remained simple and certainly such unique variations are an exception to the general rule. However, their presence may suggest that efforts were being made to help the soul after death and may have occurred in the light of the growing influence of purgatorial doctrine. Thus, these changes in burial customs may reflect a more symbolic value given to the body and its burial context and the belief that 'penance' can be carried over into the afterlife.

By the thirteenth century there were also significant shifts with regard to the preservation of buried remains. Archaeological evidence from some cemeteries of this period suggests that markedly less care was taken over the bodily preservation of individual interments.[21] Excavations at St Helens-on-the Walls, York and Kellington, Lincoln, for example, have shown that, prior to the twelfth century, special care was taken to leave burials undisturbed. After this period, the evidence suggests, graves were often disturbed by building works and later burials. For example, the extension of the east end of the church of Merton Priory, Surrey, in 1221 encroached some distance into the monastic cemetery and would have disturbed many burials.[22] At Raunds, many of the earlier graves of the ninth or tenth centuries were marked. By the twelfth century, however, there seems to be a more random distribution of graves, suggesting that markers were no longer used. These changes may reflect a shift in beliefs concerning the afterlife and the role of purgatory in the twelfth and thirteenth centuries. Prior to this, it may have been important to allow the corporal remains to survive relatively intact for the perceived eventual Day of

---

19 Thompson 2002: 231.
20 Unpublished, but a brief report can be found at: http://www.le.ac.uk/ulas/projects/ St%20Margarets/St%20Margarets.html
21 Hadley 2001.
22 Gilchrist and Sloane 2005: 194.

Judgement when, according to the Athanasian Creed, all beings would rise with their bodies and render an account of their deeds.

By the thirteenth century, it appears that many of the unique variations of burial practice, such as charcoal burial, had largely died out. One of the reasons may be that the chantry, or the personal endowment of intercessionary masses, now offered a more individual and credible strategy for the afterlife and a more logical method of obtaining remission from sins. In this period it was therefore increasingly common, particularly for ecclesiastics and wealthy patrons, to be buried within the walls of the church. One major reason behind the inclusion of the dead within the confines of the church was that burial liturgies began to focus more clearly on providing personalised contexts for intercession, particularly through the celebration of dedicated masses and prayers. The symbolic and continued presence of the dead inside the church, represented by visual memorials and tombs, was therefore of major importance.

Strategies for intercession

By 1300, many local parish churches were virtually unrecognisable from their eleventh and twelfth-century precursors. The addition and expansion of aisles, spacious naves and chancels, light-filled clerestories and ornate side chapels greatly embellished and expanded church space and fabric and reflect a distinct directional change. Such elaborations reflected a strategy for a more complex and personalised context for individual piety in the communal context. They also bear witness to the development of related artistic media in the multifarious forms of sculpture, painting, stained glass, images, artefacts, hangings and vestments. Belief in purgatory was to provide a lasting source of inspiration throughout the late Middle Ages, governing, to various extents, not just how people led their individual lives, but also how they patronised, decorated and embellished the communal space of the parish church. Furthermore, such beliefs reflected a desire to develop more varied expressions of individual piety in the communal context and attested to the importance of the visual arts in the development of strategies for the afterlife.

Generally speaking, these strategies were of two types: short-term and long-term. Short-term strategies were generally represented by a period of intensive memorial practice, initiated by the funeral of the deceased and the performance of the *placebo*, *dirige* and *Requiem*. On occasion this could be followed with the celebration of the 'Trental', or thirty masses, to be said over the ensuing month. The Trental was relatively inexpensive and therefore popular. However, for the wealthiest, requests for masses in the hundreds or even thousands were not unusual.

Long-term strategies were represented by obits or anniversary celebrations, where the name of the deceased was spoken or read out in the context of often communal ritual, in most cases celebrated once a year at a specified date (not always the date of death). In some instances, the anniversary involved an exact replication of the funeral prayers and masses held in the church at the original funeral. From the thirteenth century onwards, collective memory of the dead was also perpetually celebrated through the feast of All Souls, the 'most important festival of the dead'.[23] At the other end of the scale were the foundation and endowment of privately funded perpetual chantries, sometimes housed in their own chapel or, for the wealthiest, collegiate chapels. Long-term strategies were used to evoke memory in the context of perpetual intercessory ritual. They were devised to remind the living of the dead and to ensure that the dead were not forgotten and left languishing in the fires of purgatory.

In the later medieval period the foundation of chantries represented both the culmination of earlier processes and the ultimate personal strategy for intercession: the endowment of a mass and celebrant often housed within a defined architectural space, the chantry chapel. Some foundations, with their own altars and architectural styles and decoration (sometimes at variance with the rest of the church) represented a privatisation of church space. However, as will be later shown, such institutions, though personally founded, had a wider part to play in the religious devotions of the community as a whole. Many of the major studies of the chantry regard its origins as largely a thirteenth-century phenomenon.[24] Certainly, the *term* 'chantry', from the Latin *cantaria*, literally 'to sing', begins to appear in the documents of this period.[25] However, although the term 'chantry' certainly dates to the late medieval period, the actual *concept* of the chantry was a much earlier feature of religious life. As we have seen, notions of an afterlife and a form of purgatory had been around at least from the time of Bede, in the eighth century. We shall now examine evidence from the church fabric itself, which suggests that personalised strategies for intercession were being constructed in the centuries prior to the first official chantry foundations.

---

[23] Gilchrist and Sloane 2005: 27.
[24] Cook 1947; Wood-Legh 1965; Kreider 1979.
[25] Bond 1913; Wood-Legh 1965; Boldrick 1997.

3

Setting the Context: Early Origins and Influences on Later Medieval Chantry Foundation

Intercession and the local church in Anglo-Norman England

One of the essential questions surrounding the foundation of late medieval chantries is: why did they emerge as a phenomenon of the late thirteenth century, particularly when, as we have seen, beliefs in a penitential after-life had been current somewhat earlier? Various factors may include the breakdown of the monastic system of foundation and related expectation of commemoration, particularly with regard to the reform movement typified by the Cistercian order of the twelfth century, and the simultaneous development of purgatorial doctrine.[1] Certainly, by this period many churches and monasteries may have otherwise been fully catered for in terms of general lay patronage. Other significant events in this period include the emergence of new forms of lay experience, particularly associated with the introduction of the feast of Corpus Christi, and the formal recognition of the doctrine of transubstantiation at the Fourth Lateran Council of 1215. Significantly, this was also a period when 'every form of organised religious life, patronage, spirituality, administration and practice' had been explored'.[2] Consequently, there was only 'one further step to be taken, and that was in the direction of greater freedom from social and hierarchical pressures and a greater diversity of individual effort'.[3] Coupled with the wider social changes of the late twelfth and thirteenth centuries, these events produced a fertile environment from which the chantry chapel emerged.

Yet physical contexts for personal intercession were appearing before the formal presence of chantries in the thirteenth century. One problem, as previously noted, could be the paucity of surviving documents before the 1200s. Crouch has noted the appearance in the twelfth century of 'private extra-

---

[1]   Colvin 1991: 154.
[2]   Southern 1970: 300.
[3]   Ibid.; also see Burgess's discussion of this in his Introduction to Burgess 2004.

parochial chapels within the circuits of aristocratic manor houses'.[4] Indeed such patterns were emerging in the context of the earlier establishment of local, or so-called 'private', churches in the late Anglo-Saxon period, and it is perhaps here that the roots, or early aspirations, of the late medieval chantry chapel are found.

The tenth and eleventh centuries witnessed the rapid proliferation of private churches built by wealthy individuals, with resident priests. Lay wills of this period suggest a process whereby household priests were provided for individual churches, albeit on an informal basis.[5] These small local churches provided a place for communal worship and a more personal contact with the priest who was often hired to pray for the soul of the proprietor. Many of these churches were obvious status symbols and became an essential accoutrement of lordly status. But underlying this was a desire for intercession, and whilst they do not explain the origins of chantry chapels it is likely that their 'existence influenced the lesser aristocracy towards chantry foundation.[6] For example, the will of Richard Fitz Reiner of 1191 requested the performance of a daily mass for his soul in his newly established chapel at Broad Colney, Hertfordshire.[7]

The relatively large internal dimensions of certain private church naves indicate that they must have been designed to also accommodate a significant group of people. Many formerly 'private' churches such as the surviving examples at Alton Barnes, Wiltshire and Boarhunt and Corhampton, Hampshire (Fig. 2) and that excavated at Brighton Hill, Hampshire,[8] for example, possess internal spaces large enough to cope with a community of around forty people or more. This is the size of community that has been estimated from the excavations at the church and cemetery at Raunds, Northamptonshire.[9] These churches were more closely associated with the local settlement than many minster churches, and they therefore provided the community, potentially, with more direct and regular contact with religious practice. The local church also allowed for the formation of social relationships within the immediate community and for interaction between the living and their departed through memorial and ritual.[10] The local church catered for the religious needs of its community and the masses celebrated within such churches – churches founded by local lay lords primarily for the good of their souls as well as for local status – were, by association, intercessory and memorial foundations. Like later medieval chantry chapels, they were individually founded and, to an extent, managed, but they were also important to a wider group of individuals in that they provided a familiar context for divine worship. Within the private church, not only could the lord have a direct effect on the nature

---

4   Crouch 2001: 175.
5   Blair 1988: 8.
6   Crouch 2001: 175.
7   Ibid.
8   Fasham, Keevill and Coe: 1995.
9   Boddington, Cramp and Cadman 1996.
10   It is significant that the private churches at Faccombe Netherton, Hampshire and Trowbridge, Wiltshire were located on the boundaries *between* the manorial estate and settlement, suggesting the churches' physical relationship to both.

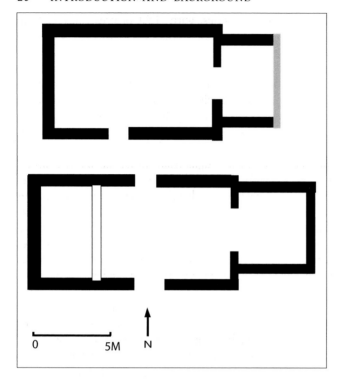

Figure 2 Plans of the Anglo-Saxon churches at Corhampton (top) and Boarhunt (bottom). Both churches still largely maintain the original plan and fabric of the period, although the east wall of Corhampton has been rebuilt since. Also note evidence for a possible western gallery at Boarhunt.

0   5M   N

and direction of eucharistic practice, but such practice itself could provide an analogy of feudal hierarchy. Far from being detrimental to local society, such conditions in effect renegotiated social relationships on a fairly regular basis. In this way, the patron's provision for a context for communal worship might be presented as a sort of 'charitable act', though with an element of selfish intent. Private churches were thus closer and therefore more accessible to the community than the less inclusive minster churches, often located several miles away. Private priests were frequently well known and integral members of the community. Over time, the private church also bound the living and the dead physically. The communal graveyards often associated with the private churches would represent the perpetual presence of the community's dead, and the church itself was a monument of collective memory and very much part of the community's history, as the parish church soon became.

The local church in the twelfth century

The late eleventh and early twelfth centuries brought about a series of institutional changes that dramatically changed the nature of lay church ownership. A series of reforms championed the 'moral superiority' of the church and as a result sought to exclude the clergy from every form of dependence on the laity. In effect, by the end of the twelfth century, secular lords were perceived more as patrons of their churches, with right of presentation, than a direct overlord and proprietor. Consequently this period witnessed 'a flood of churches, and other possessions, from the hands of laymen into those of religious houses'.[11] Blair, in a study of early medieval Surrey, noted that such gifts to existing Benedictine houses were rare, and that gifts to houses organised under Augustinian rule were particularly popular, a similar fate to that of many twelfth-century churches in southern Hampshire. This, he has suggested, was the result of the Augustinians' particular emphasis on pastoral care. It is interesting to note that in its wider social role, and the prominence given to hospitals, almshouses and education, the Augustinian order has many similarities (albeit it on a larger scale) with the social context and function of later chantries, many of which were associated with schools, the provision of alms and similar institutions of care. It is also likely that intercessory motives were a major factor behind such 'gifts', as the Augustinian canons were priests and therefore had a duty to perform regular mass. The Augustinians ran parishes – ministered, but led disciplined private lives – and could be supported by the parish tithe, a form of endowment at no cost to the founder. Likewise the foundation of a hospital provided a ready-made congregation, whose participation in prayers for the founder of their good fortune would, no doubt, be explicit. The foundation of St Katherine's by the Tower, London, in 1148 by Matilda, Stephen's queen, was served by a master, brothers and a number of poor whose 'sole duty was to offer up prayers and attend masses for the souls of the queen's two children'.[12] The bishop of Winchester, Henry of Blois, likewise founded a house of chaplains at Marwell, Hampshire, to sing masses for his soul sometime after 1128.

The church aisle: a context for private piety?

By the end of the twelfth century, the local church had become fully institutionalised and we see the emergence of a new 'parish' church. It is this period that bears witness to a significant addition to church fabric: the aisle. By the end of the twelfth century most parish churches were provided with at least one aisle. The function of the aisle has been the subject of much debate. Most commonly they have been interpreted as being a response to demographic changes,[13] to cope with a 'swelling population'[14] and more likely as a 'major response to liturgical elaboration',[15] a view supported by Morris.[16] They may also represent the emergence of the local parish as a formal collective entity that facilitated the raising of parochial finance. In this case aisles

[11]   Blair 1991: 142.
[12]   Cook 1947: 53.
[13]   A view held generally by, among others, Platt 1981; Turner 1987 and Bond 1988.
[14]   Turner 1987: 235.
[15]   Peters 1996: 72.
[16]   Morris 1989.

could function as a communal amenity. The function of the aisle, together with the relative rapidity of its introduction, may also suggest a lay reaction to proprietary changes, noted above, and the continuing influence of lay motivations within a crystallising parish church. Many aisles were added to parish churches within a relatively short time span of forty years or so after the 1150s. In Hampshire, eleven out of seventeen studied churches had aisles by 1200. In Wiltshire, seven out of eighteen churches had aisles by the end of twelfth century. In Somerset, in contrast, and due to extensive programmes of rebuilding in the fifteenth century, only three out of twenty-four churches have surviving evidence for aisles pre-1200.[17]

Could the relatively short time span of aisle development be simply ascribed to demographic changes? Surely such changes would occur gradually, and over a longer period of time, and be perhaps more noticeable in some areas than others, particularly urban areas. In London, where demographic changes were more acute, there is only evidence for one church having an aisle added in the twelfth century.[18] The almost sudden introduction of the aisle as a regular feature of church plan-forms (often originally a single addition) occurred at a time when the changes wrought by various church reforms were coming to fruition. This might be suggestive of the redirection of lay influence upon the church, manifested in a distinctly private acquisition of religious space in the form of the aisle. If so, then the aisle was a compromise between lay proprietary desires and the clerical domination of an increasingly institutionalised church. Although purgatory was foreshadowed earlier, it is claimed that a clearer *definition* of purgatory as a place in Christian theology, and the related penitential remission, was being devised in the second half of the twelfth century.[19] Such developments in Christian theology and intercessory belief coincide with the widespread addition of aisles to parish churches. However, as we have seen, such beliefs were current many centuries earlier. It is therefore likely that changes to the layout of many churches of this period reflect both individual concerns and reactions to changes in eschatological belief, and opportunity. The emergence of the new institutionalised 'parish' church and a move away from the lay-owned local, or private, churches, now meant that new contexts had to be devised. In a study of Worcestershire churches in the twelfth century, Bond has identified the construction of at least thirteen single aisles in the parish churches of this period.[20] The addition of a single aisle to parish churches runs in parallel with a perceived decrease in secular influence on the local church. Of eleven churches in Hampshire with evidence for late twelfth century aisles, six involved the construction of a single aisle, including Boldre, Stoke Charity and Tichborne. In Wiltshire, three out of seven churches exhibit this phenomenon: Bradford-on-Avon, Compton Bassett and Maiden Bradley.

17   Roffey 2004b.
18   Schofield 1994: 117.
19   Le Goff 1984.
20   Bond 1988: 144.

Thus, the second half of the twelfth century heralded a series of major changes that radically altered the topography of the local church. The addition of aisles to many parish churches of the period was influenced by similar developments occurring in greater monastic houses some decades earlier. Structural changes to both the fabric and internal organisation of the parish church also coincided with a series of ecclesiastical reforms affecting lay proprietary concerns. The period around 1170 also witnessed significant advances in purgatorial doctrine. These factors, above all else (including demographic factors), could explain the introduction and function of aisles founded within such a relatively short space of time (and well after they first appeared in monastic houses). For instance, documentary evidence from the 'Christchurch Cartulary' states that around 1090 a lay lord paid for the construction of a church at Milford-on-Sea, Hampshire, and gave half a virgate of land to Christchurch priory, who sent a priest to attend church.[21] Baldwin de Redvers in about 1160 gave over the church to Christchurch priory, with the churches at Boldre and Brockenhurst, when the priory became a house of Augustinian canons. This date also coincided with a series of structural changes at Boldre, where a south aisle was added in the second half of the twelfth century.

The foundation of aisles redefined ritual topography in the parish church. Although the doctrine of transubstantiation was not officially recognised until 1215, this period witnessed the increasing prominence of the mass as an important aspect of lay piety and a vehicle for personal intercession. Participation in various aspects of divine worship, at parish level, provided a focus for communal piety and social relationships. In particular, a major element of the mass, discussed in more depth later, was the witnessing of the elevation of the host, which traditionally took place at the high altar within the east-end or chancel of the church. Despite the importance of viewing the elevation in lay piety, the analysis of visual relationships and the reconstruction of sight lines between aisle and chancels suggest that very often the high altar was visually separate from the aisles. However, an altar within the aisle may itself have provided an alternative ritual focus. In the north aisle of Niton parish church, Isle of Wight, there exists a rare survival of a twelfth-century aisle piscina, suggesting the former presence of an altar in this location and at this time.

Ecclesiastical documents of the period are rare, particularly with reference to individual parish churches. Where they do exist, they do not provide much information about how religious practice was actually carried out within the churches. However, the examination of extant church fabric and layout may provide some insight, particularly with regard to the reconstruction of visual relationships between aisles and the rest of the church.

[21]   Hase 1994: 62.

Visual considerations of aisle liturgical topography

The location of many aisles within the general layout of the church indicates that very often their occupants had either no view, or at the very most a restricted view of the chancel area. At Bishops Cannings, Wiltshire, for example, the south aisle in particular gives the impression of a distinct liturgical area with minimal proximal relationship to the chancel (Fig. 3). The church of St Martin's, Wharram Percy, North Yorkshire has been subject to detailed archaeological research over the course of several decades, and it is a case study that can be applied to the lesser-studied churches of the south and west. Of particular relevance is the addition of a south aisle in the late twelfth century – a period particularly associated with the influence of the Norman Percy family.[22] Here, the aisle extends eastward far beyond the view of the chancel. In fact, it appears that the east end of the south aisle bears no liturgical relationship to the chancel whatsoever (Fig. 4). It can therefore be suggested that this space was a separate liturgical area with its own altar (probably on the east wall). Taking into account its association with the Percys and the significant proprietary changes of the time, it can be conjectured that this may have functioned as some sort of exclusive space or private chapel for the use of a lay lord and his family. In relation to this, architectural similarities have been noticed between this significant phase of construction and work done on the associated manor house, including the identifiable work of

[22] Beresford and Hurst 1990.

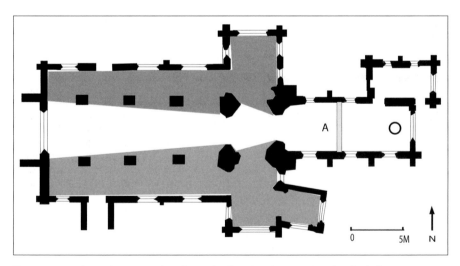

Figure 3 Bishops Cannings church in the fourteenth century. The shaded area represents areas of blocked visual access to the high altar (circle). The twelfth-century church probably consisted of a shorter chancel and an aisled nave but nonetheless vision from these areas would still have been severely restricted. (A) marks the conjectured east wall of the twelfth-century church and the site of an earlier altar.

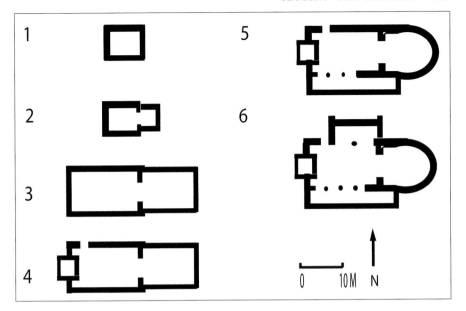

Figure 4   The early development of St Martin's, Wharram Percy, from the late Anglo-Saxon period to the early thirteenth century. The foundation of the south aisle in the late twelfth century (5) indicates that there was little visual relationship between the aisle and chancel (after Beresford and Hurst 1990).

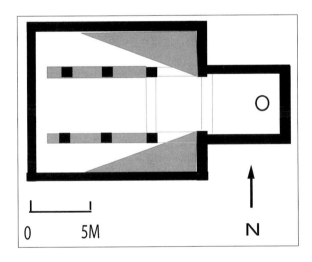

Figure 5   Reconstruction of Aldbourne church in the late twelfth century showing the visual relationship between aisles and chancel. Shaded areas represent areas of blocked visual access to the high altar.

the same mason which may indicate direct lay influence.[23] Analysis of the churches at Aldbourne, Wiltshire (Fig. 5), and Cheddar, Somerset (Fig. 6), all of whose aisles were constructed in the twelfth century, shows that the aisles, and later chapels and transepts, appear to have a limited visual relationship to the location of the high altar. Again this suggests the presence of individual

[23]   Platt 1981: 22.

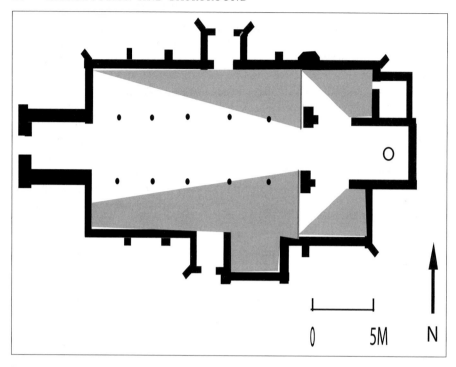

Figure 6   View-shed analysis of Cheddar parish church. Shading represents areas where visual access to the high altar is denied.

subsidiary altars. It is telling, therefore, that the aisles also had their own separate entrances, suggesting an element of exclusivity. It is perhaps significant that although there may be visual restrictions between aisle and chancel, these do not apply to nave and aisle. This could be to do with facilitating light into the body of the church. Nonetheless, the arcade had the function of making the aisle visually accessible from the nave of the church whilst maintaining a clear 'threshold' between the two. Furthermore, this may indicate that any rituals conducted in the aisles were not wholly exclusive, at least in visual terms.

The examination of visual relationships between aisles and high altars in the above examples strongly suggests that in these cases the devotional focus may have been within the aisles themselves, and probably against the east wall where many later subsidiary altars were located. The presence of an altar within the aisle of a church is a major feature of later parish churches, as is the position of chantries proper within aisles. Furthermore, the relationship of the altar to a space consciously set aside for an exclusive group of people, a family or even a guild or fraternity, suggests the altar to be a familial or common focus. The complex ritual of the mass, whilst reinforcing ancestral family bonds and social hierarchy, would by its very nature have been a device of intercession.

Overall, it should be borne in mind, however, that this discussion is not suggesting that aisles are some form of proto-chantry. What is considered here is that a series of major changes in church fabric seem, to a certain degree, to be linked to the need to develop more personalised strategies for intercession and piety in a period of doctrinal and institutional change in the context of the formation of the parish church. It is therefore suggested that such developments had some part to play in the evolution of late medieval chantries proper. Nothing exists in a vacuum. Everything comes into being through a chain of complex causes and effects, and related events. In the case of the medieval chantry movement, its origins lie in a series of causes and effects inherent within the origins and evolution of the English parish church. Though the term 'chantry' is mainly used in the context of the mid-thirteenth century onward, it can be seen that the constituents of such a phenomenon, and the directing motivations behind it, may be as old as the English 'private' or local churches of the late Anglo-Saxon period. The evolution of the chantry therefore evolved hand-in-hand with significant developments between church and community as reflected in church topography and fabric. Consequently a desire for more physical contexts for personal intercession may have played a major part in the development of the early medieval church. Such a course of developments ultimately evolved into the impressive chantries and chapels of the thirteenth century onwards. It is on these that the rest of the book will now focus.

PART II

CHANTRY CHAPELS: A PERSPECTIVE FROM THE SOUTH AND WEST OF ENGLAND

4

Sources and Approaches

Introduction

Part I examined the religious context of medieval chantry chapels. It also considered the likelihood that chantry chapels evolved from a series of events that affected the fabric of the church from at least the late Anglo-Saxon period. That being said, the chantry chapel proper, and its widespread popularity, is a phenomenon of the later medieval period, from the thirteenth century onwards. Having laid the background, it is this period that we will now focus on. Part II will examine medieval chantry chapels with special reference to the recent archaeological analysis of 80 parish church chantry chapels from the south and west of England.[1] This chapter will examine the range of sources available for the study of medieval chantry chapels. Although it will primarily refer to examples drawn from the specific study area, the class of documentary source and the methods of structural analysis can be universally applied.

Despite the dissolution of the chantries in the mid-sixteenth century, and the consequent restructuring of parish church topography, significant evidence remains for the often fragmentary survival of former chantries and chapels. With regard to the study of such structural evidence, the archaeologist Richard Morriss has suggested that in *archaeological terms*, only when a good understanding of the fabric has been established can the documentary material be assessed and 'used to aid the overall interpretation of the building'.[2] What follows is primarily an archaeological study combined with a survey of relevant documentary sources for each individual chapel. This information has formed part of an extensive survey database,[3] from which are drawn the case studies detailed in Chapter 8 and in Table 1. Where they survive, documentary sources can provide a useful source of background and incidental material to the structural survey of buildings. More specifically, such information can be used to provide evidence, in some cases, for the historical presence of chantries, dedications and chronologies and foundation provisions. In particular, churchwardens' accounts, where they survive, can provide

---

1   Roffey 2004b.
2   Morriss 2000: 165.
3   Roffey 2004b.

useful information regarding internal fixtures, fittings and goods associated with chantry foundation. Hence, in some instances, surviving documents can provide a useful source of background information for the structural investigation of former chantries and chapels.

Documentary sources

A range of primary documentary sources provides information about chapel and chantry foundations and their goods. Particularly important are the documents relating to the Statutes of Mortmain in 1279, a piece of legislation which declared that all chantry foundations must have a royal licence.[4] It has been claimed that no fewer than 2182 such licences were issued between 1281 and 1547.[5] However, one has to be careful of an over-reliance on the licences alone. The amount of licences issued almost certainly exceeds the actual foundations themselves as for one reason or another the actual endowment of chantries may never have happened. Licences could also be ignored or evaded by legal means. There were also exemptions, many of which are listed in patent rolls. Overall, these documents, though identifying some chantry chapels, are not particularly detailed and like many legal documents are rather standardised. They can therefore tell us very little about individual foundations and how they operated. Chantry instructions, such as those found in the royal licences, and, importantly, wills, can be used to identify and locate former chantries. However, Dobson has pointed out that wills can be potentially problematical in that they 'frequently emerge as declarations of intent rather than evidence of creation'.[6] Wills can be limited in that they are too specific. This has been noted by Burgess,[7] and by French, who observes that they 'do not inform on a lifetime of religious involvement'.[8] They can, however, provide some useful information about particular burial arrangements in chapels.

With regard to the wider social context, both Burgess and French have indicated, and demonstrated, that churchwardens' accounts may be a particularly fruitful source of information in that 'they address lay priorities and [the] community concerns' of chantry foundation and intercessory endowments.[9] Surviving churchwardens' accounts for England are detailed both by Hutton and Kümin.[10] However their survival is sporadic. For example, the survival rate in the research area for the medieval and post-medieval period is for the diocese of Winchester, 9%; for Bath and Wells, 11%; and for Salisbury, 15%.[11]

---

4   The Statutes of Mortmain were introduced to prevent land continuing to fall into the 'dead hand' of the church.
5   Pounds 2000: 104.
6   Dobson 1996: 268.
7   Burgess 2000.
8   French 2001: 11.
9   Ibid.
10   Hutton 1994; Kümin 1996.
11   Foster 1997: 78.

The survival of accounts for the medieval period alone is more fragmentary. For the eighty chantries and chapels that were subject to detailed recording and analysis, accounts only survive for six relevant parishes prior to 1547; at Stoke Charity, Hampshire; Bridgwater, Ilminster, Nettlecombe and Yatton, Somerset and St Thomas's, Salisbury, Wiltshire. Some churchwardens' accounts have been published for the recorded examples at Stoke Charity;[12] St Thomas's, Salisbury,[13] and Yatton.[14] Other churchwardens' accounts from churches outside the immediate research area[15] can also provide potentially useful comparative information.

The documents that relate to the dissolution of the chantries in the mid-sixteenth century (the so-called chantry certificates) are also a valuable source of information about individual chantry foundations, their goods, services and location within the church. Chantries were first surveyed in 1546 in response to Statute 37 Henry VIII, c.4. As a result, commissioners in each county were required to discover and certify to the court of Augmentations the landhold-ings of such institutions on 4 February 1536. In February 1548, a second survey (Statute Edward VI, c.4) was carried out. Under this second act, all chantries, colleges, religious brotherhoods and hospitals were surrendered to the king by 1 April 1548. As a result of this process a second set of chantry certificates was sent to the court of Augmentations by local commissioners. Documents for the counties of Hampshire, Somerset and Wiltshire (among others) survive and are currently held in the National Archive, Kew (E 301). The chantry certificates for the counties of Somerset (E 302/42) and Wiltshire (E 301/56; E 301/58) have been published,[16] but not those for Hampshire (E 301/51). It is important to remember, however, that they only provide information about chantries surviving in 1547. They do not generally contain information about those founded in monasteries and those in parish churches that had already been dissolved or declined prior to this date. This may be particularly true of early foundations,[17] though the context for chantry foundation such as side-chapels and altars may have still had some ritual function. It is also possible that certain chantries were overlooked or concealed and therefore do not feature in the surveys.

Further published material discussing the local effects of the dissolution of the chantries can be generally found for other counties in the south and west of England, including Devon[18] and Dorset.[19] Evidence for the research area for the period of dissolution can be found in documents relating to the dispersal of chantry lands,[20] and also within general inventories of church goods, receipts, accounts letters and surveys for the sixteenth-century dissolutions of religious

12 Williams 1913.
13 Swayne 1896.
14 Hobhouse 1890.
15 For example, Burgess 1995; Butcher 1870; Doree 1994.
16 Green 1888; Jackson 1885.
17 Kreider 1979: 89.
18 Snell 1960; Hanham 1967; Orme 1979.
19 Fry 1905–1909.
20 Woodward 1982; 1983.

houses and chantries.[21] Primary information can also be found in documents relating to chantry priests' pensions, for example, for Wiltshire (E 301/101).

For a review of primary and secondary sources and general background information, the *Victoria County History* volumes provide an analysis of individual parish churches, including evidence for the foundation of chantries and private chapels, as well as information regarding relevant primary sources.[22] Likewise, for the sample area, *The Buildings of England Series*[23] offers invaluable art-historical and architectural information for parish churches and chantries as well as for liturgical features, such as piscinas, aumbries, sculpture and tombs. The series also provides a useful on-site reference guide; providing descriptive accounts, dates and comparative information for relevant architectural features.[24] Individual notes and reports survive for certain parish churches that make some reference to chantries and chapels. They are referred to where relevant on the individual chapel recording templates contained in the appendices. They can be found in the respective county journals: *Proceedings of the Hampshire Field Club*, *Wiltshire Archaeological and Natural History Magazine* and the papers of the Somerset Record Society, Somerset Archaeological Society and Bristol and Gloucestershire Historical and Archaeological Society.

Archaeological approaches to standing fabric

The archaeological examination of the surviving physical structure and topography of former chapels can provide an insight into the form and fabric of religious belief that, in many cases, remains largely 'invisible' from the historical sources. Archaeological examination allows for the investigation of the physical context of chantry-based religious practice and how various strategies for intercession were enacted in chapel form and fabric. It also allows for the reconstruction and analysis of related art and architectural media that may, in some instances, survive wholly or partially. Three key principles that can be applied to the study of standing structures are: *sequences defined by straight joints, stratification by partial destruction* and *typological study*.[25] To this can be added *sequences defined by building materials*.[26]

---

21   In primary form (E 117) for Hampshire (E 117: 13/19; 14/36/1; 14/36/2; 14/36/3 14/36/5; 14/37; 14/38; 14/39; 14/160; 14/184), for Somerset (E 117: 14/23; 14/90; 14/91; 14/92; 14/94; 14/172; 14/180; 14/190; 14/192) and Wiltshire (E 117: 13/74; 13/98; 13/125; 14/37; 14/38; 14/103; 14/104; 14/105; 14/187) and in published form (Walcott 1876; Williams 1913).

22   *Victoria County History* (VCH) 1919–1995.

23   Pevsner 1958a; 1958b; Pevsner and Cherry 1975; Pevsner and Lloyd 1967.

24   However, it should also be pointed out that many chantry chapels are omitted from these studies. In fact, the presence of some former chapels can only be revealed or indeed 're-discovered', in many cases, by the examination of the individual churches and their fabric themselves.

25   Taylor 1976.

26   These methods and techniques are, of course, generally well known to buildings archaeologists. However, for the non-archaeologically trained reader it may be wise for

Figure 7   South chapel, Basingstoke, showing the constructional relationship between the chancel south chapel and the south aisle of the church.

Sequences defined by straight joints involves the analysis of the relationship between particular parts of buildings or episodes of construction. It is concerned primarily with the way in which the various elements of the fabric 'proclaim sequences defined in time by the way they are joined'.[27] Essentially, this works on the principle that later additions to the building can be identified by the fact that they generally abut an earlier structure, often forming what is termed a 'straight joint'. Contemporary phases of building will, more often than not, present a uniform fabric – various elements of the building being keyed in to each other. Abutments revealed by straight joints can be seen, for example, at Basingstoke, Hampshire, (Fig. 7) where the south chapel of rough rubble construction clearly abuts the fine ashlar work of the south aisle, as well as blocking its former east window.

Abutment of structures, as at Basingstoke, can provide both a *terminus ante quem* ('date before which') and *terminus post quem* ('date after which') in the form of datable architectural features such as windows. These *typological features* will provide two chronological reference points. Typology, as applied to buildings, uses an art-historical approach by identifying features that are characteristic of an architectural period, such as windows or forms of buttress, for instance. An example of this can be seen at Stoke Charity, where the north aisle abuts the chancel chapel. The aisle contains a Romanesque, or Norman, doorway and thus informs us that the chapel must be earlier than this date (Fig. 69). *Typological features* can include such datable elements as

us to consider these briefly so as to understand the basic principles that underlie the interpretation of church fabric, and how it relates specifically to chantry chapels.
[27]   Taylor 1976: 4.

Figure 8   South chapel, Bishopstone, showing sequences of construction.

architectural features, as well as give more generalised dates or periods such as those provided by tool marks or masonry types.

Sometimes a series of features can be identified which provides a sequence of phases of destruction and rebuilding. The presence of a datable feature in any sequence can provide either a *terminus ante quem* or *terminus post quem* for the changes in fabric. This *stratification by partial destruction* can clearly be seen in the internal fabric of the south chapel, Bishopstone. Here, two windows of the twelfth and thirteenth century pre-date the fourteenth-century arch through to the nave. The sequence indicates, not only the period of changes, but the various stages of development, culminating with the chapel's construction in the fourteenth century (Fig. 8).

Often the reconstruction or extension of chapels will involve the use of new and different materials. The use of different types of stone often provides a clear indicator of change and, sometimes, the status of the structure. An example of this can be seen in the south chapel at Godshill, where the grey ashlar stone of the diagonal buttresses clearly contrasts with the rubble fabric of the chapel. In Somerset, the common use of highly contrasting stones, such as the greyish Blue Lias, gold Ham Hill limestone and red sandstone, can provide clear indicators of structural change. Examples, examined below, include the reconstruction of the north aisle and porch at Bridgwater, where the division between the original fabric of red sandstone construction and the

Figure 9 St Mary Bridgwater. The rebuilding of the north porch and aisle, probably as a result of chantry foundation, can clearly be seen in the use of different building materials.

rebuild in Blue Lias can clearly be seen (Fig. 9). On occasion, the change in building materials may indicate internal structural change, as for example with the red sandstone easternmost piers of the north aisle at St Mary Magdalene, Taunton. Here, the external fabric of the aisle is of the same material, but the other arcade piers are of Ham Hill limestone, suggesting a reconstruction and eastern extension of a pre-existing structure. Changes in fabric can also be less obvious. Sometimes subtle differences with regard to tooling techniques, brick bonds and different types of mortar may identify phases of constructional change.

As illustrated above, the principles of stratigraphy, evidence for constructional change and typology can be used to examine internal changes within individual chapels. For example, archaeological evidence in the western arcade of the north chapel at Rodney Stoke, in the form of a base moulding behind the Rodney tomb of 1651, suggests that this blocked wall was once an open arcade. Former features may often leave structural traces such as slots or inserts on piers and walls, that may suggest the former presence of medieval screens. This can be seen clearly in the north chapel at King's Somborne, where the filled slots on the south pier base and the dark shadow on the north wall clearly denote the location and dimensions of the former screen (Fig. 10). At Basingstoke, referred to earlier, the fine ashlar work of the south aisle is in strong contrast to the rough flint-work and rather functional-looking later south-east chapel. Since this new chapel had replaced the earlier aisle chapel it suggests some change in the fortunes of the church patrons. Here, perhaps, local people were not willing to spend as much money on the embellishment on their church in comparison with earlier times.

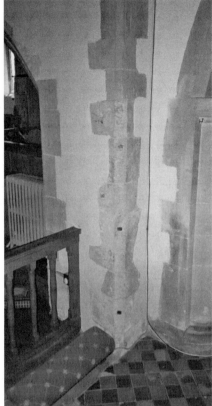

Figure 10   Evidence for a former screen in the south chapel, Kings Somborne.

Floors can be examined and their relationships to datable features, such as tombs, may indicate their originality. This works on the common assumption that, similar to abutments and straight joints, that which lies underneath must be, generally speaking, contemporary or earlier. For example, the tombs and ledgers that are cut into the floor of the north chapel at Montacute indicate its medieval date. They are clearly cut into an existing floor. Similarly, in the south chapel of Boyton, the central tomb clearly lies on the surface of the medieval floor. By contrast, later floors will often abut earlier features. In the Hampton chapel, Stoke Charity, the medieval floor tiles are laid against pre-existing features, such as a post-medieval tomb, clearly indicating that they were reset after this period.

The structural analysis of building stratigraphy can be tied together with datable features, such as windows, which can provide chronological reference points for major structural change. Such changes in fabric can then be compared with surviving documents and comparative changes to reconstruct the former spatial organisation of chantry chapels. All this information can be combined to build up an overall picture of chapel development.

Spatial and visual analysis

The examination of space, layout and conjectured former sight lines can, in some instances, provide an insight into how the chapel's space was used. Inferences can be made about the relationships between related areas of both church and chapel and used to develop an understanding about the spatial relationships between monuments such as tombs, altars, windows and doorways. In effect, this helps interpret why certain features were placed where they were. The basis of this approach lies within the field of what can be termed 'informed observation'. Spatially, this involves the examination of, for example, datable features such as doorways and screens, and the conjectured level of exclusivity – were they accessible only to a specific group of people or the wider parish community? The size and location of the chapel are taken into consideration; i.e. whether or not chapels are associated with, or entered from, chancels or more public areas, such as the nave or aisle. The size of the chapel may also indicate the extent of access as well as the number of people potentially involved. Smaller chapels may suggest a more select congregation, for example. As noted, vision was the most important medium for religious experience in medieval religious practice. The application of viewshed analysis, or the examination of lines of sight, discussed later, has been previously carried out mainly in landscape contexts.[28] Such an approach is nonetheless helpful in investigating the visual relationship between altars and other areas and features in the church. Viewshed analysis may also help to articulate the nature and extent of visual participation in the ritual of the mass carried out within the confines of the chapel. Analysis of lines of sight within buildings has been formerly carried out by Markus,[29] who applied the concepts of the access analysis – the examination of spatial segregation and routes of access demonstrated by the work of Hillier and Hanson[30] – to vision. This method has been applied to medieval buildings to good effect by Graves, who examines how religious ideas were visually encountered by the laity, and how light and sight worked within the parish church.[31] Such an approach is invaluable in analysing the spatial relationship between chapels and chantries and the parish church and community. It assists our understanding of why monuments are placed in particular areas of chapel topography. It indicates the importance of public visual access to the symbols, images and features of chapel space and fabric; it also suggests the nature and level of visual participation in the rituals enacted within them. Visual relationships in chapel and church topography can be examined by reconstructing lines of sight, or viewsheds. The basis of this approach involves the archaeologist moving around the church and establishing what could have been seen from certain areas and how features or structural elements, such as tombs, squints, walls and windows,

---

28 Fisher *et al.* 1997; Lake *et al.* 1998; Pollard and Reynolds 2002.
29 Markus 1993.
30 Hillier and Hanson 1984.
31 Graves 2000.

for example, may support, inhibit or obstruct former sight lines in church.[32] Again, this approach assumes a level of informed observation – the knowledge of what parts of the church or architectural elements may have existed in the medieval period, and what has been reconstructed, blocked or moved since. This approach is designed to answer particular questions, such as whether it was important for chapel altars to be viewed from public areas of the church; or if subsidiary altars had a clear view of the high altar. Also, it may reveal to what extent personal and religious symbols, tombs and monuments were deliberately located to place them in public or clerical lines-of-sight, and what this can reveal about the importance of vision within religious ritual. The standing fabric and chapel topography need to be examined together. This then establishes the basis for a wider interpretation of the form, fabric and function of medieval chapels, individually and collectively.

Elements of chapel structure

The two essential elements of the chantry chapel are therefore, firstly, the *fabric*: the material context of chapel construction – its definition, constructional materials and fixtures and fittings (including, of course, the all-important altar) and, secondly, its *space*. This second element includes the physical topography of chantries and chapels and the relationship between features (such as tombs, altars and images, where evidence for them survives) that inhabit this space. It also includes the way that vision was facilitated within this space; between the laity and clergy and areas of ritual importance.

Fabric

Internal features include evidence for screens, squints, tombs, altars, liturgical features such as aumbries, piscinas and light fittings, as well as elaboration and other relevant features. Such elements allow for the reconstruction and analysis of former chapel space and visual relationships between features and the church in general. Medieval tombs, for example, have been said to provide 'a reflective index of social or economic trends'.[33] The location and positioning of tombs within chapels, particularly with regard to groups of tombs, is thus arguably significant. Importantly, they may be datable and often provide a fixed chronological point of reference. The reconstruction of internal features of the medieval chapel based on the recording and analysis of the surviving evidence can expose how 'ceremonial was enacted in spaces provided in and defined by the building' and how the use of symbolism and decoration reinforced this message.[34] The position of altars, windows, symbols, niches and heraldic devices, and how they were used and perceived, are likewise

---

[32] Roffey 2004a; 2007 (forthcoming).
[33] Finch 2000: 115.
[34] Burgess 2000: 47.

of relevance, as such architectural features are often linked into a common ritual topography. Such data also allow for a chronological interpretation of individual chapels and their features to be built up, to facilitate comparison and contrast with other elements of the church, such as whether individual chapels were constructed as part of a general programme of work or were individual and unique additions to church fabric.

Space

It has been stated that 'a mode of analysis which demands a really close under-standing of chronology is that of the use of space'.[35] This includes analysis of chapel space, location of a chapel within a church and the examination of spatial relationships between features such as altars and tombs, and chapel and high altar. Visual relationships are also significant, particularly with regard to the visibility of ritual foci, religious images and, importantly, the mass. Access to and from chapels is also important. Furthermore, spatial information collected from chapels can cast light on the level of personal and collective participation in intercessory practice. As Duffy has recently noted, and as will be discussed in depth later, one of the key issues in the study of the late medi-eval church is the privatisation of lay religious experience afforded by chantry foundation.[36] Here, one of the main questions is: to what extent were chantry chapels wholly 'private' enclaves? Like Duffy, this study seeks to highlight that such monuments reflected a 'personalization' and not a privatisation of church space. Hence, chantry chapels were public monuments inasmuch as they nourished everyone's religious experience and cannot be seen as a symptom of privatisation. Therefore, lines of sight can be reconstructed and viewed in the context of the development of collectively accessible spatial geographies. As will be seen, vision was the most important medium for religious experience. Therefore the analysis of lines of sight and visual relationships is crucial – one might say indispensable – to our understanding of medieval religious practice. It may be able to inform us to what extent chantry masses were visible from the body of the parish church, particularly the more publicly accessible areas, such as the nave and aisles, or only from within the chapels themselves. The reconstruction of visual relationships also takes into account the placing of monuments to obstruct lines of sight, the association between personal and religious images and the use of light and the consequent location of windows. Importantly, it also can also provide an insight into how chapel space was reorganised over time, particularly with regard to the Reformation, which, as will be seen, brought about an iconoclasm of former ritual space.

We will now move on to consider the range and nature of the archaeo-logical evidence drawn from the eighty chapels that form the basis for this work.

---

[35]   Grenville 2001: 19.
[36]   Duffy: 2003.

5

Medieval Chantry Chapels: Form and Fabric

Introduction

This chapter is directly related to the recording and analysis of 80 chapels, drawn from 63 churches in the counties of Hampshire, Somerset and Wiltshire.[1] As such it provides a detailed and comprehensive insight into the structural evidence for former chantries and chapels extracted from some of the more extensive surviving examples in the south and west of England. This was drawn from an initial pilot survey of over 100 medieval parish churches in the three counties. The research area, therefore, offers significant surviving evidence and a range of chapel types and provides a fairly representative and extensive sample for detailed investigation. This allows various general patterns and trends to be recognised, as well as the identification of unique individual features. The examples were selected on the survival of physical evidence alone and therefore comprise some of the best extant chapels in the south of England. All three counties, particularly Somerset, provide a wealth of physical evidence and a range of both primary and secondary documentary sources. Based on the original recording methodology utilising *pro-forma* recording sheets,[2] this chapter will present the range and types of surviving evidence for chapels and their related features, fixtures and fittings. It will also draw in relevant comparative examples to further illustrate some of the major points. Part III will then place this material in a wider context by providing a broader comparative discussion of the evidence.

The structural evidence

The word 'chapel' is medieval in origin and comes from the Latin *capella* referring to the 'little cloak' of St Martin that belonged to the Frankish kings.[3] Chapels could be components of church buildings, or free-standing, and were normally constructed to house altars. Examples of the former

[1]   Roffey 2004b.
[2]   Ibid.
[3]   Orme 1996: 76

include chantry chapels, and chapels dedicated to the worship of particular saints, such as Lady chapels.[4] Free-standing chapels might come in the form of rural chapelries, bridge or churchyard chapels. Though this book concentrates primarily on chapels directly associated with parish churches, it is worth noting that all chapels were intended to house both worship and intercessory services. The famous chantry chapel on Wakefield bridge, North Yorkshire, or the Battlefield college at Shrewsbury, Shropshire, or the impressive churchyard chantry chapel at Buckfastleigh, Devon were all founded both for memorial purposes and for use by the laity as places of worship. Although it should also be noted, of course, that the majority of chantry foundations would have appropriated existing altars, chapels and chantry foundations can be found in various locations, both within the body of the church and as separate adjuncts or additions to parish church fabric. Examples of the latter include side-chapels, transepts and aisles. Many of these used existing church space and required elements of reorganisation or rebuilding, or indeed involved the complete construction of a new structure. Although there are numerous examples of chantry chapels constructed between the piers of arcades, particularly of the 'stone cage' type found at Winchester and Salisbury cathedrals, for example, they are generally not found in parish churches, possibly due to spatial restrictions. A rare surviving example can be found in the church of St Mary Magdalene, Newark, Nottinghamshire. Here, the Markham and Meyring chapels located in the chancel arcades are of the stone-cage variety. Both date from the first decade of the sixteenth century. Surviving examples such as these may indicate that, at least in larger parish churches, these structures may have been more common than generally thought. At Burford, Oxfordshire, the small parclosed chapel of St Peter, placed against the east respond of the north aisle, is made up largely of wooden screens, dismantled at the Reformation. However, at its east end is a fourteenth-century stone canopy, which formed part of a chantry chapel that adjoined the rood screen. At Chipping Norton, in the same county, a chapel may have been located in front of the north pillar of the chancel arch, where the carved reredos, with three canopied niches, exists. The chapel probably extended southwards as far as the next pillar and there would have been timber screens around three sides, perhaps with a decorated canopy above in a similar arrangement to that at Burford.

Often the external fabric of the parish church provides structural information that is internally hidden by plastered walls, or tombs and monuments. External fabric is often stripped off the plaster or render that formerly covered it, and evidence for joins or changes in fabric is more readily visible. Hence, evidence for structural relationships, changes in fabric and building materials and the insertion of doors and windows is often more evident upon external examination. As discussed in Chapter 4, structural analysis of stratigraphic relationships between various elements of the chapel and parish church can reveal evidence for rebuilding, extension or relative chronology between building phases. Abutments revealed by straight joints, as seen clearly at

---

4   Though very often, in time, these were also used for chantry foundation.

Figure 11 The west wall of the south chapel at Boyton, illustrating evidence for a former aisle in the form of a blocked arch. Also note the trace of a later buttress.

Basingstoke, where the south chapel abuts the south aisle as well as blocking its former east window, provide a *terminus post quem* for the construction of the chapel (Fig. 7). At Montacute, the small lobby-like feature between the porch and south chapel is revealed as a later insertion since it appears to abut both structures. A straight joint indicating an abutment is clearly visible in the fabric. At Boyton, evidence for the earlier aisle survives in the fabric of the west wall, where the remains of a blocked arch can be seen. Before the insertion of the unusual round window, this side of the chapel was also supported by a slim buttress, the outline of which is similarly visible in the fabric (Fig. 11). Here, the rebuilding of the chapel and addition of the large round window probably relate to the establishment of a college of priests in the late thirteenth century, the house of which survives today to the south of the church.

Changes in building materials, as at Basingstoke, can also indicate structural change and stratigraphic relationships. At Bridgwater, where red sandstone is replaced by new work using Blue Lias stone, the external fabric of the aisle and porch clearly reveals an episode of rebuilding. This, as will be seen in the case study of Bridgwater in Chapter 8, may relate to the re-foundation of two chantries there around 1400. Similarly, in the external fabric of the north

Figure 12   The east end of Old Basing parish church showing the change in building materials from rough masonry to brick. Here the rebuilding of the chancel and north chapel (with insertion of a new window) was probably due to the construction of the brick south chapel shown on the left.

chapel at Ilchester, the reconstruction and extension of what was possibly a porch made of local Ham Hill stone, can be marked in the new use of Blue Lias. At Old Basing the use of brick alerts us to the fact that the rebuilding of the chancel and north chapel was probably related to the construction of the brick south chapel (Fig. 12). In contrast, building phases that are contemporary, as can be seen with regard to the chapels and south transept at Bishops Cannings, are exhibited as all one build; their constructional elements are keyed-in. Here, there are no straight joints and the construction courses and materials are all common and uniform.

The study of structural relationships can also elucidate the processes involved in the rebuilding and extending of many chapels. In this respect, examination has shown that many chapels display evidence for having been extended eastwards at some point. At Yatton, the north transept chapel appears to have been widened by a metre or so. Here, the drip mould running along the external face of the chapel terminates about a metre from the eastern corner, suggesting a rebuild. In this case, this may have been the result of repair, or more likely to incorporate it in the building of a later chapel to the east (Fig. 13). At St Thomas's, Salisbury, archaeological evidence indicates that the south aisle was probably extended by three bays in the fifteenth century. Here the former end of the south chapel can be seen in the present fabric. This was probably to facilitate the founding of two chantries in the chapel at this period. Many other examples from the study area indicate evidence for the eastern extension of aisles or pre-existing chapels, as at Brympton d'Evercy,

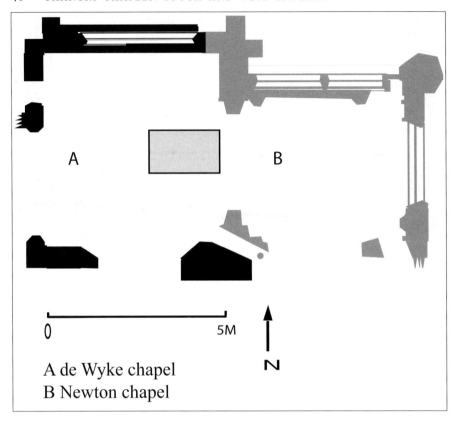

A

B

0   5M

N

A de Wyke chapel
B Newton chapel

Figure 13   The north chapels at Yatton showing extension of de Wyke chapel in the fifteenth century (outlined in grey).

King's Somborne, Mere, Minehead, Montacute and Old Basing. At Corsham, the chancel of the church appears to have been extended by half a bay as a result of the construction of a chapel to the north. At Binsted, the eastern extension of the north transept can clearly be seen in the irregular coursing of the east wall. Archaeological evidence at Mere suggests that the aisles on both sides of the church were widened to align with the construction of the eastern chapels. On the aisle-side of the west wall of the south chapel, however, there is a roof-line. This suggests that the south chapel predates the south aisle, which was built and then widened at a later date. Many chapels have evidence for roof heightening, probably associated with the insertion of a ceiling. Often this is only in the nature of a few courses, but it can clearly be seen by the use of different stone and mortar types, as seen at Stoke Charity, the chapel of Holy Trinity at St Cuthbert's, Wells, and Curry Rivel.

In addition to documentary evidence, archaeological traces survive for the foundation of chapels in churchyards, such as the chantry of Our Lady at Chew Magna, and the chantry of St Katherine, Frome. At Chew Magna, a churchyard chantry chapel is referred to in the will of John Bartelet

Figure 14   Possible location of former churchyard chantry chapel of Our Lady, Chew
Magna.

in 1517.[5] To the north of the church the earthwork remains of a former
masonry structure aligned with the church indicate the likely site of this
former chapel (Fig. 14). At Frome, significant medieval fabric survives from
what may be the former chapel of St Katherine situated a few hundred
metres uphill from the parish church. A good surviving example is the former
chantry chapel of Our Lady that stands in the churchyard of St Michael's,
Bray, Berkshire.

Some chapels have evidence for integral associated structures. At Bromham,
the Tocotes and Beauchamp chapel of the fifteenth century was entered via
the rebuilt south transept, where an elaborate pendant vault suggests that some
importance was attached to this structure. It may have been used as some
form of anteroom or lobby, and the stone seating along its south wall supports
this suggestion. The anteroom may have been used as a separate chamber, or
even 'over-flow', from which the chapel mass could be viewed. Alternatively its
purpose may have been to provide a waiting area for timed masses.[6] A similar
arrangement can be found at another Beauchamp chapel, at Warwick, where
there was a small lobby north of the chapel with benches. At Brympton,
Montacute and Yatton (Fig. 13), a series of chapels are connected with each
other. It is likely that the north-west chapel at Brympton d'Evercy functioned
as the burial chapel for an individual and also as part of the church where the
laity gathered at intervals (discussed in next chapter) and that the north-east
chapel contained the altar and later tomb memorials. A similar pattern may

5   Weaver 1913: 194.
6   See Chapter 6.

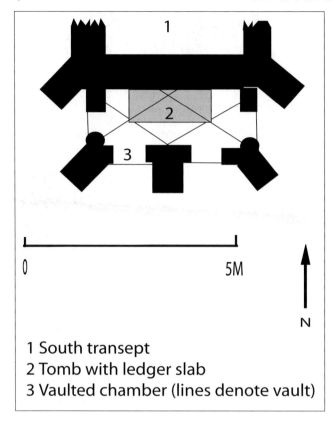

1 South transept
2 Tomb with ledger slab
3 Vaulted chamber (lines denote vault)

Figure 15 Plan of the burial cloister with tomb, attached to the south chapel at Bishopstone.

have existed in the north chapels at Yatton and Montacute. At Brympton, Yatton, and possibly Montacute, these eastern chapels are later additions, or indeed extensions. Such initiatives may suggest a deliberate attempt to expand areas of lay control in the fifteenth century. Furthermore, certain chapels with chantry foundations may have been associated with separate memorial chapels, as with the Clopton chapel and chantry at Long Melford, Suffolk.[7] It is also possible that both chantry and memorial chapel could be in separate churches. At Corsham, the tombs of Thomas and John Tropenell reside in their chantry chapel within the north chapel. At Great Chalfield, close to the manor house constructed by Thomas Tropenell in the fifteenth century, there is another chapel on the south side. This latter chapel is divided from the nave by an ornate masonry screen decorated with family emblems and shields. It can be suggested that both chapels may have reflected different functions. That at Corsham is primarily for intercession, whilst that at Great Chalfield served as a mortuary chapel within the parish church. It is also of possible significance, for reasons to be discussed, that the chantry chapel at

7   The Clopton chapel (c.1490s) is a large chamber east of the north aisle. The chantry chapel is to the east of this and approached by a tiny vestibule or priest's room with panelled ceiling.

Figure 16   The Lamb chapel, St John's, Devizes. Note the foreshortened east window of the chapel and the blocked small window in the wall of the chancel indicating the probable presence of a former anchorite cell.

Corsham is situated to the north of the church, whilst the burial chapel at Great Chalfield lies to the south.

In certain cases, there were auxiliary buildings and other features associated with medieval chapels. The elaborate burial cloister at Bishopstone is one example of this, as is evidence for an anchorite cell on the east wall of the Lamb chapel at St John's, Devizes. Regarding the first, the small burial cloister outside the south wall of the south chapel at Bishopstone is unusual (Fig. 15). The structure has two entranceways to the east and west, is vaulted, and contains a damaged tomb. It appears to be integral with the construction of the south transept in the fourteenth century. Whilst the function of the cloister is hard to interpret, it was certainly a highly visible monument to those entering the church via the south porch. Its position and accessibility suggest that it may have been a shrine of some form, the burial place of some local hermit or holy man. Alternatively, it could have been used for church processions at Easter and other feasts, or to house a relic.

At Devizes, the external elevations of the Lamb chapel reveal several interesting and unique features (Fig. 16). These are a blocked 'low-side' window, evidence for beam-slots or 'put-logs', the blind lower half of the east window (internally a reredos fills this space), and a possible roof-line of a 'lean-to' structure. This evidence strongly suggests a former anchorite cell. The 'low-side' window was a common feature of anchorite cells and provided visual access to the mass inside the church, as can be found at the extant examples at Yateley, Hampshire, and Compton, Surrey. Similar features can be found

at Leatherhead, Surrey,[8] and Britford, Wiltshire. Interestingly, the 'low-side' window at Britford is situated in the west wall of the south transept and provided a view to the south chapel altar, not the high altar, as was usually the case. The east window of the Lamb chapel at Devizes is of particular interest. That it is half blind suggests that this type of window was originally planned, and inserted, to take into account the construction of an anchorite cell outside, against the east wall. It can be further postulated therefore that this building was in some way integral to the foundation of the chapel and chantry within. Here the connection of the chapel and associated cell would be seen as particularly efficacious for the founder, both in its connection with a 'holy man' or woman, as well as the act of charitable provision itself.

External fabric

Secular and religious symbols and decoration

In some cases the external fabric of the parish church was often highly decorated with symbols of both a secular and religious nature, often denoting status, familial affiliations and religious sensibilities. As such, the external fabric could potentially represent a form of 'canvas' upon which architectural 'messages' could be inscribed. This was particularly relevant with regard to chapels where the use of overt decoration and symbolism could be used to draw attention to such structures as monuments associated with individuals desiring a statement or context for intercessory practice, such as chantry foundation. The three-storey porch associated with the Savage chapel at Macclesfield, Cheshire, has the shields of Rochester, London and York – the three places where Thomas Savage was a bishop before becoming an Archbishop. At Old Basing, the north external elevation of the north chapel is embellished with label stops containing the emblems of both the Paulets and at least seven other connected families. Such devices could be seen as intercessory markers and/or statements of the family's religious fervour for personal or social gain. By contrast, at Devizes and Bromham, the external elevations of the south chapels are adorned with heraldic symbols, canopied niches and angels grasping shields depicting the instruments of the passion, designed to attract attention and prayers from people outside the chapel. Here the founders are directly linked to intercessory motifs. The outstanding examples at Old Basing, Bromham (Fig. 17), Devizes and Lacock attest to the intricacy and complexity of architectural detail that could be invested in such monuments. Significantly, the majority of these examples date from the mid-fifteenth century, which may suggest a change in the use of architectural sculpture at this period.

Many chapels display some form of rudimentary embellishment, particularly the use of gargoyles or beast heads, as at St Thomas's, Salisbury, at Sherston,

8   Gilchrist 1995.

Figure 17   The elaborate north elevation of the Tocotes and Beauchamp chapel, Bromham.

in the Trinity chapel at Cheddar, or in the north chapel, Old Basing. In some instances, chapels show evidence for selective embellishment in that only a particular side of the chapel is decorated. In all cases this is either the town side of the chapel or the side situated near a public entrance. At St Andrew's, Cullompton, Devon, an inscription commemorating John Lane (c.1525) runs at low level along the west wall of the aisle he built, close to the porch so that it could be viewed by all those entering the church. Often, as in the case of the churches of All Cannings, Brading, Bromham and Devizes, for example, the chapels situated in visible areas were highly decorated in comparison with their counterparts on the north side. Many chapels display external niches in highly visual positions. At Bromham and Devizes, large canopied niches domi-nate the eastern gables of the respective chapels. At Bridgwater, the porch, associated with two chantries in the north aisle, has two large canopied niches either side of the entrance. Elsewhere, at St Luke's, Gaddesby, Leicestershire, the highly decorated western façade contains a row of narrow blank gables accompanying three niches, central doorway and decorated battlements. The carved stone cornice contains a variety of interesting and imaginative subjects, such as human and animal heads, chickens, hens and mermaids.

Windows

The position of windows in relation to the possible internal arrangements of chapels and chantry spaces has often been overlooked in published studies. When considered with other evidence, the insertion of windows can often provide datable information for chapel construction or reconstruction. However, it should be noted that examples do exist of windows being copies of earlier ones, as at Fotheringhay, Northamptonshire, for example. Clear examples can also be seen at Stoke Charity, Curry Rivel and Nettlecombe. Evidence for an Anglo-Saxon window at Stoke Charity and for late twelfth or early thirteenth-century lancets in the second and third of these chapels, indicates significantly earlier dates than formerly recognised for these structures. The recording and analysis of windows also allows typological comparison with other parts of the church, to identify similar and related episodes of rebuilding. Such evidence can indicate whether the chapel was constructed as part of general church building, as seen at Bishop's Canning, where the architectural style of windows matches that of the south transept. At Crewkerne, Somerset, the use of similar style windows indicates that the north-east chapel was added at the same time as the north transept and chancel aisle. At Long Ashton, Somerset, windows of comparable style suggest that the north chapel was constructed at the same time as the aisle. At Binsted, the insertion of a fourteenth-century window allows for a dating of the chapel extension. As noted, at Bishopstone, the three windows of the twelfth, thirteenth and fourteenth centuries are visible in the fabric of the wall between the south chapel and nave and detail the various stages of development, culminating with the construction of the chapel in the fourteenth century. Some windows exhibit dated inscriptions, such as at Minehead and Sherborne St John, and these permit a closer dating of chapel rebuilding or reuse. In the case of Sherborne St John, the insertion of the chapel east window in the early sixteenth century, with its decorated 'R' and 'P' device, probably reflects the appropriation of the former Brocas chapel by Ralph Pexall at this time.

Of particular significance is the actual positioning of windows. This may indicate the former location of important areas of church and chapel space. Windows can provide a backdrop to highlight internal features such as tombs, as seen at North Bradley and Limington. They were also inserted to high-light particular areas, such as the skewing of the east windows in the north chapel at Montacute (Fig. 27). At All Cannings, the east window sill of the Beauchamp chapel slopes down significantly to direct light onto a low altar. At Stoke Charity, the east window is misaligned with the central apex of the roof to highlight the position of the Hampton tomb in the chancel arcade. Here also a new window was inserted in the north wall in the early fifteenth century to accentuate an Easter sepulchre (Fig. 71). The Reformation seems to have put an end to the use of some windows to illuminate or highlight litur-gical areas. During this period structural evidence suggests that many windows were blocked, such as at Alton, Lacock, the south chapel at St Thomas's in Salisbury, Stogumber and Tichborne.

The chapel and its church

In certain cases the construction of a chapel might take into account the architectural requirements of the parish church. The addition of chantry chapels provided extra liturgical space and the setting for an additional altar (and therefore an additional mass). As in the case of the Paulet chapels at Old Basing, or the two chancel chapels at St Thomas's, Salisbury, this could be a significant and sizeable addition. The foundation of some chantry chapels also provided for a porch. Perhaps one of the best examples of this arrangement can be seen in Greenway Chapel, St Peter's, Tiverton, Devon. Here, the south porch and chapel, built by the merchant and ship-owner John Greenway in 1517, are decorated with niches and friezes of ships that possibly refer to Greenway's own vessels, which operated out of Dartmouth. Porch structures integral with chapel construction can be found in many examples from the study area. At Cheddar, the chapel of St Nectan is joined onto the side of the porch. At Montacute, the chapel is joined to the church porch by a narrow lobby. At Wedmore, the guild chapel is squeezed in between the south transept and the porch. Here, however, a separate entrance leads from the porch into the chapel and two internal windows provide a view into the chapel. In both these latter examples, there was a conscious desire to make the chapels accessible from communal areas. At Bridgwater, the reconstruction of the north aisle, sometime around 1400 for the foundation of two chantry chapels, also made provision for a large two-storey porch.

Chapels were often one element of a series of associated structures. The Phelips north chapels at Montacute comprised a complex of chapels, vestibule and porch with priest room. Possible 'vestibules' attached to chapels can also be found at Bromham and Devizes. Many chapels in the Middle Ages were founded as corporate ventures, for guilds and fraternities, such as the north chapel at Aldbourne and the elaborate two-storied chapel of St Katherine at St Andrew's, Chippenham, in Wiltshire, with a communal chapel on the first floor and meeting rooms on the ground floor. This kind of arrangement generally dates to the late fifteenth and early sixteenth centuries. It may suggest that during this period, members of a strong mercantile class were making publicly visible monuments and creating an exchange with the church by constructing

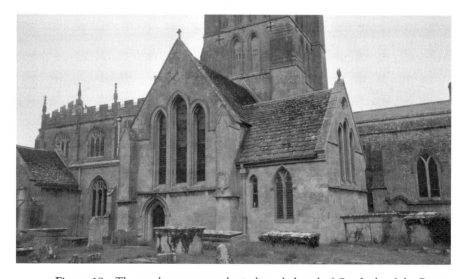

Figure 18   The south transept and misaligned chapel of Our Lady of the Bower, Bishops Cannings.

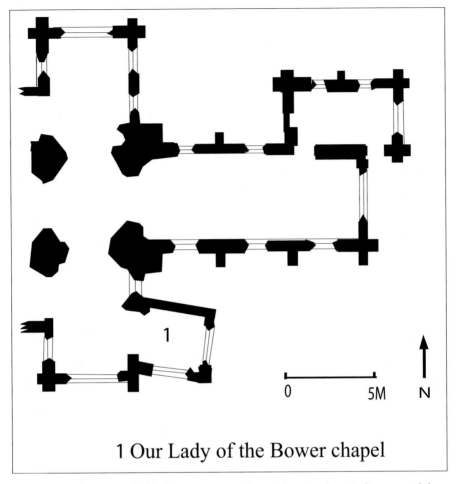

1 Our Lady of the Bower chapel

Figure 19   The east end of Bishops Cannings church showing the misalignment of the south chapel (1) so as not to obstruct the south-west window of the chancel.

spaces that provided access; on entering the church, their presence in a memorial context could not be missed.

In one case, the construction of a chapel respected the pre-existing architectural or spatial arrangements of the church. In the late thirteenth or early fourteenth century, the chapel of Our Lady of the Bower at Bishops Cannings was aligned slightly to the south-east and away from the church (Fig. 18). Such an arrangement suggests a contingency to prevent obstruction of the south window of the chancel and therefore to prevent unnecessary impediment of light into this ritually important area (Fig. 19). Sometimes the construction of chapels was part of a larger building campaign. At All Cannings and Bishops Cannings, the south chapels were constructed at the same time as the south transept. At Crewkerne and Ilminster, the chapels were integral components of the construction of the transepts. Similarly, at Lacock the drip mould of the north chapel is continuous with that of the chancel, indicating that the two were contemporary. These types of chapel may suggest planning on the part of local wealthy laity to provide extra church space.

Internal fabric, fixtures and fittings

The internal space of chapels would often be defined by screens and contain a range of decorative and liturgical features, such as piscinas, tombs, images and other related architectural features. Furthermore, each aspect of internal space was ordered and contributed to a planned ritual topography with the chantry altar as its focus. Overall, the chapel was organised and decorated to provide a sacred context for individual intercession and communal worship. These elements, and the spatial relationships between them, can be investigated and often reconstructed by archaeological examination.

Screens

The chapel screen was normally a parclose, divided between a 'blind' lower section and a partially open upper section. This arrangement had the dual role of providing a barrier, but only a partial one, and therefore controlled visual access to chantry ritual – in particular the all-important elevation of the host. It has been declared that no parish church screens survive from before the twelfth century in this country.[9] Examples pre-dating the fourteenth century are few and far between so that those that do survive, such as the thirteenth-century wooden screen in the south transept chapel at Sparsholt, Berkshire, may truly be said to be of an 'exceptionally rare date'.[10] In the 80 chapels studied here, not one chapel screen dates from before 1400. Elsewhere, there are rare examples of pre-1400 rood screens such as at Lavenham, Suffolk (c.1340) and at North Leigh, Oxfordshire.

The vast majority of chapel screens, where they survive, are from the fifteenth century. The issue here could of course be one of survival or replacement. But there could be other socially oriented issues at work, such as the increased physical restriction (though not necessarily exclusion) of chapel and chantry space from the fifteenth century onwards, which is examined in the next chapter. There is widespread evidence for the presence of former screens in the study area. Out of the 80 examples, evidence survives in varying forms for 35 former screens. In Somerset, there is evidence for 20 screens, in Hampshire 2, and in Wiltshire 13. Evidence for screens can come in two forms: surviving examples and structural evidence within church fabric for their former presence. Due to restoration of many churches, particularly in the nineteenth-century rebuilding or re-tooling of medieval stonework, such structural evidence may often be lost, as is likely for the south chapel at

9   Brooke 1971: 67.
10   Pevsner 1966: 223.

All Cannings. Wooden parcloses survive in some cases. Good examples can be seen in the St Andrew's and Huse chapels, Cheddar, the north chapel at Curry Rivel, Long Ashton, Mere, Minehead, and St John's, Winchester. Masonry screens survive in the chapels at Corsham and Great Chalfield and Whitestaunton.

More commonly, the evidence for lost screens consists of insertions and slots in pier and arcade bases. This can be seen clearly in the north chapel, King's Somborne, where the filled slots on the south pier base and the dark shadow on the north wall clearly denote the location and dimensions of the former screen (Fig. 10), in this case of a height of approximately 1.80 metres. Other forms of structural evidence can be found in the Holy Trinity chapel, St Cuthbert's, Wells. Here, the bases of the central pier have been carved away to allow for the fitting of a screen. Filled slots for former screen fixtures survive on piers of many chapels including Godshill and Mottistone, Isle of Wight, and in the north chapels at Aldbourne and Lacock. At Montacute, a fragment of a former screen may survive *ex situ* in the chapel. At Limington, a doorway cut through the dividing wall leading from the nave to the chapel may suggest the former presence of a screen to the west, as otherwise one could simply gain access through the arcade unless it was blocked by a now removed tomb.

There is also evidence to suggest that some chapels may not have been screened at all. In the chapel of St Nectan, Cheddar, a screen would have obstructed a view of the image niches. At Stoke Charity, Old Basing and Sherborne St John, the presence of tombs positioned within arcades makes the existence of former screens unlikely. Some post-Reformation examples exist at Stogumber and Farleigh Hungerford, and consist of railings which seem to have been intended to provide more of a physical barrier. It is worth noting that the 'curtains' referred to in some accounts and inventories, such as for Bradford-on-Avon, Wiltshire and Mere,[11] may have also served as a barrier, albeit temporary, to some chapels. It can also be argued that the placing of tombs in arcades may have acted as a form of obstruction, as at Stoke Charity and Old Basing. A similar arrangement can be seen in the Kirkham chantry chapel in Paignton, Devon, where the south transept chapel is divided by a screen with two wide-arched openings within which sit large tomb chests and central opening. At Old Basing, the walls dividing the chancel from both north and south chapels contain large tombs as well as a central doorway (Fig. 20). Here the tombs and their architectural setting would have acted as a screen with the lower half blind, whilst the open recesses above each of the tombs gave restricted visual access into the chapels from the rest of the church. A similar example can be found in the Brocas chapel at Sherborne St John, where the entire tomb fills almost all of the space of the arcade. Such arrangements, it can be argued, had a powerfully intercessory motive behind them. The memorial of the founder formed part of the 'screen' and framed the liturgical drama performed within the chapel itself: one could not but have

[11]   Jackson 1885.

Figure 20 The tomb arrangement in the south chapel, Old Basing. Such a composite arrangement can be seen to act as a screen with the tombs forming a highly visible component.

seen the memorial when witnessing the elevation within the chapel. In this way it acted as a form of presencing device within the fabric of the chapel.

Squints

The nature and function of 'squints', or internal 'windows', common to many later medieval parish churches, require further investigation and form a neglected area of study. Such features are found in many of the parish churches of southern and western England, and comprise a variety of types. There is widespread evidence for the presence of squints in the study area. Out of the 80 examples, evidence survives in varying forms for 28 squints. In Somerset, evidence for 13 squints survives; in Hampshire 4; and in Wiltshire 11. As such, a strict definition of the squint is not possible except to say that they generally facilitated vision to an altar. Moreover, though hard to date due to lack of architectural embellishment, squints in parish churches appear to be largely a phenomenon of the late fourteenth to early sixteenth centuries. Within the increasingly busy and complex topography of the parish church, the squint would have facilitated clear lines of sight, and in the case of 'passage' squints, physical access also, between the various parts of the expanding church. In some cases, they also allowed priests at subsidiary altars (such as chantry altars) to view the high altar in an attempt to synchronise the rituals. Squints, therefore, can be found in many forms. Some, such as at St John's, Winchester, provided a view to the high altar only for the priest officiating in a side chapel. Others, as at Ilminster, provided a view to the high altar for the general parishioners from the aisle and transepts. Double squints,

Figure 21   Types of squint. From top left: chapel squint from Ilminster; 'private squint' at Yatton; 'double squint', north chapel, Aldbourne and 'priest' squint from south chapel, St John's, Winchester.

such as that at north chapel, Aldbourne, facilitated views for parishioners and a celebrating priest, or to distinct areas of the church (Fig. 21). At Stoke Charity the double squint provided a view from the nave to the north chapel and to the chancel from the north aisle. On the other hand, 'private' squints, as in the north chapel, Yatton (Fig. 21), provided an exclusive view for a small group of people only. The squints at Brympton d'Evercy, Great Chalfield and Yatton are barely a metre from the floor surface, with no evidence for the floors being raised. At Brympton d'Evercy, the position of a low squint in the north-west corner of the late fifteenth-century chapel is again of particular interest. Here, the squint is not situated near the location of a former altar. Instead, as at Yatton, its position provided a view of the chancel from the back of the chapel. The squint is situated at waist level (with no evidence for significant change in floor level) and therefore suggests that the observants were either sitting or kneeling. Furthermore, from this position every other altar within the church could be viewed – within the east end of this chapel, the altar in the north chapel and in the south transept.

So-called 'passage squints', which were also a sort of internal doorway used for processionals, can be found at Basingstoke, Churchill, Portbury, Sherston (Fig. 22) and Yatton. Although many squints are plain functional features, the six-metre long squint between the Horton chapel and the chancel at Holy Trinity, Bradford-on-Avon, is a significant feat of engineering, and was cut through solid masonry. This particular example indicates the lengths that people would go to make sure vision between altars was achieved. The majority of squints in the study area was oriented roughly east-west to provide a view to high altars, for reasons that will be discussed later. However, examples from the north aisles at Bradford-on-Avon (Fig. 56) and Churchill (Fig. 57), and the south chapels at Urchfont and Whitestaunton (Fig. 59), were oriented north-south and provide a view *across* the church, and not to the east-end of the chancel, suggesting a visual relationship between subsidiary altars.

Figure 22   Passage squints from Churchill, left, and Sherston.

Tombs

Although in the context of intercession it was not necessary for the corpse to be present, tombs often formed a major feature of chapel topography. A broad variety of tombs and memorials can be found in the area under study. Some of the earliest are what can be termed 'recess burials'. Here, a wall alcove provided an architectural setting for a tomb. Examples can be found at Bishopstone, Bridgwater, Freshwater and at West Lavington. Elsewhere, on the south wall of the Savage chapel at Macclesfield, there are two large decorated arches, the easternmost one opening into a small, lit recess containing the alabaster effigy tombs of John and Elizabeth Savage, c.1528. At Nettlecombe, the recesses took the form of two small chambers attached to the side of the south chapel. Nettlecombe and Crewkerne also furnish evidence for individual burials within the fabric of chapel walls. At Nettlecombe, in the east external wall of the chapel, a vertical ledger memorial suggests that the individual may have been buried standing up (Fig. 23). At Bridgwater, the link between the position of tombs and public visibility was more explicit, with the recess tombs being positioned outside the chapel. Here the tombs were adjacent to the public entrance of the church.

Ledger slabs and brasses often mark the position of burials under the floor and were the most common form of church burial in the medieval period.

Figure 23   East wall of Ralegh chapel, Nettlecombe, showing ledger stone of a possible wall burial.

Figure 24   Raised ledgers in the north chapel at Buckland Dinham.

Examples can be found at Boyton, Mere and Tichborne. In the north chapel at Brympton d'Evercy, a group of ledger slabs are clustered around a central Purbeck marble ledger inscribed with a cross, perhaps marking the burial of the founder. In the chapels of Buckland Dinham (Fig. 24) and South Wraxall, Wiltshire, the ledger slabs are raised several centimetres above ground level. Here, a desire to make these memorials more prominent may lie behind their arrangement.

Several large table or altar tombs survive in the research area, like those at Stoke Charity, Corsham, Ilchester and Long Ashton. At Ilminster, the tomb altar of William Wadham is highly elaborate, decorated with crocketed niches and the figures of Christ in Majesty surrounded by donors. Here, the use of decorative symbolism reinforced the link between such individuals, the tomb, and Christ and the saints as saviour and intercessors. The Oglander tomb at Brading is decorated with depictions of charitable acts on its north or 'public' side, and family members on its south chapel side, suggesting that its location may have particular visual implications (Fig. 25). At Corsham, the Tropenell tomb is inordinately large, suggesting that, in this example at least, a tomb may have also had a dual function, possibly as a 'table' on which to place liturgical objects, or as a subsidiary altar. In light of this, it may be significant that the construction of the Waller tomb in the early sixteenth century at Stoke Charity necessitated the insertion of a squint to provide a view of the tomb from the nave (Fig. 71).

Another form of tomb present in many chapels is the effigy tomb, probably the most expensive and most conspicuous mode of burial of the period and often made of high-quality materials. These tombs portrayed a real or idealised life-size representation of the entombed individual and were often highly deco-rated and painted. Evidence for painted effigies survives in the north chapel,

Figure 25 The Oglander tomb from the north chapel, Brading, showing depictions of charitable deeds juxtaposed with the Oglander family shields.

Yatton and south chapel, Bromham. Particularly fine individual examples of effigy tombs can be found at Godshill, Old Basing, Titchfield and Yatton. These types of tomb, as discussed below, may be an attempt to provide a visual reminder of the deceased in the context of the religious practices associated with chapels. Many tombs may have also acted as Easter sepulchres. They are usually found on the north side of the church, either in the chancel or in north chapels. Although many Easter sepulchres may have been temporary wooden structures, such as the 'box frame draped with cloths' at All Saints, Bristol,[12] some were more permanent. The presence of what may have been an elaborately decorated Easter sepulchre was integral with the construction of the north aisle at Bradford-on-Avon for the Birde and Horton chantries. Examples of tombs used as Easter sepulchres also survive at North Bradley, Ramsbury, Rodney Stoke and Stoke Charity (Fig. 26). Elsewhere, the tomb of John Clopton at Long Melford doubled as an Easter sepulchre.

Very often the Easter sepulchre was covered during Easter week. The churchwardens' accounts from All Saints, Bristol refer to iron 'riddels' which may have been used for altar or wall hangings.[13] At Stoke Charity, a large iron hook associated with the Waller canopied altar tomb on the north wall may suggest a similar fitting for the hanging of a cloth over this monument

---

[12] Burgess 1995: xxix.
[13] Burgess 1995: 35.

Figure 26 The Waller tomb and possible Easter sepulchre, Stoke Charity. This photo, taken from the chancel, shows that it was clearly visible from the high altar. It was also visible from the nave and north aisle. Note the small iron 'riddel' on the wall next to the tomb's top right-hand corner.

when used as an Easter sepulchre during Holy Week. It may also have been used for a hanging on anniversaries. Similarly, in the north chapel at Boldre, a series of metal fixtures on the north side of the east wall close to the site of the altar may have been used for the support of a wall hanging of some form, though in this case probably not an Easter sepulchre because of its proximity to the chapel altar. Certainly the location of the Boldre fittings, both close to the altar and in a highly visible setting, may suggest that they were used to suspend some form of 'curtains' or Lenten veil, used in many parish churches and testified to in some churchwardens' accounts and inventories, as at Mere.[14] A few Easter sepulchres have been displaced and are now to be found in other locations around the church, which is probably the case at Bradford-on-Avon. It is possible that many large recess tombs, such as those found in the south chapel at Bishopstone and the north chapel in North Bradley, may have also served as Easter sepulchres. In the north chapel at Portbury there is, unusually, no east window. However, the presence of an elaborate north window may suggest a former architectural emphasis in this area of the chapel. This may have been the location of an Easter sepulchre, or the 'St Helen sarcophagus' referred to in an early sixteenth-century will.[15]

As already seen at Montacute, many tombs and monuments were subject to removal or relocating. The two table tombs in the south chapel at

14 Jackson 1885.
15 Weaver 1903:108.

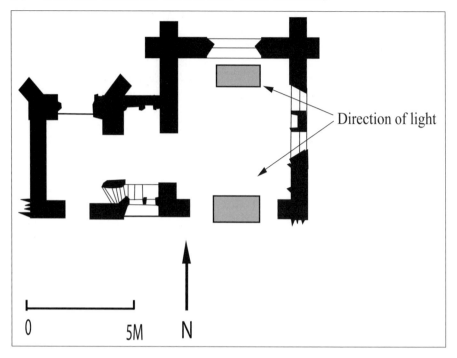

Direction of light

0   5M   N

Figure 27 The north chapel, Montacute, showing skewed east windows, direction of light and conjectured original location of tombs.

Whitestaunton are examples of this. Here, post-medieval flooring lies underneath at least one of the tombs, indicating that they have been moved. Another factor that aids reconstruction of former tomb location is that changes or additions evident within the church fabric might reflect what has been termed by Richard Morris a 'technical determinism'.[16] One example of this is the placing of church windows to act as natural spotlights in areas of liturgical or commemorative importance, such as an altar or tombs. The 'skew' in the chancel east window at Rivenhall, Essex, for example, was possibly an attempt to direct light onto an altar.[17] Similarly, the position of windows within particular areas may indicate the former position of tombs. In the north chapel at Montacute, two lancet windows in the east wall were skewed so as to direct light onto the north wall of the chapel and the south arcade. It is likely that the present medieval tombs within this chapel have been moved from their original positions. They were probably originally on the north wall and between the arcade to the chancel respectively. If this were the case, then the skewed arrangement of the windows was devised to highlight these areas (Fig. 27).

16 Morris 1989: 296.
17 Rodwell and Rodwell 1985: 133.

Evidence for the removal of a chapel tomb may also be found at Bradford-on-Avon.[18] Here, the brass and ledger stone to Thomas Horton is now displayed on the east wall of his former chantry in the north aisle. In the churchyard there is a table tomb, probably dating to the fifteenth or early sixteenth century. On one side of this tomb is the depiction of the crucifixion and it is likely that this tomb originally came from inside the church. There can be no doubt that many chapels contained more tombs than they do at present and, as a result of the Reformation or restoration, many have been displaced, destroyed or lost.

Altars

The altar was the fundamental element and the ritual focus of the chantry chapel. Essentially, it provided a physical setting for the celebration of mass and therefore the main focus for lay piety and devotion. Often richly adorned with cloths, lights, images and symbols, the altar played an essential role in eucharistic ritual. It was the stage for the complex symbolic re-enactment of Christ's passion and presence and the implicit promise of universal salvation. Pre-Reformation altars are rare. Many were dismantled, destroyed and sometimes used as floor slabs in the immediate Reformation period because of their association with the Catholic mass. A rare survival can be seen in the chantry under-crypt of St Alphege, Solihull, Warwickshire. Fragments of an altar stone also survive in the south chapel at Wedmore. In the chapel of St Nectan at Cheddar, an intact example survives complete with two consecration crosses still visible on the surface. Early Post-Reformation traditionalist altars survive in the Trinity chapel, Cheddar, where the Laudian altar of 1631 occupies the site of an earlier one. In the north chapel at Tichborne, there is a late sixteenth-century (and therefore forbidden) portable altar, replete with IHS motif and crosses. At Corsham, the stone screen from the north aisle into the chapel contains a ledge on either side of the entrance that may indicate the former presence of subsidiary altars or, alternatively, two *prie-dieus* within the screen itself.

The location of former altars can be reconstructed by examining the survival of related features such as piscinas, aumbries and sedilias. Evidence for plinths or wall supports and corbels may also suggest a former altar. Plinths survive at Buckland Dinham and Nettlecombe. Large ledges, as seen on the east windows of the chapels at Boldre and All Cannings, may also indicate the former presence of an altar, as does evidence of fittings for wall hangings, as seen at Boldre and Boyton. Areas surrounding former altars may also have been emphasised architecturally, for instance by the insertion of windows. At Urchfont, moreover, the likely site of the medieval altar was highlighted by the presence of decorated pilasters and figural sculpture. At Lacock, the ledges, niches and decorated recess on the chapel east wall would seem to suggest an emphasis on this area. Reredoses may indicate the site of a former altar as they were used as a decorated backdrop, as in the chapel of St Katherine

18   Doubtless many more were removed and are now lost.

at St Cuthbert's, Wells, and in the Lamb chapel at St John's, Devizes. At Mere, the site of a possible former altar in the south chapel is indicated by a raised platform containing ledger slabs. At Nettlecombe, a surviving patch of encaustic tiles at the east end of the Ralegh chapel may indicate the location of the chapel altar. The eastern panels of the wooden barrel ceiling in the north chancel chapel at Minehead contain significantly more panelling than the west, and are probably a deliberate decorative emphasis above the site of a former altar. Similarly, in the Sharrington chapel at Lacock, the eastern bay of the fifteenth-century lierne vault contains decorative and painted garlands and angels with the instruments of the passion, again to emphasise the setting of the altar. Such evidence not only reveals the architectural emphasis provided for the space of the altar, but also enables the reconstruction of ritually important areas (Fig. 28).

The presence of squints, to provide views of altars from different areas of the church, can also reveal both the former presence and position of an altar. In the north and south chapels at Old Basing the dimensions of the small squints indicate that, in all probability, they were for the use of a single individual, in this particular instance a priest. More importantly, this suggests the position of the altar that he was serving. At Old Basing the altar appears to have been located in the centre of the chapel and not at the east end. The reason was probably to provide a visual connection with the high altar in the adjacent chancel as well as in the opposite south chapel. The social implications of these features are discussed in more detail in the following chapter. At Boyton, the remarkable circular window in the west wall of the Giffard chapel was probably added at around the same time as the large

Figure 28 Detail of vaulting in the Sharrington chapel, Lacock. Note the architectural emphasis on the eastern panel above the site of the former altar (on right) using 'rosary' decoration on the ribs, and more elaborate bosses.

central tomb of Margaret Giffard in the second quarter of the fourteenth century, and hence possibly to accentuate this new memorial focus (Fig. 11). At Buckland Dinham, the large fourteenth-century window in the east wall of the north chapel is inserted off-centre, in the south side of the wall, to throw light directly upon the two Dinham tombs within, and possibly onto an associated altar that may have stood before them. At North Bradley, the fifteenth-century tomb of Emma de Stafford was a structural component of the recessed window above it.

Piscinas and aumbries

The piscina, a common feature of many parish churches, is a basin for washing mass vessels. Normally provided with a drain, they were usually set in or against the wall to the south of an altar. There is widespread evidence for the presence of piscinas in the study area. Out of the 80 examples, evidence survives in varying forms for 34 examples. In Somerset, evidence for 10 piscinas survives; in Hampshire 7 and in Wiltshire 17. Many piscinas from the study area are architecturally quite plain, such as the simple rectangular piscina from Bishops Cannings and the small Romanesque example from the north chapel, Minehead. Interestingly, this latter example must have been reused from somewhere else, as architecturally it predates the construction of the chapel. Decorated piscinas can be found in the Huse chapel, Cheddar, and in the north chapel at Brympton d'Evercy. This latter example consists of a hexagonal base corbel with trefoil arch head. That in the Huse chapel is a 'double-piscina'. Evidence from the south chapel at Great Chalfield indicates that some piscinas may have been painted. Some piscinas also contained a shelf (thereby doubling as an aumbry). Examples of this can be seen at Curry Rivel, the north chapel at Bishopstone, and in the south chapel at Mere. Certain chapels do not contain a surviving piscina, such as the Beauchamp chapel at St John, Devizes. This may be due to destruction, or obstruction, by later tombs and memorials, as in the Goddard chapel, Aldbourne. Furthermore, many piscinas may have been freestanding, an example of which partially survives at Stoke Charity. Like some windows, referred to above, a number of piscinas show evidence of being blocked (probably at the Reformation). Examples of this can be found at Ludgershall and in the south chapel, Aldbourne, where the former piscina is blocked by an early sixteenth-century tomb. Many chapel altars were dismantled at the Reformation, and hence many piscinas became defunct. This almost certainly accounts for the fact that so many have been lost.

An aumbry is a recess or cupboard to hold the sacred vessels used to celebrate the mass. In the research area there is surviving evidence for 11 examples, ranging from plain square cupboard-like features, such as found at Ilchester, to the more decorated types such as the ogee-arched decorated example from St Andrew's chapel, Cheddar. The example from St John's, Winchester appears to be incorporated into a squint from chapel to chancel. It is rare to find squints and aumbries together in the sample area. The only chapels containing both aumbries and squints are the north chapel at

Aldbourne and the south chapel at Lacock. However, the respective squints are so-called 'double' squints and may suggest more regular use. The south chapel at St John's, Winchester may contain a composite aumbry and squint, which may 'hold a key' to the alternative functions of some squints discussed in the next chapter.

Other fixtures and fittings

Evidence for some form of seating arrangement survives from many of the sampled chapels. One form of seating is the sedilia. These are seating arrangements normally reserved for priests or perhaps servers. Often they come in the form of three composite masonry seats positioned on the south side of the chancel, but some can also be found in chapels. Examples can be found at Boyton, Titchfield and St John's, Winchester. These are all on the south side of their respective structures. The sedilia in the south chapel at Boyton – perhaps unusually for a small rural church – has three seats. However, this particular arrangement is linked to the foundation of a college of priests here in the thirteenth century and may also relate to the number of people required for a high mass, rather than a votive one.

Evidence for substantial seating arrangements survive in the Tocotes and Beauchamp chapel at Bromham, and in the south chapel at Bishopstone. These seats appear to have been integral with the construction of these chapels and were clearly able to seat a dozen or so people. This may suggest, in these cases, the presence of the laity or a choir on certain occasions. In the guild chapel of Our Lady at Wedmore, where membership was open to all townspeople,[19] the bases of the arcade piers incorporate masonry seats. Furthermore, many chapels contain surviving evidence for bell-cotes, as in the south chapels at Bishopstone and Godshill. The small slits in the gables of the east ends of the chapels at Brading and Corsham may reveal the positions of former sacring bells. Such features may have been used to herald the elevation of the host within the chapels and to make those outside the chapels or in the town aware of this important moment. If so, the parish community was indirectly involved in that most important of religious celebrations (much like the 'call to prayer' in Islamic communities). In the south chapel at Mere, the stairwell in the centre of the south wall is intriguing. It appears to serve no obvious function other than to give access to the roof. Alternatively, it may have provided access to a screen that may have divided the chapel. It may also have provided access to a small bell tower or platform. A similar feature exists at Yatton in the north-east corner of the de Wyke chapel and may have served a similar function. In the north chapel at Curry Rivel, a possible blocked upper door has an external stair turret in the north-west corner of the chapel, suggesting the presence of a former screen and/or rood loft.

---

[19]   *VCH, Somerset* 1975.

Decorative and architectural features

The presence of masonry vaulting in many chapels, for instance at Bishopstone, Limington and Portbury, has been noted as being a comparatively 'unusual thing in parish churches',[20] particularly since in all these cases these are the only parts of the church to have such a feature. Impressive chapel fan vaults survive at Limington and Lacock, and ribbed vaults from Bishops Cannings, Bishopstone and Portbury. Other examples elsewhere include the masonry vault of the Wilcote chantry, North Leigh, Oxfordshire, which is unique to the county. In the Spencer chapel, Great Brington, Northamptonshire, the magnificent fan-vaulted polygonal-recessed bay window has clearly been influenced by that in the Henry VII chapel at Westminster abbey and perhaps serves to illustrate the dynastic pretensions of this particular family. Many masonry vaults have been victim to post-Reformation changes or 'restoration'. However, evidence can often survive. A vaulting shaft fragment in the north-west corner of Our Lady of the Bower chapel at Bishops Cannings reveals the presence of a former vault, as do the fragments of what must have been quite an impressive fan vault at Ilchester. Many chapels also contained wooden ceilings. Fifteenth-century examples survive from Stoke Charity and the chapel of Holy Trinity at St Cuthbert's, Wells. Evidence for painted ceilings survives, for example at Lacock and in the Swayne chapel at St Thomas, Salisbury. Elsewhere, a good example, though restored, can be seen in the Rose chapel at Salle, Norfolk. Apart from ledger slabs, floors were often tiled, as at Limington, Nettlecombe and Stoke Charity. It is likely that at Brympton d'Evercy, and possibly at Bromham, Mere and Tichborne, much of the floor space was taken up by ledger slabs, in these cases (no doubt highly polished) Purbeck marble.

A wealth of architectural detail, fixtures and fittings as well as decoration thus survives from the sampled chapels and chantries in the research area. But much is lost, especially in the form of pre-Reformation imagery and movable or temporary decorations, such as hangings, altar cloths and vestments. In many places, the location of former icons is evident in the form of image corbels, for example at Boyton and at St John's, Winchester. Elaborate canopied niches survive at Cheddar and Montacute, Stoke Charity and Ramsbury. Within the chapel of St Katherine at St Cuthbert's, Wells, there is a carved reredos, containing several niches, which was originally defaced, hidden behind the east wall, and only revealed again in the nineteenth century.[21] The placing of niches, as will be shown in the next chapter, can reveal much about the ritual topography of such chapels. Images acted as the focus for either personal or collective devotion. In some cases, the chapel altar may have been associated with the image as a devotional focus, rather than the other way around. In the south chapel, Droxford, the statue that such a niche was meant to display was intended to be highly visible, and may have been directly visually associated with the altar (Fig. 29). At Urchfont, the niche formed part

[20]   Biver and Howard 1909: 7.
[21]   Ferrey 1851.

Figure 29
Canopied niche and
altar in the south
chapel, Droxford.

Figure 30
The remains of the
'Jesse' reredos in the
Tanner chapel, St
Cuthbert's, Wells.

of sculptured reredos, which would have been part of a composite setting for the chapel altar. Painted images survive on screens at Long Ashton, while evidence for sculptural depictions of biblical scenes and stories survive at Brympton d'Evercy. There is a defaced 'Jesse Reredos' in the Lady or 'Tanner' chapel at St Cuthbert's, Wells (Fig. 30).

At St Bartholomew's, Ducklington, Oxfordshire, the north aisle, possibly the chapel of the Dyve family in the thirteenth and fourteenth centuries, was decorated with elaborate flowing tracery on windows with a continuous string course of ballflowers and motifs of the coronation of the virgin in tracery of the east window (which would have linked with stained glass). There are also some disfigured sculptures depicting the life of Mary. The aisle contains two ogee-recesses decorated with vines and grapes which issue from a crouched figure in the point where the canopies meet, possibly representing the biblical Jesse. In the Lane aisle at Cullompton, the slim internal buttresses are beautifully carved with various personal and religious symbols. The interior of the Sharrington chapel at Lacock was decorated with sculptured and painted images of plants and flowers and small animals that dangled and crawled around its arches, piers and shafts (Fig. 31). Such an effect may have promoted a sort of natural forest glade effect to the chapel's interior, and may have

Figure 31
Detail of pier shafts in Sharrington chapel, Lacock, showing defaced painted animal carvings.

Figure 32   'Lily-cross' from south 'Leigh' chapel, Godshill.

sought a particular aesthetic response. Many other chapels in the research area contain, to various extents, rich decoration in the form of canopied niches (no doubt once containing beautiful devotional images), sculptures and wall paintings.

The survival of images in painted form is particularly rare, though examples do survive from a number of the sample chapels. It seems that this sort of decoration really does appear to have been common, but was to become a major casualty of the Reformation. Where examples do survive they testify

Figure 33
Detail of glass from the Dauncey
chapel, West Lavington, showing
the juxtaposition of the family
initial 'D' in the quatrefoil design
with chalice and Eucharistic bread.

to the importance and quality of such adornment. The north wall of the
Swayne chapel at St Thomas's in Salisbury depicted scenes from the life of
the Virgin, while that at Great Chalfield depicted St Katherine. The east wall
of the Hampton chapel at Stoke Charity was painted with various religious
scenes. On the north wall of the chapel of St Anne, Farleigh Hungerford, is
a remarkable painting of a warlike St George, an image which may particularly reflect the martial connections of the Hungerford founders. In the Leigh
chapel at Godshill, the elaborate painting of Christ on the lily cross depicted
on the east wall is particularly striking (Fig. 32). However, it is interesting
to conjecture that what we might have here is a form of rebus. Is the 'lily'
a play on words for the name Leigh, such as 'Leigh, Leigh' or 'le Leigh'? If
so, then the usage of this depiction becomes more obvious, in that it identi-
fies the chapel's founder whilst juxtaposing his name with that of the image
of Christ – a potentially powerful intercessory tool. At Ewleme, and in the
Frowyk chantry chapel at South Mimms, Middlesex, evidence survives for the
use of IHS motifs on the walls. Medieval stained glass rarely survives from
chapels and chantries of the period, though images do survive in this medium
at All Cannings, Farleigh Hungerford, Nettlecombe and Stoke Charity. In
the Trevelyan chapel at Nettlecombe, a stained-glass heraldic device of the
Walesburg family is reversed and may indicate that it was to be viewed from
the outside, although such inconsistencies in stained-glass design and placement may be relatively common.[22] A significant stained-glass survival is that
in the west window of the Dauncey chapel at West Lavington. Though the
glass has doubtlessly been moved to its present position, its imagery is nonetheless intact, and depicts the ornate gothic 'D' of the founder's family juxtaposed
with a chalice and eucharistic bread (Fig. 33). This indicates an earlier inter-

[22]   Caroline Barron pers. comm: 2002.

cessory function for what has been termed a post-Reformation private chapel for the Dauncey family.[23] It thus calls into question the dating of the arcade emblazoned with the 'D' motif, to the late sixteenth century, as well as the tombs, and suggests a pre-Reformation date for this chapel.

Spatial analysis

Location

Analysis of chapel location can reveal patterns with regard to the placing of chapels in particular areas of the parish church. Trends within the sample area indicate that the placement of chapels towards the east end of the parish church was becoming increasingly common in the fifteenth century (Figs 34–36). Such patterns, which may be due to restrictions in space, liturgical change or a desire for a more 'exclusive' location, will be discussed more fully in the next chapter.

[23] VCH Wilts 1953: 203.

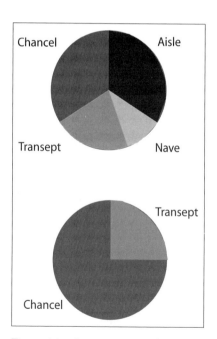

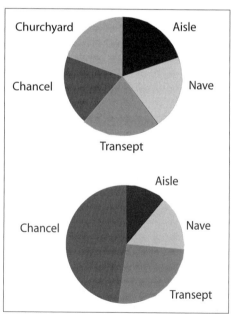

Figure 34 Comparative graphs showing the location of sample foundations pre-1400 (top) and post-1400 (bottom) in Hampshire.

Figure 35 Comparative graphs showing the location of sample foundations pre-1400 (top) and post-1400 (bottom) in Somerset.

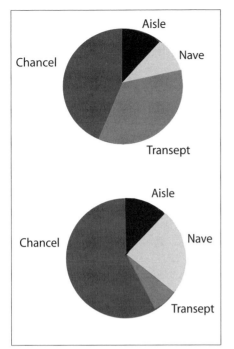

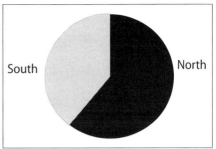

Figure 37 Orientation of sample chapels in Hampshire (17).

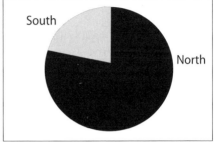

Figure 38 Orientation of sample chapels in Somerset (36).

Figure 36 Comparative graphs showing the location of sample foundations pre-1400 (top) and post-1400 (bottom) in Wiltshire.

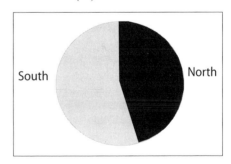

Figure 39 Orientation of sample chapels in Wiltshire (27).

Orientation

The particular orientation of chapels, with regard to locations on the north or south side of the church, may be of interest and may reveal evidence for other trends in chapel foundation. In Somerset, almost 75% of the sampled chapels were situated on the north side of the church (Fig. 38). In Hampshire the percentage is close to 60% (Fig. 37). However, in Wiltshire the figure is under 50% (Fig. 39). Nevertheless, in this latter case, around 50% of this percentage may have had already pre-existing chapels to the north, such as at Aldbourne, All Cannings, Bishopstone, Ludgershall and Mere.

View-sheds

View-shed analysis is the examination of former sight lines within the parish church. It can allow for the reconstruction of relationships between subsidiary altars, the conscious positioning of tombs within lines of sight, and the visual relationship between chapels and parish church. Spatial analysis of chapels and chantries and their relationships to the church indicates the potential for private and public participation, in particular with regard to visual relationships. Informed observation can be used to reconstruct parish topography and relevant lines of sight, particularly with regard to the placing of altars, monuments and squints. This reconstruction also allows for the consideration of proxemics, or proximal relationships between tombs, altars and windows, and may reveal how these were consciously positioned in relationship to other monuments or religious foci (Figs 40, 41). The implications of these reconstructions, highlighted by further examples, will be discussed in more detail in the next chapter.

Access

Spatial analysis of chapel topography also involves the consideration of doorways and how access may be restricted or otherwise to chapels from various parts of the church. The results from the research area are inconclusive but nonetheless provide information regarding structural evidence for the insertion

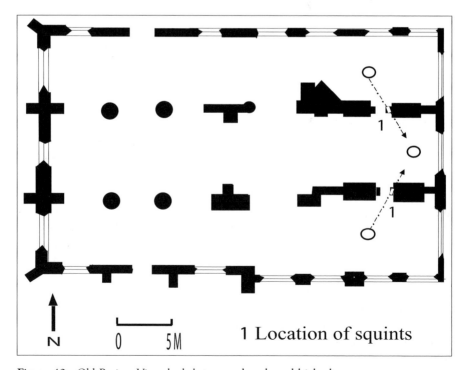

Figure 40 Old Basing. View-sheds between chapels and high altar.

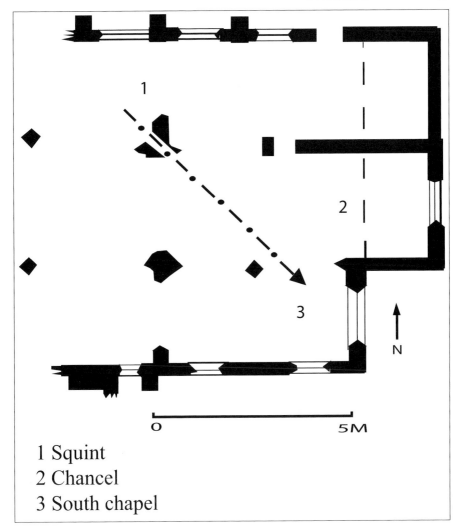

1 Squint
2 Chancel
3 South chapel

Figure 41 St James's, Taunton. View-sheds between chapels.

and blocking of doorways, which may be suggestive of changes in the use of chapels over time. Fourteen chapels in the research area have evidence for separate doorways, for example, Binsted, Crewkerne, Devizes, Ilchester and Stogumber. Archaeological evidence exists for the presence of former doorways at some sites. At West Lavington and Whitestaunton, the doorways were clearly blocked up at some point. In the north chapel at Aldbourne, a gap in the base mould that predates the fifteenth-century window suggests the presence of a former doorway. At Ramsbury, the eighteenth-century doorway clearly had a predecessor. Here, the medieval mouldings have finished terminals, suggesting an earlier door. Some chapels, such as the Spencer chapel at Great Brington, Northamptonshire, were clearly off-limits to the general parishioners. Here the separate doorway and wrought-iron railings indicate that, in this instance, the chapel was for the exclusive use of the family. However, on the whole, wider evidence suggests that many chapels were generally accessible from public areas of the church, either from the nave or aisles, and even where screens exist, doors are often present.

In conclusion, despite the destruction and re-organisation of medieval chapels and chantries in the centuries after the Reformation, much survives to enable the reconstruction of the form, fabric and fittings of such structures, especially when examined collectively. Archaeological study can therefore reveal the various types of chapels and how they involved reconstruction or innovation in ritual space. Importantly, an archaeological approach allows for the examination of what can be termed strategies for intercession – that is, how the location, fabric and physical environment of the chapels were arranged and manipulated to express the religious and intercessory motivations of both founders and local communities. Having analysed the component parts of chapels in the sample area, it is now worthwhile to give an overview of the material gathered and to place it in its wider context.

PART III

CHANTRY CHAPELS:
THE WIDER CONTEXT

6

The Social and Religious Context of Chantry Chapels in the Medieval Parish Church

Introduction

This chapter assesses and interprets the evidence presented in the previous chapter in light of relevant documentary sources and, particularly, comparative studies, and will consider the foundation of chantry chapels in a wider social and religious context. In particular, it will assess what the previous analysis of chapel fabric, fixtures and fittings can tell us about how the chantry chapel worked in practice. First, this chapter will consider the social dimension of chantry and chapel foundation, specifically considering the evidence for the actual presence of the laity in chapels, and the overall contribution of chapel and chantry foundation to communal religious practice in the parish church. The various forms of chapel will then be discussed and the spatial relationships between chapel monuments, such as altars and tombs, and chapel orientation. This will provide an insight into how so-called strategies for intercession were created and enacted within chapel fabric and layout. Finally, the importance of vision in chapel religious practice will be investigated.

Chapels and chantries: the social dimension

Central to the foundation of a chantry was the mass, indeed the *raison d'être* of the chapel was to provide a physical context for eucharistic celebration. As we have seen previously, an association with the ritual of the mass with personal intercession had been long-standing by the late medieval period and overall it indicates the quantitative value of the mass as a unit of direct beneficial merit. During this period, therefore, the mass was paramount. As well as being the central Christian rite, its performance was also seen in the context of intercession as a unit of cumulative merit: the more masses said, the less time spent in purgatory. This relationship between the number of masses and time spent in purgatory led Richard Weyvyle in 1417, for example, to request 3,000 masses to be said for his soul in the three days immediately after the day of his death.[1] Quite how this feat was actually accomplished, however, is not known. Linked with the popularity of the mass was the important theme of Christ's sacrifice or passion re-enacted symbolically at the elevation of the host, the most important element of the mass. Visual representations of the passion, from wall paintings and hangings through to glass and sculpture, set it in full visual context and were intended to 'remind the onlooker of the judgement when the individual's response to Christ's sacrifice would be decided'.[2] As a result, and coupled with images of the Doom and scenes from the lives of saints, they would act as a set of visual stimuli to prompt action in pious devotion and works of good.

By the sixteenth century, at the very least, it has been claimed that the low mass was the typical form of eucharistic practice.[3] Certainly this was also the most common form of chantry mass and it can therefore be argued that chantry foundation played a major role in promoting the prominence of the low mass within church practices. Saying a low mass also helped fulfil priestly obligation to celebrate once a day. In fact, as a priest could only celebrate mass once a day, new livings were created to provide for these extra chantry masses. The low mass was relatively short and could be performed by the priest himself assisted by a single minister, or even 'just answered by the congregation themselves'.[4] This latter factor also facilitated the fact that a living founder could actually assist in his or her own devotion in a very real way, by actively participating in the ritual itself. Consequently, it has been argued that it offered the laity a context for saying vernacular prayers, which they might substitute for the Latin text of the liturgy as part of their own personal worship.[5] Founders undoubtedly exercised a major influence on the form and location of their respective chapels and chantries, and also on the liturgy performed within them. For example, Thomas Lord Burgh of Gainsborough, Lincolnshire, was able to specify which masses he wished to be performed in his chapel, namely to the Holy Trinity (Sunday); Holy Spirit (Monday); Mary Magdalene (Tuesday); Requiem (Wednesday); All Saints (Thursday); Jesus (Friday) and the Blessed Virgin on the Sunday.[6] In contrast, the will of John Maudeley of Wells on the eve of the Reformation in 1540 specified 'a virtuous priest' to perform for a specific period a 'Masse of Requiem and Masse of (the) fyve Wounds with this psalme "miserere mei Deus and De Profundis"', as well as every Friday to sing psalms of the Passion, and David's psalm once in the Advent and once at Lent.[7] Other stipulations included the precise timing of services. The instructions for the chaplain of Simon Ralegh's chantry at Nettlecombe specified that the mass was not to be celebrated before 10 o'clock to enable his wife and heirs to attend it.[8] As well as the mass, some priests

1   Weaver 1903: 80.
2   Burgess 2000: 47.
3   Cobb 1978: 437.
4   Dix 1945: 599.
5   Dix 1945: 599.
6   Richmond 1994: 198 – 9.
7   Weaver 1903: 59.
8   Wood-Legh 1965: 293.

were requested to also perform other celebrations, more commonly the *placebo* – the service normally appointed to be said on the eve of the funeral – and the accompanying *dirige*. They may have been carried out as regularly as once a day or whenever else stipulated.

It would appear that, should they wish to, the laity may also have attended these celebrations, particularly the mass. Several churchwardens' accounts testify to the presence of seating arrangements in chapels. At Ashburton, Devon, for example, money was provided for the making of 'a seat' in 'the aisle of St Thomas'[9] and later in the 'aisle of St Mary'.[10] We are also informed that at Ashburton, money was provided in 1539 for 'a deske'.[11] Butcher describes this feature as a lectern, but it is equally possible that it was a *prie-dieu*. Certainly there is evidence that the Islip chantry chapel at Westminster Abbey had such a feature at this period. At All Saints, Bristol, the churchwardens recorded that 'they made seats in the church before St Dunstan's altar',[12] very likely the site of the Halleway chantry.[13] At Mere, we hear of tables, seats and a 'desk',[14] and in the will of John Stourton we are informed of the installation at his request of a 'reading desk' by his tomb'.[15]

Despite the fact that certain later chantries and chapels were located closer to the chancel, they were still accessible from more public areas of the church. Furthermore, it can be suggested that in some instances, and perhaps only on special occasions, the general laity may have obtained access to the chapel itself. Evidence for substantial seating arrangements survive in the Tocotes and Beauchamp chapel at Bromham, and in the south chapel at Bishopstone. These seats appear to have been integral with the construction of these chapels and were clearly able to seat a sizable number of people, suggesting, in these cases, the presence of the laity on certain occasions. In the guild chapel of Our Lady at Wedmore, the bases of the arcade piers contain masonry seats. It is possible that the 'seats' referred to as being in front of St Dunstan's altar, or the Halleway chantry at All Saints, Bristol, may have been of the same, albeit more temporary, form.

The space and size of certain chapels indicate that they were built to accommodate more than a priest and a few exclusive individuals. In many urban churches, significant space was appropriated by chapels and chantries. Almost half of the internal space of Holy Trinity church, Coventry, was taken up by chantry and guild chapels. The latter included the Mercers', Tanners' and Butchers' chapels. At St Thomas's, Salisbury, there were already fourteen chantry priests attached to the church by 1394.[16] This implies a potentially crowded and busy church in which lay access and participation could hardly be restricted in practice. In a smaller town like Old Basing, the north and

9   Butcher 1870: 19.
10   Ibid.: 20.
11   Butcher 1870: 26.
12   Burgess 1995: 14.
13   Ibid.: 28.
14   Jackson 1885: 326.
15   Weaver 1901: 145.
16   Tatton-Brown 1997: 104.

south Paulet chapels are over two-thirds the size of the nave. At West Dean, Wiltshire, the Borbach chantry, which comprised the south aisle, accounted for nearly half of church space and in fact the aisle remains the parish church presently due to the destruction of the old nave in the nineteenth century. It is likely, therefore, that many chapels and chantries were not necessarily totally off-limits to the laity. At Ashburton, the 'separate altars' were often surrounded by 'minute bodies called lights sustained by groups such as "the maidens", "the bachelors" and the "married wives"'.[17] This indicates the indirect influence of the laity on the ceremonial setting of these altars, and its intimate contact with it. More specifically, William Caxton in the *Doctrinal of Sapyence* informs us that the laity 'stand so nyghe the aulter that they trouble oftimes the preest'.[18] The will of John Pympe of Nettleshead, Kent, requested that his parclosed chapel 'be of no more widnesse than is needful that oon halfe for the prest and his clerke that other halfe for theme that shall knel wtin'.[19] This indicates that there were participants besides those directly involved in the liturgy being celebrated within the chapel.

From the fifteenth century, chantry founders increasingly relied on parish churchwardens, as well as worthy members of the community, for the welfare and running of their chantries and chapels.[20] By 1500, the laity, in the form of churchwardens, were commonly the trustees of parish chapels and chantries and often integrated other institutions, such as municipal bodies, in the 'complex web of supervision mechanism'.[21] At St James's, Bristol, the Spicer chantry was sustained by a long-term investment strategy devised and controlled by the churchwardens.[22] As a result of such public involvement, chantries could, as in the case of St Mary-at-Hill in London, 'yield a healthy annual income' for the parish,[23] although the chantries and chapels themselves often had a more direct role in the spiritual welfare of the laity. Vestments, vessels and books could be loaned from the chapels and chantries on feast days.[24] Chantry priests were indispensable during particular busy times in the parish calendar, particularly Easter.[25] They may have also acted as confessors, as from the Fourth Lateran Council of 1215 confession was obligatory at least once a year.[26] Admittedly though, we have no direct evidence that it was necessarily strictly adhered to in all instances.

17   Rubin 1991: 141.
18   Duffy 1992: 112.
19   Livett 1909; Graves 2000: 80.
20   Burgess 1996: 250.
21   Kümin 1996: 16.
22   Burgess 1985: 60.
23   Burgess 1996: 278.
24   Duffy 1992: 122.
25   Kümin 1996: 160.
26   Brooke and Brooke 1984: 118.

On a wider social scale, many chantry foundations involved the provision for a school or institutions of welfare. At Ewelme, Oxfordshire, a school was founded in 1437 by the earl and countess of Suffolk, and the priests of the Buckingham chapel, Buckinghamshire, are believed to have been the first schoolmasters of what became known as The Royal Latin School. At Dennington, Suffolk, the chantry in the south aisle was also used as a school room and the original abacus and a sand word-tray still survive.[27] There are no similar survivals in the study area, although schools were certainly founded as a part of chantry foundations at Ramsbury[28] and Ilminster,[29] as well as at Crewkerne and Bradford-on Avon.[30] In Alton, the chantry commissioners noted 'a stipendiary priest, founded by one John Champflour to teach children grammar'.[31] At Bradford-on-Avon, the school associated with the chantry foundation of Thomas Horton in the early sixteenth century was governed by Carthusian monks from nearby Hinton charterhouse.[32] In this case, it can be seen that such a school, and thereby the parish community, would have benefited from the influence of the Carthusians, a particularly austere and scholarly order. At Godshill, the extant chantry certificate states that the chantry priest was also to teach grammar to the local children.[33] Chantry priests also had a wider religious role in their parishes, often helping out with or supplementing the work of the parish priest, particularly on busy occasions. At the dissolution of the chantries at Bradford-on-Avon it was reported by the commissioners that there were no priests to help the vicar apart from the chantry priest.[34]

Other examples of broader social activity occur at Bishop's Stortford, Hertfordshire, for instance, where the chantry priest paid for repairs to the church battlements. On one occasion at Bishop Stortford the chantry priest organised a 'drinking' for his parishioners.[35] The chantry inventories for the chapels at Mere include, among other items, tables, boards, dripping pans and 'brass posts',[36] suggesting perhaps similar organised communal events here. In the 1470s, Richard Choke founded a chantry in the chapel of St Mary, also called 'Meryattes chapel' in the parish church at Long Ashton, Somerset.[37] The foundation required a priest to sing masses 'solemnly by note' and also provided for the repair of local bridges and roads. At Ilminster, the chapel founded by John Wadham and dedicated to St Catherine, provided yearly payments to poor prisoners.[38]

---

[27]   Thompson 1947: 144.
[28]   VCH *Wilts* 1986: 44.
[29]   Gowring 1886: 38.
[30]   Orme 1976.
[31]   VCH *Hants* 1903: 480.
[32]   Orme 1976: 117.
[33]   Chantry Certificate E301/51.
[34]   Walcott 1876: 22.
[35]   Doree: 1994: 46.
[36]   Jackson 1885: 326.
[37]   Green 1888: 93, 275–277; Weaver 1901: 240.
[38]   Green 1888: 1–2.

The primary function of either chapel or chantry – as a context for personal intercession – was to provide a context for public piety. It depended on forming a relationship between the founder and the ordinary laity, and a relationship with the mass as its central and pivotal medium. The foundation of a chantry provided more masses in a period when the increase in divine service was particularly valued. The prayers of the community were valued: the more prayers, the more powerfully enhanced the ritual. The public, in turn, benefited from even more elaborate and plentiful ceremonies, the protective powers of the eucharistic ritual and the spiritual efficacy of the mass in general. Some of these effects, for example, are detailed in the *Lay-Folks Mass Book* written by John Myrc in the fifteenth century and include, amongst other benefits, protection from sudden death, ageing and lack of food.[39] Masses could also be said for protection against storms, trouble of the heart and temptations of the flesh.[40] Such benefits indicate a belief in the ability to influence both natural and personal predicaments. Some chantry foundations perhaps served as a context for personal reflection and prompted even more assiduous intercession for members of one's own community. Intercession itself offered access to temporal as well as spiritual favours when associated with alms and education and other systems of communal welfare, which provisions were inherent in many chantry foundations. Intercession also offered protection and reduced a psychological sense of helplessness. It provided security in a time of uncertainty. Very often the chantry mass was the 'morrow mass', a mass held at dawn for those who would be working during the day when the parish mass was celebrated. As such it would have provided spiritual succour for a significant number of the laity who would otherwise have been deprived of a chance to participate.[41] In some examples, bell-cotes, such as those in the chapels at Bishopstone, Godshill and Mere, may have been used to give notice of religious observances for those nearby. The location of some chantries, often in the aisles or side chapels, also brought the mysteries of Christ's passion closer to the worshippers, bringing the celebration of the mass, that most important of Christian rites, out of the exclusive confines of the chancels and into the inclusive body of the church itself. As a consequence, this allowed closer visual communion with what was seen as the real presence of Christ and its inherent promise of salvation.

At another level, chantries and chapels played an important role in the highly symbolic world of late medieval spirituality, which was made progressively more accessible to the laity. Chantries and chapels were the setting for the highly ritualised celebration of the mass, and provided a medium of communication between the laity and Christ's passion, as well as that between the living and the dead. There was something for everyone in the elevation of the host; 'for the mystic and the irretrievably mundane, the devout individualist and the communal fanatic'.[42] Transubstantiation itself offered not only

---

39   Peacock 1902: 10.
40   Warren 1913.
41   Duffy 1992: 140.
42   Bossy 1991: 148.

the potential of salvation, but also the very act itself of the bread turning to flesh offered a very real message of transformation. One could aspire to change. The mass therefore offered a message both inspirational and relevant to all. The association of the chapel, and therefore its founder, with intercessory images, as well as the juxtaposition of intercessory images or symbolism with familial devices, acted as an associative catalyst for intercession. Thus, at the north Paulet chapel at Old Basing, the symbols of St Peter and the Virgin Mary, juxtaposed with those of the founder, forged a link between the perpetual ritual and the soul of the deceased. The same applies to the synthesis of religious image and the play on words of the Christ on the lily cross in the Leigh chapel, Godshill. In a sense, intercessory ritual inevitably prompted a sort of sub-conscious remembrance in the observer. Pamela Graves calls the use of such methods and devices a 'powerful technology for salvation' and a means by which prayers are 'tricked' or indeed 'stolen' from people.[43] To the medieval mind, the association of the individual with the ritual of the mass acted as an *aide mémoire* and as such would be an indirect and mnemonic petition for prayer. However, this relationship was not purely one-way, as the spiritual benefits of the mass, the increase in divine service afforded by individually founded chantry altars and the introduction of new and varied forms of devotional practice were beneficial to the whole community. They contributed to a varied and colourful religious experience. Furthermore, the associated embellishment and sometimes expansion of church space and fabric, afforded by personal endowments and related gifts, also indicate that the relationship was mutually beneficial.

This co-existence of both individual and communal dimensions emerged, it has been claimed, as a '*leitmotiv* of all parochial religion: personal efforts were indispensable elements in the quest for salvation, but many of their features contributed to the strengthening of communal ties'.[44] The mass was not just a sacrament, but also an important social institution in Pre-Reformation society, providing a focus for communal piety and group relationships.[45] In a society where world views were dominated by religion, shared participation in the mass provided a unifying principle to medieval communities and a universally understood proclamation of salvation. Chapels and chantries were pivotal to the inter-relationships between inward and public religion and indicative of the growing influence of lay priorities within parish life and structure. In this sense, the shared action of mutual prayers for the dead, as encouraged by the chantry, provided a 'state of pre-political, undifferentiated human affinity'. This universal state, it has been claimed, dissolved social tensions and bound people together, despite their inherent social differences.[46] Similarly, the state of purgatory, and therefore its remission, was open to everyone; rich or poor alike. This universal state was promoted by the use of ritual and symbolism. Far from being vain ostentation, the overt decoration of many chapels and

43   Graves 2000: 143.
44   Kümin 1996: 181.
45   Bossy 1983; Graves 1989.
46   Rubin 1991: 2.

chantries was used to reinforce a message,[47] a message that was essentially 'a sophisticated intellectual construction containing a vision of heaven, and a celebration of the history of salvation'.[48] More significantly, this was a message that was universally applied and understood by medieval communities. Decoration defined sacred space, providing a metaphysical setting for the rituals of intercession, and a colourful and emotive context for lay piety. One only has to go into a modern Eastern Orthodox church or indeed a Tibetan Buddhist temple, for example, to see the effect that light, colour, display and symbolism can have on the rituals enacted within, and on the way these rituals can be perceived by those observing or participating. The physical structure and decoration of medieval chapels was partly devised to induce a mood of reverence, to refine or sharpen the senses, and to engage the emotions with the spiritual truth that was both stated and enacted. The parishioners formed the congregation for which the celebration of the mass in chantries and at the high altar had significant meaning. But there was also a 'spiritual congregation' present in the various forms and images of the saints.

The cult of saints was an essential element of medieval religious practice and their images would have been visually prominent, and diverse, within many parish churches. They were therefore an important feature of everyday life and their role was 'not so much exemplary as that of helpers and intercessors in daily life'.[49] Their role as intercessors was often viewed in very practical terms, as is dramatically illustrated, for example, by the wall painting of the Day of Judgement in the parish church of South Leigh, Oxfordshire. The wall painting, which dates to only a few decades before the Reformation, shows St Michael literally weighing a soul on a set of scales. To his right is the watchful figure of the Virgin Mary who is clearly seen tipping the scales with her hand in favour of the examined soul. Such depictions provide a very visual indication of the role of certain saints as intercessors, particularly the Virgin Mary, who, being seen as a human being as well as the mother of Christ, was therefore viewed as being particularly empathetic to the human condition. At the well known example of Morebath, Devon, the icon of the local saint, Sidwell, was the subject of numerous gifts, in particular a set of silver shoes.[50] Images were also subject to regular bathing and dressing. Some images of the Virgin Mary in particular seem to have had quite an extensive wardrobe, and they were often dressed according to particular feast and religious days.[51]

Another important element in chantry ritual was sound. It is likely that such masses would have been sung (instead of recited), consequently providing a 'compound mnemonic effect' to chantry ritual[52] that would act as the verbal element to the visual setting. 'Unadorned plainsong', it has been claimed, 'formed the backbone of the liturgy and was customary in all

47   Burgess 2000: 46.
48   Goodall 2001: 165.
49   Marks 2004: 91.
50   Duffy 2001.
51   Marks 2004: 165.
52   Burgess 2000: 47.

parish churches'.[53] Chantry priests themselves, in some cases, were able to sing and play music, particularly organs.[54] Music lent 'liturgical distinction' to the rituals as well as compounding the mnemonic effect of the chapel's architectural features, symbols and images. Documentary evidence for organs exists for Andover, Hampshire,[55] though archaeological evidence is predictably scant at present. Many chapels contain post-Reformation organs, such as Alton and Binsted. A particularly early example survives at Brympton d'Evercy and may arguably (though admittedly tenuously) represent an early musical emphasis in this area.

Chapels and chantries, therefore, introduced a set of shared symbols for communal interactions. Indeed, it is perhaps no coincidence that the popularity of chantry-centred eucharistic practice, and particularly the lay influence behind them, coincides, to an extent, with the introduction of new types of devotions, such as that to the Five Wounds and the Rosary. Although such foundations were not directly responsible for their introduction, they certainly assisted in their widespread diffusion and popularity. Significantly, the main evidence that we have for such devotions is from chantry foundations,[56] and it has been claimed that one of the reasons why chantries were valued in parish churches was that they provided not merely *more* masses, but *particular* masses.[57]

An important element of chantry and chapel foundation was the construction, layout and ordering of church space. Archaeological examination of the architectural and structural setting and location of chapels can reveal how and why space was constructed or adapted to provide various strategies for intercession and, no less importantly, provide a context for communal religious practice.

Strategies for intercession I: Form and fabric

Documentary records, particularly wills, reveal the relative freedom of choice that testators exercised in the request for intercessory masses, burial and funeral arrangements. Likewise, surviving medieval chapels indicate a freedom of choice in the matter of their structure, location, appropriation and decoration. As Rosenthal has pointed out, they provide a context for 'individualized forms of institutionalised religion'[58] and suggest that those who commissioned them revelled in a diversity of expression. An important element of this (primarily archaeological) research is that not only does it consider the use of space in chantries and chapels, but also the fabric of space: the structural setting

---

[53]   Kümin 2001: 70.
[54]   Burgess 1996: 248.
[55]   Williams 1913: 4.
[56]   Michael Hicks pers. comm: 2002.
[57]   Duffy 1992: 370.
[58]   Rosenthal 1972: 49.

that encompasses and defines religious practice. Structural analysis enables an examination of the form of individual chapels and the processes of building, alteration, extension and rebuilding to which they have been subject over time. Such changes, it is argued, took into account both the needs of the founders *and* the community. Archaeologically, the constructional and material form of a chapel can be defined here as either an *adaptive* or *constructive* type. *Adaptive* chapels involved the appropriation, modification or reconstruction of existing areas, whilst *constructive* types involved the construction or creation of new church space.

Adaptive types

Adaptive chapels and chantries involved the reuse of existing space. This might mean the use of transepts, found for example at Binsted, Bishopstone and Crewkerne, or aisles, as at Bridgwater and South Wraxall. Certain of these *adaptive* types necessitated significant rebuilding, often visible in the surviving fabric; ironically, new work 'speaks' of much older use in these circumstances. At All Cannings and Bridgwater, the respective chapels have been rebuilt in superior materials. In the case of the Beauchamp chapel at All Cannings, the decorated parapet has been extended to encompass the parish church. Not only has the construction of the chapel provided more church space, it has also directly contributed to its overall embellishment. At Bridgwater, rebuilding phases can be seen quite clearly in the surviving fabric, largely via a change from roughly coursed red sandstone to Blue Lias (Fig. 9). Here it is likely that the former mortuary use of this part of the church, as shown by the crypt entrances and external recesses, was respected, if not deliberately maintained, in the consequent rebuilding phase. At Boyton, the remains of a slim buttress on the west wall cut by the insertion of the late thirteenth-century window (which coincide with the addition of sedilia, piscina and central tomb inside), would seem to indicate a change in use or purpose of this building as a collegiate chapel (Fig. 11).

Further significant factors might include the extension of pre-existing chapels, as noted at Brympton d'Evercy, Buckland Dinham and Yatton (Fig. 13). In each case, eastern adjuncts have been added to north chapels. Furthermore, there is evidence for separate altars founded within these extensions, with direct physical access between the old and new structures. These extensions may be indicative of a reaction to demographic change, or could have been meant to provide new ritual areas, or, more likely, to extend the chapels closer to the high altar as a place of particular spiritual efficacy – a trend that can be witnessed in other examples discussed below. In some cases, the foundation of a chapel or chantry necessitated the extension of an aisle, arguably to bring the chantry closer to the perhaps more exclusive, and certainly more spiritually potent, chancel. As discussed below, the south aisle at St Thomas's Salisbury was extended in the fifteenth century. Elsewhere, the extension of an aisle to facilitate chantry foundation can be seen at St Mary's, North Leigh, Oxfordshire, where the north aisle was extended, and provided with an impressive fan vault to form the Wilcote chapel. A similar pattern can be noted at Mere and possibly at Old Basing. In the latter, the position of a blocked squint in the west end of the chancel north wall may mark the position of a former altar situated at the east end of an earlier and shorter aisle. At Mere, the north chapel was extended in the late fourteenth century, probably as a result of the foundation of a chantry for the Bettisthorne family.[59] This change is marked internally by the presence of a late thirteenth-century door, now leading into the chapel, which was probably an original external entrance. Above this is a window of slightly earlier date as its sill is partially cut by the door arch, which likewise is now an internal feature. It is possible that these features were maintained to provide both physical and possibly visual access to the north chapel and chancel. At Ilchester, the small north chapel is of particular interest as it appears to have been extended eastwards by half a bay. Internally, there is evidence for vaulting in the western bay, but not in the eastern extension. It could be, in this case, that a vaulted porch or vestry has been extended and reused as a chapel.

Although arguably it may have been a cheaper option, a major factor behind the adaptive use of church space may have been the prominence given to existing sacred or important areas such as crypts, chapels or Lady chapels. At Cheddar and Corsham, for example, former Lady chapels were adapted to become chapels or chantry foundations. Many chapels, such as the south chapel at Wells and the north chapel at Lacock, were dedicated to the Virgin Mary, providing a dual, though not mutually exclusive, use as chapels and a focus for Marian devotion in the public sphere. At Bridgwater and Binsted, the former crypts of earlier structures were incorporated into the new foundations, perhaps suggesting a continuation of mortuary tradition.

Such changes may also have been necessitated by the foundation of further chantries and altars. Structural alterations, as a result of re-foundation or appropriation, can be reconstructed by examining changes within chapel fabric and topography. In the south chapel at St Thomas's, Salisbury, for instance, the chantry of William Swayne founded in the fifteenth century led to the rebuilding and extension of the old St Stephen's chapel. The probable reason behind the extension of the chapel space at this time was for the provision of an altar for the Taylors' Guild.[60] By the Dissolution, the south chapel had also been the site for the Brodgate and Warwick chantries. As will be seen below, similar changes in religious focus occurred three times over the space of 150 years at Stoke Charity. At Sherborne St John, appropriation of the former fourteenth-century Brocas north chapel led both to the insertion of the tomb of Ralph Perall, or 'Pexall' (c.1525), in the south arcade and the addition of a new window in the east wall of the chapel with the initials of its new patron emblazoned on the label stops.

Given that different chantries might be celebrated at the same altar, two or more chantries often used the same location, as at St Thomas's, Salisbury. In the case of St Thomas's, the extension of the space may have been meant to provide space for a larger group of people, or alternatively for the

[59] See Chapter 8 for a more in-depth discussion of this.
[60] VCH Wilts 1962: 149.

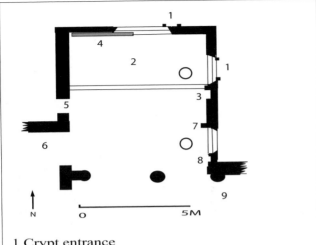

Figure 42
De la Bere chapel, Binsted. Note how the position of the two altars is revealed by the location of the two east windows and associated piscinas.

1 Crypt entrance
2 Raised dias
3 Piscina
4 Tomb recess with effigy of Richard de la Bere
5 Doorway
6 North aisle
7 Image pedestal
8 Piscina
9 Chancel

Figure 43
Wadham chapel, Ilminster, showing conjectured position of altars. Also note how both altars would be visible from other areas of the church via the north aisle and crossing.

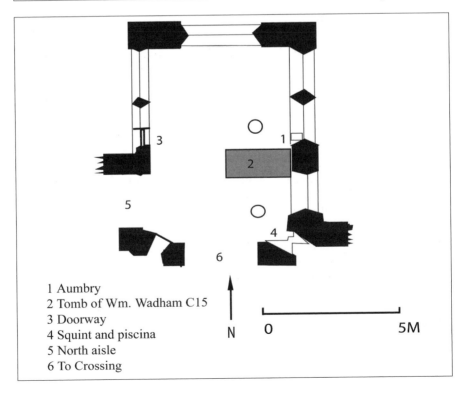

1 Aumbry
2 Tomb of Wm. Wadham C15
3 Doorway
4 Squint and piscina
5 North aisle
6 To Crossing

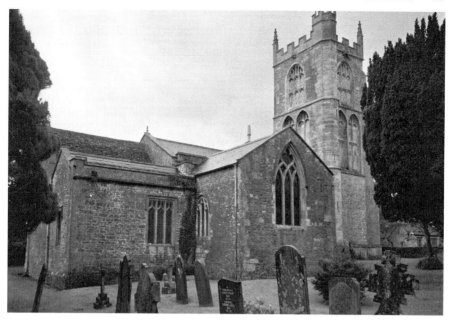

Figure 44   Buckland Dinham. Note the off-centre window in the east wall of the north chapel located to emphasize the area of altar/tombs in the south of the chapel.

two aforementioned altars. At Holy Trinity, Bradford-on-Avon, at least three chantries were founded in the north aisle: at the west-end by Reginald de Aula in 1420, from 1524 to 1540 by William Birde, and at the east end of the aisle by Thomas Horton who died in 1530.[61] Hence the reredos that is situated in the centre of the north wall of the north aisle represents either an altar, or, more likely, an Easter sepulchre associated with the Birde chapel. Similarly, two chantries were founded in the north transept at Bridgwater, and separated by a north-south running partition, now removed. The same arrangement seems to have been employed at St James's, Taunton, Somerset.[62] At Binsted, the north transept was rebuilt, probably in the fourteenth century. The presence of two piscinas indicates the presence of two former altars; that to the north, probably founded by Richard de la Bere, was arguably situated in the more prominent position, since it is placed on a raised platform above the crypt (Fig. 42). At Ilminster, evidence for two former altars also exists in the Wadham north chapel (Fig. 43).

Changes in the status or use of chapels sometimes afforded the architectural emphasis of new areas within them. In the early sixteenth century, a new window was inserted in the north wall of the Hampton chapel at Stoke Charity to emphasise the Easter sepulchre and tomb of John Waller. A squint was probably constructed at this time to give a view from the nave to this new

[61]   VCH *Wilts* 1953: 26.
[62]   Woodward 1982: 28,35.

ritual focus. In the north chapel at Buckland Dinham, a new west window probably emphasised the area occupied by the two slightly raised Dinham tombs of the fourteenth century. At a slightly later date, a further window was inserted in the east wall. This window is not centrally placed in the chapel wall and is slightly misaligned with the aforementioned opposite window in the west wall, as a result of the presence of the north chancel wall. A piscina and tomb in this area of the chapel suggest that the window was inserted to emphasise an altar formerly positioned here (Fig. 44). As noted, the large circular window at Boyton was probably inserted in the fourteenth century to emphasise the central area of the chapel where the effigy tomb of Margaret Giffard was placed (Fig. 11).

Constructive types

Constructive chapels are those that necessitated a purpose-built structure and in some instances represented a major structural undertaking. These sometimes involved the specific construction of aisles, for example at Bradford-on-Avon. Often an extra or outer aisle might be constructed to provide extra ritual space and to house chantries. The Lane aisle at St Andrew's, Cullompton, Devon, comprises an outer south aisle built by John Lane, a local wool merchant, around 1525. A new porch was also added in place of the west bay of the inner south aisle. Many chapels were founded in newly constructed transepts, such as the fourteenth-century de la Bere transept at Binsted. A unique arrangement can be seen at St Mary's, Scarborough, North Yorkshire. Here four chapels were constructed at the end of the fourteenth century which, unusually, were built side by side at right angles to the south aisle, extending from transept to porch. Generally speaking, the most impressive type of constructive chapel is the side-chapel,[63] like the impressive examples found at St John's, Devizes, and the Beauchamp chapel at St Mary's, Warwick, among many others. Of the 80 chapels sampled in the counties of Hampshire, Somerset and Wiltshire, nearly 70% (53) were of the *constructive* type. Prime examples would include the chapels at Basingstoke, Bromham, Godshill, Stogumber and Whitestaunton. Furthermore, in the research area all chapels constructed before 1300 were of the *constructive* type, such as Boldre, Boyton and Nettlecombe. This may indicate the direct input of the laity determining the early development of the parish church layout and use of space (as noted with earlier developments discussed in Chapter 3). The construction of such chapels represented a significant extension of church liturgical space, as well as the introduction of an increased lay influence within parish church structure and topography. At West Lavington, the construction of the Dauncey chapel

---

[63]   The labelling of chapel types can be problematic as the use of such architectural terms as 'side-chapel', and 'transept' and 'chancel aisle', are often interchangeable (with regard to chantry chapels). The issue is one of semantics and here such words only serve as a general guide to chapel location and not a difference in spatial function.

of the late fifteenth or early sixteenth century resulted in the complete demolition of the south transept.[64]

The construction of chapels reveals both the influence the laity exercised on the embellishment and expansion of church ritual space and its acquaintance with current architectural style. For instance, the Tocotes and Beauchamp chapel at Bromham far surpassed its parish church, both in embellishment and architectural sophistication. At Old Basing, the north and south chapels expanded ritual space in the parish church by at least a third. Moreover, at Old Basing, the fifteenth-century south chapel, constructed in brick, introduced a relatively new form of building material to an essentially rural parish church (Fig. 12). The impressive three-bay south aisle chapel at St Luke's, Gaddesby, Leicestershire is in stark contrast to the rest of the church, with its superior-quality stonework and elaborately decorated exterior containing a variety of interesting and imaginative architectural motifs.

Some of the more important chantry chapels in monastic foundations comprised two stories, often with a first-floor chantry and a tomb area below. Examples include the Henry V chapel at Westminster Abbey and the Edward IV chapel at St George's, Windsor. There are, in some rare instances, examples of two-storey chapels in parish churches, though of a slightly different arrangement. At Compton, Surrey, the east-end of the church comprised a sanctuary, with first-floor chapel above, and a connecting stairwell which may have also formed part of an anchorite cell. At St Alphege, Solihull, Warwickshire, the north chancel chantry chapel of Holywell consisted of a chapel with an undercroft, below which may have originally been a priest's chamber. At All Saints, East Horndon, Essex, there is a brick-built two-storey shallow south transept with a south gallery that leads to a priest's room with a fireplace.

As noted, many chapels and chantries were associated with porches, or indeed, as at Bridgwater, the construction of the north aisle chapels facilitated the construction of a porch. Here there may be a more explicit link between the foundation and construction of chapels and the expansion of communal space. At St Peter's, Tiverton, Devon, the south porch and chapel built by John Greenway in 1517 were clearly made to be seen as one composite structure. Both are highly decorated with personal motifs and religious symbols. Graves has noted that in the case of Cullompton, Devon, the construction of the porch created 'an architectural emphasis' on the south of the church and provided a 'kind of foregathering space'.[65] Such an emphasis would of course highlight the significance of the chapel as it is associated with the porch. At Bridgwater, the porch contained an internal window that allowed those in the porch to view the rituals held in the north aisle chantries. At the entrance to the porch are two large canopied niches and it could be posited that these may have contained an image, or possibly even two, connected with the chantry dedications. In some cases, where founders constructed multiple chapels in separate churches, one motivation may be associated with good works, as the foundation of chapels often provided more church space and extra priests

[64] *VCH Wilts* 1953: 203.
[65] Graves 2000: 143.

to often busy parish churches. Lord of the manor Richard Beauchamp may have had a major role in the construction of three chapels in Wiltshire, at All Cannings, Bromham and St John's, Devizes.[66] Certainly the architectural features at Bromham and Devizes suggest the same architect was used. In these cases the primary motivation may be to provide several contexts for accumulating intercession, but especially in the case of Bromham and Devizes, parish topography is also greatly expanded, and beautified, as a result.

As noted above, the parish church at Godshill has an unusual double nave and chancel. On the north side of the south chancel is the tomb of Sir John Leigh dated c.1529, although his chantry was within the south transept, off the south nave. The chancel and the Leigh chapel appear to be of the same date (late fifteenth or early sixteenth century); possibly the second chancel was constructed by Leigh as a form of public works to provide much needed extra space for the parish community. It is interesting that his tomb is in the chancel and not his chantry chapel, perhaps offering a gentle reminder to the parishioners of their most beneficent patron.

Chantries and chapels: personalised monuments in the public context

As noted previously, *surviving* archaeological evidence for chapels and chantries founded before the fifteenth century appears to show that they were generally located in the more publicly accessible parts of the parish church, such as in the churchyard, nave or aisles. From the fifteenth century onward, a period that coincides both with growing evidence for the enclosure of the countryside and parclosing,[67] the majority of chapels was constructed at the east end of churches, specifically near the chancel (see graphs detailed in Figs 34–36). Such a trend, it could be claimed, may reveal a move towards the 'privatisation' of religion as posited, for example, by Richmond and Carpenter among others,[68] as well as perhaps a shift in the traditional emphasis placed on public participation. However, it should be borne in mind that such available evidence concerns the issue of *surviving* features as opposed to a *representative* sample and does not take into account the number of altars and temporary chantries that did not survive physically. According to Thomson, the years after 1450 saw the greatest pressure of land enclosures.[69] Such social trends, it could be argued, may be reflected in increased privatisation of parish church space. Consequently, it may indicate, on one level, a trend towards exclusivity – a pattern that came to dominate the role of the chapel in the post-Reformation period. As noted above, a vast majority of surviving chapel screens date from the fifteenth century and could therefore reflect an increasing desire to separate chapels from other areas of the church and in

66 VCH *Wilts* 1975: 30.
67 Graves 2000: 81.
68 Richmond 1984; Carpenter 1987.
69 Thomson 1983: 43.

Figure 45
Detail of the screen
to Huse chapel,
Cheddar, showing
elevation squints.

effect provided a barrier to public religious practice – in effect, 'enclosing' one's chapel. However, archaeological study of screens reveals that in nearly all cases the height of the screen hid both the altar and most of the celebrant priest, but did not hide the elevation, the most essential element. Evidence for the insertion of 'peep-holes' or elevation squints in some church screens to allow those kneeling close to the screen, or children, to observe the elevation, supports this interpretation. They can also reveal both the public renegotiation of such barriers as well as the resultant tolerance and flexibility given over to it. To demonstrate this, some examples of 'peep-holes' in screens such as at St John's, Winchester, the Huse chapel, Cheddar (Fig. 45), and in the south chapel at Mere, indicate that the insertion of such breaches was reasonably unrestrained. In these examples the comparative intricacy, and therefore the time taken to insert these, could not have gone unnoticed. This is not to say that they were countenanced, but they were probably tolerated and it suggests how such potential obstructions could be renegotiated by the laity. There is even evidence that this factor was incorporated into later screen design, such as at Roxton, Derbyshire, and Cherry Hinton, Cambridgeshire.[70] At St Cuthbert's, Wells, the wall between the chapel of the Holy Trinity and the chapel of St Katherine to its east contains a window. This window was formerly external (before the latter chapel was added), but was possibly kept to provide visual access into the new chapel. A similar arrangement may also be found in the south chapel of St Thomas at Burford, Oxfordshire.

With regard to chapel location, as already noted, many chapels from the fifteenth century onward appear to have been placed even closer to the more prestigious east end of parish churches. This may suggest an element of exclusivity. In the research area, the Ralegh chapel at Nettlecombe, founded as a chapel possibly as early as the late thirteenth century, took the form of a wide south aisle open to the nave of the church. It was visually and physically a part of the church body. However, an additional chapel, added in the 1530s at the east end of the north aisle and connected to the chancel, was of a different nature. It was divided from the aisle by a screen and its location places priority in its association with the chancel. Likewise the two early

[70]   Vallance 1936: 41.

sixteenth-century north chapels at Minehead are integral to the chancel and were divided from the body of the church by a series of screens. At Montacute, entrance to the chapel was via the north porch that led into a small lobby to the west of the family chapel, which, like Nettlecombe, was positioned next to the chancel. A stairway from the lobby gave exclusive access to a room above the porch. The Spencer chapel at Great Brington, Northamptonshire, was sectioned off from the main body of the church with iron railings. It also had its own private entrance.

However, many chapels and chantries were nevertheless founded in more public areas of the church, such as the Horton and Birde chantries in the north nave aisle at Bradford-on-Avon and the Leigh chantry at Godshill. Undoubtedly, evidence for chantry chapels founded within church naves, such as at Burford and Chipping Norton, Oxfordshire, suggests the former presence of many more. More significantly, although some chapels and chantries may have been more *topographically* disconnected from the traditional public areas of the church, they were still accessible both *physically* and, more significantly, *visually*. Furthermore, it may be remembered, there is evidence to suggest the presence of the laity inside chapels at certain times. In many fifteenth and early sixteenth-century chapels – such as those at Bromham, Mere, Mottistone,

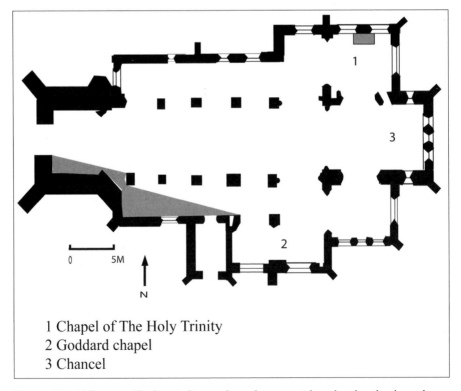

1 Chapel of The Holy Trinity
2 Goddard chapel
3 Chancel

Figure 46 Aldbourne. Shading indicates the only areas within the church where the view of all the altars is denied.

Nettlecombe, Old Basing, and Stogumber – access to the chapels was gained from public areas. Access to the Darrell chapel at Ramsbury could only be gained via the north aisle, as the chapel was separated from the chancel. But in all these examples, visual accessibility to the chapel altars, and ultimately the elevation, was in no way compromised. Where it may have been compromised, such as at Stoke Charity and Sherston, squints were constructed to provide a view of the chapel altars from the nave and aisle respectively.

In other examples, such as the Tropenell chapel at Corsham, and Sherborne St John, physical access from the chapel was obstructed by tombs, and at St John's, Devizes, by a masonry screen. In these cases, however, physical access was still from the primarily public areas. In those chapels that sought proximity to the east end, the motive may have been status or a desire to get close to the high altar as a place of particular spiritual efficacy. Nonetheless, the chapels and chantries within them still recognised and relied upon the public. Their location only had significance insofar as the associated rituals and ceremonies were valued by the whole community. The obvious visual obstruction caused by people situated close to piers aside, many chancel chapels, such as at Nettlecombe and Bromham, were visible from most areas of the church. At Aldbourne, examination and reconstruction of lines of sight within the parish church reveal that only from the very back of the church could a view of *all* altars within the church *not* be obtained (Fig. 46).

Location and orientation

The location, reconstruction and orientation of chantries and chapels reveal the direct influence of individual motivations on church fabric as well as the underlying concerns for intercession and how this could best be provided for. Analysis of chapel location or orientation – that is, its particular location either to the north or south, or to the east or west of the church – may reveal the motives and implications behind particular settings. For example, on one level, the location of a chapel in the east or west part of the church proves to be informative about its relationship to areas of public or clerical access, possibly emphasising the high altar as a place of particular significance. However, the motivations behind the location of chapels in either the north or south side of the church may be more complex and not immediately obvious. In some cases, such as the south chapels at Ludgershall and Old Basing, orientation of the structure may have been dictated by the pre-existence of a chapel already to the north. Similarly, the location of the chapel may also have been influenced by the location of burial plots, the site of the porch or on which side the town was situated, such as at Mottistone, where only the east wall of the Cheke chantry is decorated because this is the aspect that faces towards the town. In such cases, a priority may have been to make the chapel a highly visual monument. It is perhaps no coincidence that chapels like those at Bromham, Crewkerne and West Lavington were highly decorated externally with intercessory and secular motifs, such as heraldic shields juxtaposed with

Figure 47   The highly decorated and prominent canopied niche on the Tocotes and Beauchamp chapel, Bromham.

religious symbols. It is interesting that the entrance to the chantry chapel at Gaddesby, Leicestershire, is via a door encased in a highly decorated façade. At Bromham and Devizes, large image niches alert any observer to the function and status of the chapel. In a sense, the large niches and particularly their former images may have suggested the spiritual prominence of the chapel when compared with the rest of the church (Fig. 47). As noted above, some chapels may have been associated with porches, perhaps to attract public attention to them as well as to provide communal space.

Considerations underlying chapel location may therefore be of a practical as well as a religious nature. However, there is some evidence, particularly in Somerset and to an extent in Hampshire, that suggests that there was a desire to found chantries and chapels specifically on the north side of the church for eschatological reasons. As illustrated in the previous chapter, in Somerset almost 75% of the sampled chapels are situated on the north side of the church (Fig. 38); in Hampshire the percentage is close to 60%. One reason behind this may be the traditional association of the north side of the church with devotion to the Blessed Virgin Mary, as revealed by the foundation of Lady chapels, for example. However, it may also be argued that chantries and chapels founded on the north side of parish churches reflect, on the part of individual founders, an importance ascribed to the north side of the church in relation to death, memorial or traditional lay activity. Those found on the south side may reflect the presence of existing buildings in the north. They may also, in examples such as at Crewkerne and Bromham, demonstrate motives that were more status-driven, or alternatively placed especial emphasis on external display in a highly visual context. Hence, emphasis placed on the north side of churches for eschatological purposes may explain the intentions behind the foundations of chapels and chantries there. Evidence from wills also indicates that certain testators specifically requested burial within the north side of churches in the sample area. For example, at Yatton, in 1491, Thomas Browne specified that he was to be buried in the north side of the parish church, whilst at Portbury, Somerset, in 1457, John Bedill requested burial in the 'north part of the said church'.[71]

Motivations behind the specific orientation of chapels, possibly more spiritually driven than functional, may be hard to interpret. However, within an archaeological approach to the built environment, the concept of structuralism, derived largely from social theory, may be useful in the analysis of buildings, and the levels of meaning inherent within the use of space.[72] Essentially, structuralism is used in these instances to help articulate 'the essential theoretical position that the space defined by architecture does more than simply represent society'.[73] In this light, the location of chantries and chapels may reflect a sub-conscious categorisation of information about religious belief. Consequently, this may be reflected in the relevance given to physical location and particular orientation. Structuralist, and indeed post-structuralist, approaches to the study of buildings may reveal how sub-conscious motivations affect spatial and architectural arrangement. Specifically, Bourdieu's famous study of the Kabilye house has revealed that the spatial layout of domestic accommodation is subject to a set of binary oppositions, such as light and darkness, death and life, male and female.[74] Though there may be issues of over-generalising the data in such approaches, the categorisation of spatial phenomena may show possible sub-conscious patterns and directives that can be reconstructed by archaeological investigation. Using such perspectives, Gilchrist's study of gender and material culture has highlighted engendered elements of church topography.[75] In particular, she has commented on the location of the cloister on the north side of a significant number of nunnery churches (as opposed to male monasteries, where the cloister is in general on the southern side), and positioning of statues to the Blessed Virgin Mary and other female icons within north chapels and aisles.[76] Gilchrist, however, also discusses the importance given to the north side of the church in relation to death and commemoration and that the church can be seen as a metaphor for the body of Christ crucified.[77] According to this ideology, the wound in Christ's right side could correspond with the north of the church and was said to issue blood and water, so that it came to represent the eucharist (ibid). Gilchrist's recent research into the spatial use of the cloister and monastic church at Norwich has revealed similar patterns.[78] The roof bosses in the northern and eastern cloister are dedicated to the depiction of the

[71] Weaver 1901: 295 and 172.
[72] E.g. Ferguson 1996; Graves 2000; Giles 2000.
[73] Ferguson 1996: 3.
[74] Bourdieu 1977.
[75] Gilchrist 1989, 1994.
[76] Gilchrist 1994: 133.
[77] Ibid.: 140.
[78] Gilchrist 2005.

apocalypse and the salvation as well as the instruments of the passion. This may explain why we find the depictions of the instruments of the passion adorning the north aisle of churches such as at Churchill, as well as on tombs and monuments, such as at St John's, Winchester, (though this can in some instances also be found in several southerly placed chapels such as Bromham). Comparatively, in Scotland, Richard Fawcett notes: 'even as early as the later thirteenth century, many patrons of church building operations were choosing to have their tombs on the north side of the presbytery'.[79] One reason behind this practice, further indicating the importance of the north in memorial and eschatological practice, is the presence of Easter sepulchres. Generally, the north side of parish churches was the focus for the most important of Christian celebrations, that of Easter, where for a whole week, in many parish churches, an Easter sepulchre was erected. The Easter sepulchres, discussed later, were the symbolic stage for the re-enactment of Christ's entombment and resurrection, and therefore their association with the north side of the church, and the connection between intercession and burial practice, is of significance. For example, the aforementioned will of John Bedill in 1457 specifically requests burial at Portbury parish church 'in (the) north part of church before St Anne'.[80] This area of the church is also associated with a likely Easter sepulchre, the 'St Helen sarcophagus' in the 'chancel'.[81] This latter reference may actually refer to the north chancel chapel, also referred to as the Holy Sepulchre chapel. The importance of this area of the church is also highlighted by the presence of the passage squint, connecting the chapel both physically and visually with the rest of the church.

Another significant factor may be the association of chapel foundations on the north side of churches with crypts. From the studied chapels in the studied area, examples can be found at Alton, Binsted, Bridgwater, Castle Eaton, Farleigh Hungerford and Sherston. All are uniquely associated with north chapels. The reuse of areas associated with earlier mortuary practice may be a factor in the construction of some of these chapels. At Binsted, changes in the external fabric and the presence of two low-level doorways suggest that an earlier crypt was possibly incorporated into the reconstruction of the north chapel. Inside, an elevated area in the north part of the chapel is the result of the presence of the crypt below.

Another factor regarding the location of chapels on the north side of churches may be a traditional association of the laity with the north side of the church. There are several early examples of the importance given to the north side of churches in the context of lay piety. In the tenth century, for instance, it has been suggested that the construction of the New Minster to the north of the Old Minster, Winchester, was to provide a place for lay worship.[82] At Crowland, Cambridgeshire, in the Middle Ages lay parishioners worshipped in the abbey church in a chapel to the north of the church

79 Fawcett: 2002: 305.
80 Weaver 1901: 172.
81 Weaver 1903: 108.
82 Rosser 1992: 273.

which has been claimed to reflect earlier importance given to the north by the laity during the pre-Conquest period.[83] Similarly, at Hereford, the focus in the parish church of St John was a chapel in the north transept[84] and at St Frideswide's, Oxford, the north transept was the site of the parochial altar. The Hampton north chapel at Stoke Charity, and possibly the north chapel at Brympton d'Evercy, may have served as earlier manorial churches before the construction of the later church to the south. Research elsewhere has shown that very often north aisles were constructed before south aisles within many twelfth-century parish churches in Worcestershire.[85] Here, in thirteen cases only a single aisle was constructed, and of these, nine were in the north of the church.[86] As noted, in the sample area churches of Hampshire, at least four out of six churches with single aisles built before 1200 positioned these aisles on the north side. As discussed previously, many aisles may have been founded primarily as a space for 'private' chapels with intercessory motivations. Consequently, the present analysis reveals a level of independence, or freedom, in chapel foundation. Location and orientation of chapels may have been determined by an emphasis on visual accessibility, as at Bromham, and its relationship to areas of common use such as church entrances, as at Cheddar and at Bridgwater, or by a desire to place one's chapel closer to the high altar, as in the eastern extensions of chapels or aisles at Mere and St Thomas's, Salisbury and Yatton. Most chapels and chantries were, it seems, located for eschatological motives and the desire to found the chapel within an area of the church traditionally associated with death and commemoration or a certain spiritual potency.

Chapels and chantry foundation formed a physical context for lay piety and intercession. Their location is therefore of utmost importance in their relationship to both church and public. But equally, if not more important is the internal geography of the chapels themselves and the way that space is used and negotiated to provide a fitting setting for that most important of Christian rites, the mass. As we have seen from the previous chapter, the internal layout and fabric of chantry chapels was often rich and varied. If the context for intercessory ritual was the chapel itself, then its ceremonial focus was the altar, the *spiritus locus* for eucharistic celebration. Secondly, the founder's corporal remains were not technically required for the rites of intercession. Nonetheless, the presence of the founder's tomb was often an integral element to many chantry chapels.

---

[83]   Ibid.: 271.
[84]   Ibid.: 271.
[85]   Bond 1988.
[86]   Ibid.: 144.

Strategies for intercession II: Altars and tombs

The altar and its immediate setting were part of a 'symbolic system operating within a history of salvation and it was lived as a drama re-enacted during mass'.[87] But, this was a drama that required framing, its confines being set by physical as well as spiritual barriers. It was for this role that many chapels were screened, not necessarily to provide an area of exclusivity or private piety, but to provide definition to the rituals enacted within. Far from being just a vehicle for eucharistic celebration, the altar also symbolically represented 'a symbol of our Lord's tomb', and the bread and wine 'the body of the Lord which was embalmed and buried' within.[88] In effect, the chapel altar therefore symbolised the tomb from which Christ had risen and, in the form of the host, emphasised the underlying promise of salvation, a message whose relevance would have been clear to all. The link between the chapel and chantry tombs and the altar was significant, leading to one chantry founder, William Terumber of Trowbridge, to specify that his priest should celebrate mass and matins 'byfore the tombe of Johane late my wife, called Jhesus auter'.[89] Here the link between a specific tomb and altar is identified and often the two may have served the same purpose. Tomb altars can be found at many of the sample chapels, including Corsham, Ilminster and Ramsbury. At Cheddar, the will of Thomas More in 1493 requests burial specifically 'before the altar of St Nectan'.[90] Many tombs present in chapels may have doubled as Easter sepulchres, a link that no doubt would have been regarded as particularly efficacious. Examples include the Waller tomb at Stoke Charity and the Clopton tomb at Long Melford, Suffolk. In these cases the connection of one's mortal remains with the symbolised tomb of Christ could be coupled with the communal focus of Easter time.

Before the thirteenth century, monasteries were the favoured place for burial for the nobility and landed gentry.[91] After this period it became increasingly common, if not 'habitual practice', for the wealthy to seek commemoration in the form of providing an effigy of themselves.[92] It is also in this period that we begin to see the increased use of churches and chapels as a context for burial, a period that coincides with the earliest documentary evidence for chantries. Tomb-chests or tomb-altars of the fifteenth century have been identified as an 'abbreviated version' of tombs with life-sized effigies 'crossed with the older traditional tombs set in low wall niches'.[93] It is unclear whether or not tomb altars, or table tombs as they are sometimes called, functioned specifically as altars in the strict sense. Nonetheless, they seemed to have been, in many

87   Rubin 1991: 14.
88   Hardison 1965: 36–7.
89   Jones 1867: 248.
90   Weaver 1901: 304.
91   Golding 1986: 37.
92   Saul 1992: 45.
93   Cherry 1984: 89.

cases, an essential element of ritual topography. It could be suggested that by the fifteenth century there was an increased emphasis placed on the connection between individual burial and eucharistic and intercessory ritual – the setting of the ritual, the altar and the founder's tomb is one and the same. While certain tomb-altars may have symbolically acted as altars, they may also have been used for the placement of vessels, books or similar items of a liturgical nature; the inordinately large table-tomb at Corsham is an example. Without wishing to stretch the analogy too far, if the altar reflected the stage, then the tomb (particularly those that contained effigies, it could be argued) formed the *dramatis persona* of the performance. Medieval tombs, as noted, provided a reflective index of various social and economic factors.[94] But their presence is often thought integral to the perceived efficacy of intercessory ritual, in that, either by use of symbol or effigy, they acted both as a memorial and as evidence for the presence of the individual within such ritual. As such, they may have provided a physical presence or mnemonic for associated chantry practice, or at the very least anniversaries, that would have helped to 'stimulate the continual intercession of the living by the careful repetition of their own funeral service at least once a year'.[95] At St Giles, Edinburgh, the chantry priest of the Boroun chapel was required to sprinkle holy water on the founder's tomb prior to celebrating the chantry mass.[96] Moreover, it is pretty clear that some tombs were constructed before the death of the individual. As noted, the will of John Stourton specifies the placing of a 'reading desk' by his tomb,[97] suggesting that his tomb was constructed at the period that his will was being drawn up. In these cases, the tomb served as a *memento mori*, reminding individuals still living of the impermanence and fragility of life and the need to prepare spiritually for death.

Many early effigies, such as those of the Raleghs at Nettlecombe, provide a rudimentary depiction of the deceased. But by the fifteenth century there was a desire to provide very real life-size and life-like depictions of the founders. These effigies would often occupy a central part of their chapel and would often be attired in the clothing and regalia befitting their rank – hands often held piously in post-mortem prayer. The location and visibility of tombs is of particular significance. Many tombs in chapels and chantries, especially those of the founders, were situated in highly visible areas, as at Bromham and Yatton. One of the functions of monumental tombs, therefore, may have been to 'presence' the individual within the rituals enacted within the chapels.[98] In a sense, they would act as a form of mnemonic serving to evoke the individual in the minds of the chapel priest and the attending laity. In the Bettisthorne south chapel at Mere, the ledger and brass to John Bettisthorne (c.1398) was placed in the centre of the chapel. Unusually, his brass image and inscription face to the west and were designed to be 'read' by an individual or individuals

94   Finch 2000: 115.
95   Burgess 1988: 67.
96   Wood-Legh 1965: 295.
97   Weaver 1901: 145.
98   Graves 2000: 142.

situated to the west of the chapel. This arrangement, it can be argued, 'presenced' the individual in the minds of those involved in the eucharistic rituals, placing him firmly in their minds and memories. In other examples, tombs acted as visible obstructions because they were situated close to ritual areas, or within the arcades dividing chapel and chancel (Fig. 61).

Likewise, the position of tombs can also act as a deliberate physical obstruction. In the north or 'Dinham' chapel at Buckland Dinham, for example, the two ledger slabs of Sir John and Lady Dinham (c.1322), placed in the centre of the chapel, are raised several centimetres off the ground. Such an arrangement (with, incidentally, no evidence that they were not originally so arranged) indicates that they provided a very real obstruction (Fig. 24). Individuals in the chapel would be aware of such monuments as obstacles; they thus acted as a form of physical mnemonic, alerting individuals using the chapel, such as the priest, to their symbolic presence. The location of ledger slabs and brasses near entranceways is also of significance. At Boyton, the ledger and brass to John Giffard (c.1322) are situated on the threshold of the Giffard chapel and effectively cover the whole entranceway; they would have been viewed regularly by the collegiate chaplains there. Recent studies by the author have revealed similar arrangements in the former chapel of John Gower at the former priory of St Marie Overie, Southwark.[99] Here, both tomb and chapel were deliberately placed in the north aisle next to the entranceway from the priory cloister, an arrangement designed both to be highly visible to the canons, who would file past several times a day, as well as to the public. In many cases, throughout the medieval period and well into the sixteenth century, tombs were located not just in highly visible areas but also in central areas, such as the tombs and effigies at Yatton and Bromham and the ledger slabs at Tichborne, and the tomb at Brympton d'Evercy with its Lombardic inscription. Such placements indicate not just a desire to appropriate space, making them the dominant or 'central' monuments within the chapel space, but also, more importantly, a very real and central presence in the intercessory rituals acted out (in many cases, on their behalf) within the chapels. One particularly rare example of a highly visual memorial is that of Thomas Babington (c.1540) at St Winifred's, Kingston-on-Soar, Nottinghamshire. Here, the memorial is either a sort of setting for a chantry and/or a now lost tomb and consists of an ornate canopy constructed of columns with a network of hexagonal panels which have religious figures and tracery. It is clearly a visually impressive monument and one, no doubt, designed to draw attention to itself.

Sometimes such visual memorials could have more subtle, symbolic levels of meaning. At Godshill, the arcade between the south chapel and chancel contains an effigy of John Leigh and his wife dating to the early sixteenth century. Here, the couple are dressed in formal attire, hands clasped in prayer towards the site of both chapel and high altar. They were very much a presence, highly visible from both the body of the church and the chapel itself. On the soles of the knight's feet, largely hidden from public view, are

99 Roffey 1998; Hines, Cohen and Roffey 2004.

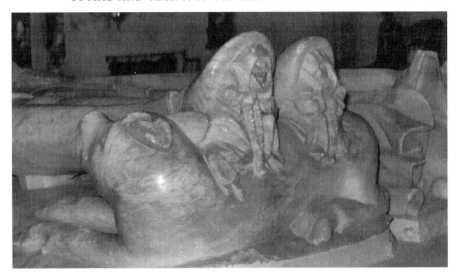

Figure 48   Tomb of John Leigh c.1529, Godshill, showing the depiction of bedesmen
with rosaries on the soles of the effigy's feet.

the sculptured images of a 'bedesman' with a rosary (Fig. 48). Such a feature
provided an interesting play on words, with the sole or Soul of the deceased
being associated with a representation of a particular act of charity. Another
example of this device can be found on the Fitzherbert tomb at Norbury
church, Derbyshire.

The importance of both location and the use of mnemonic devices can
be further demonstrated at Rodney Stoke. Here the fifteenth-century tomb-
chest of Thomas Rodney, located between chapel and chancel, consists of
an armoured effigy under a cusped arched canopy. On the south, or public,
side of the tomb are heraldic devices, and on the north side, or more private
face, are icons of St Erasmus, St Anne and the Virgin and child, as well as
St Leonard, the patron saint of the parish church. This arrangement illus-
trates the dual function of this particular tomb: the side associated with the
chapel and individual intercession contains images of the intercessors, whilst
the other side demonstrates the more earthly and status-driven nature of the
tomb. Such heraldic devices may not just reflect issues of social standing and
hierarchy, but may also serve to provoke awareness of the individual entombed
and therefore connect him or her with any rituals that were being observed
within. At Brading, the tomb of Oliver Oglander (c.1530) is one of a number
of Oglander tombs clustered around the area of the former medieval altar.
Depicted on the north or 'public' side of the tomb are images of beggars
and cripples (Fig. 25). The south or 'private' side of the tomb has images of
Oglander and his wife looking in the direction of the altar surrounded by
family members. This type of display is of course a precursor of later post-
Reformation tombs, which use similar devices, but what is interesting here
are the two different types of imagery – one promoting the moral standing

of Oglander and his suggested association with works of mercy, and the other suggestive of a more inward, family-based piety, with Oglander and his wife at the centre of the family. Likewise, at Minehead the tomb of Richard Bruton, positioned between the north chapel and chancel, was comparatively more decorated on its south, public facing, side.

Another significant feature of the Oglander chapel is the cluster of family tombs around the altar, with the earliest ones, those of Oliver and his father John, nearer the centre of the chapel, suggesting in this case an emphasis on public visibility as opposed to proximity to the chapel altar. The relevance of such visual relationships and how they are negotiated is discussed in detail in a later section. Further family 'clusters' can be found in the north chapel of Curry Rivel, where the arrangement of six recess tombs of the thirteenth and fourteenth centuries is suggestive of what can be read as a gathering of deceased family members lined up along the north wall of their ancestral chapel. Here they symbolically and visually constituted a very real and continued presence. Their presence would also form an effective backdrop to any rituals carried out in the chapel.

Another noteworthy arrangement for tombs and burials in the north chapel at Curry Rivel is the predilection for wall, or recess, tombs. This emerges as a commonly encountered characteristic, generally in pre-fifteenth-century chapels. Examples of recess burials can be found in Bishopstone, for instance, where the recess takes up almost the entire north wall of the chapel. More striking however are those at Curry Rivel. Here the central recess tomb (possibly that of the founder Sabina de Revel c.1254) is, like the others, cut into the fabric of the wall, but in this instance it projects externally from the wall, where a small masonry adjunct can be seen outside the chapel (Fig. 49).

Figure 49 The north chapel, Curry Rivel, showing the wall adjunct for the possible founder's tomb.

Figure 50   Burial 'cloister' at Bishopstone.

A similar example of a later date also survives at North Bradley. A comparable feature can be found in the Ralegh chapel at Nettlecombe, where the recesses of two tombs are actually adjunct compartments, again projecting externally. At St Michael's, Macclesfield, Cheshire, the south wall of the Savage chapel has a large decorated niche opening into a small lit chamber containing alabaster effigy tombs of John and Elizabeth Savage (c.1528). Bishopstone's vaulted burial cloister on the external south wall of the south chapel may also be an example of such practices (Figs 15, 50), as could the external recess tombs along the outside of the north aisle at Bridgwater. These latter examples are positioned close to church porches and are suggestive of a deliberate attempt to attract visual attention to themselves.

At Nettlecombe and Crewkerne, there is evidence for individual burials within the fabric of chapel walls. As noted earlier, at Nettlecombe, in the east external wall of the chapel, a vertical ledger memorial suggests that the individual may have been buried standing up. All of these examples, except for the adjunct burial at North Bradley, date before 1400 and may suggest an early practice of individuals, possibly founders, consciously desiring to be part of the actual fabric of their chapels. Here a conscious link is forged between the material fabric of the chapel (as a context for intercessory practice) and the remains of the deceased. Similar associations between physical structures and burials have been noted recently by Williams with regard to Sandwell priory, West Midlands, in the fourteenth century.[100] Here the burial of monastic patrons was linked to the construction of a family chantry in the south transept. Consequently it is argued that this provided a strategy of commemoration

[100]   Williams 2003

'providing material means by which memories were inscribed'.[101] Such an emphasis may suggest a particular significance given to the direct relationship between human remains and intercessory practice during this period. To take this further, it may be possible that the popularity of life-size effigy tombs in the later period may reflect a move away from the actual *material* presence of the deceased to a more *symbolic* one.

That personal requirements formed part of church fabric can also be argued for the relationship between chapels and crypts as referred to above. As seen at Binsted, rebuilding of the chapel incorporated the earlier crypt, suggesting an element of continuity associated with traditional family places of burial. Likewise, in the chapel of St Thomas at Burford, the floor of the chapel was raised so as to compensate for the crypt underneath. In these cases, wall burials and association with crypts reveal a desire both to associate places of burial with chapel and chantry space, but more importantly, and particularly in the case of wall burials, they provided a very real and physical link between the individual and the chapel and its rituals – arguably, like the rituals of intercession themselves, in perpetuity.

An important aspect of the religious practices performed within the chapels and chantries, and a factor that was crucial in the interactions between the laity and the intercessory rituals enacted, was the association of the masses celebrated in the chapels with specified individuals, especially the chapel or chantry founders. Very broadly speaking, the attraction of the chapels and chantries on a purely spiritual level was that they were a context for the mass. As has been noted above, the use of 'presencing mechanisms' allowed the mass to be associated with the individual or individuals by the use of various devices, such as tombs, heraldic devices and symbols and in the form of inscribed altar cloths and wall hangings. Although many chapels were in use before the death of the founder, the fact that many chapels and chantries were used by founders and later family members should not detract from the fact that such institutions were primarily intercessory foundations. The 'active' role and presence of the founder, it can be argued, could have continued *post-mortem*, in that the deceased ensured a presence in their chapel by symbolism, memorials and especially the ritual itself – 'the pronunciation of the name of the dead was more than simply recollection: it was the means by which the dead were made present'.[102]

Chantries, chapels and visual topography

As noted above, the role of founder's or family tombs was a significant factor in certain intercessory rituals. At Yatton, as shown in the below plan (Fig. 53), the tomb of Richard Newton and wife was highly visible and therefore symbolically present. Here the tomb deliberately obstructed the line of sight to the chapel

[101] Williams 2003: 236.
[102] Geary 1994: 87.

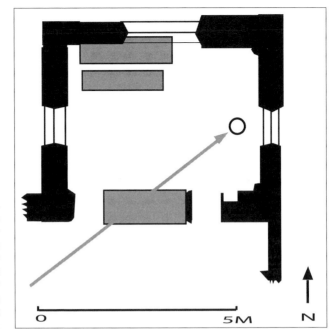

Figure 51 Limington, reconstructing the view of the laity to the altar in the chapel. Note how the line of sight is 'obstructed' by Gyvernay tomb in the arcade between chancel and chapel.

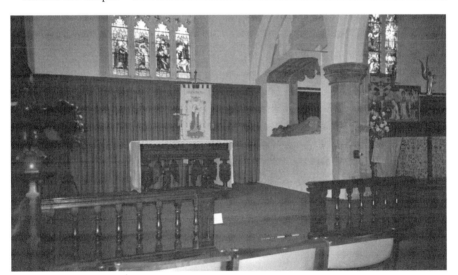

Figure 52   Recess tomb between the north chapel and chancel, Minehead.

altar, acting as an insistent reminder to those in the chapel. In the south chapel, Mere, in the second half of the fifteenth century, the tomb chest of John, Lord Stourton, was inserted within the arcade between chapel and chancel (Fig. 61). It is tempting to conjecture that perhaps another motive for placing the tomb in this position, besides proximity to the high altar, was to obstruct the line of sight from the chapel to the high altar to act as a presencing mechanism.

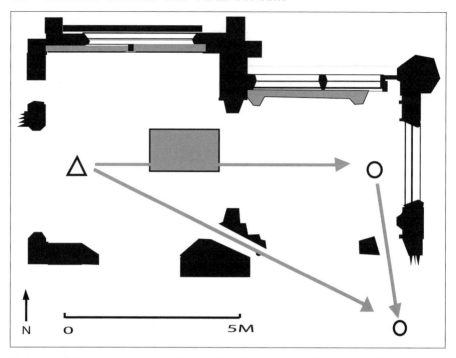

Figure 53　The north chapels at Yatton. The lines represent the views to the chapel and chancel altars from the back of the chapel for laity present in the chapel, and the visual relationship between the altars themselves (for celebrants).

This strategy would place the tomb and its occupant not only within the minds of the observing laity or priest, but actually within the physical sphere of the rituals observed. At Limington (Fig. 51), visual access for the laity to the chapel altar is via the fourteenth-century tomb. At North Bradley and in the north chapel at Bishopstone, for example, the tombs would have acted as a mnemonic backdrop to religious ritual. A prime example can be seen be seen at Montacute, with regard to the conjectured position of the tombs against the north wall and between the arcade through to the chancel, as discussed previously (Fig. 27). In this case the north tomb acted as a backdrop for the mass performed in the chapel. The tomb in the arcade effectively breached the line of sight into the chapel and therefore may have acted as an 'intercessory trigger' to presence the individual within the performed rituals.[103] At Minehead, the insertion of a small open recess and tomb in the wall between north chapel and chancel wall not only facilitated a visual connection between altars, but placed, or 'presenced', the individual memorial within this visual relationship (Fig. 52). Here, the entombed individual is particularly commemorated in the context of associated eucharistic practice.

What can be seen in these instances is that an essential requirement of chantry and chapel planning is a provision for clear sight lines within ritual

---

[103]　Graves 2000: 143.

topography, particularly with regard to the spatial arrangement of tombs and visual accessibility to eucharist celebration. Rituals enacted within the chapels and chantries called all the senses into play – the hearing of bells and litanies, the smell of incense, the oral murmuring of supplications, and the feeling of sensuous discomfort at kneeling for the elevation. But, while words and music were the integral elements of lay participation, the visual aspect was perhaps paramount. Consequently, it has been claimed that there was a 'whole emphasis in western lay devotion upon seeing'.[104] Importance was placed upon direct visual communion with the host at the point of elevation, but also upon indirect visual contact with the symbolic elements of the chapel, through its rituals, its decoration and its architectural embellishment.

Facilitating a vision of salvation: the squint

Chapter 5 briefly considered the nature and function of 'squints', or internal 'windows'. We have seen that they are often common, if enigmatic, additions to parish churches and are especially related to the presence of chapels. They have been little studied but some traditional interpretations suggest that squints afforded clear lines of sight for the laity within aisles which were built to contain a 'swelling population'.[105] Other interpretations concerning the use of squints have considered their function as confessional windows,[106] their relationship to the use of sacring bells,[107] as well as the possibility that they were used for offertories, or were a symbol for Christ's wounds.[108] Certain squints may have been used in processions, and it has also been suggested that squints allowed priests at subsidiary altars (such as chantry altars) to view the high altar.[109] (A study of squints in the county of Warwickshire, for example, has indicated a clear connection between squints and altars.[110]) However, the latter interpretation presupposes the presence of a chapel altar, but fails to explain why the priest there would need to see the high altar. One reason may be to give the priest celebrating at such altars a view of the pyx hanging above the high altar. It is possible, however, as a result of the multiplication of masses within the church, that the high altar was beginning to lose precedence. Squints may have facilitated the 'staggering' of eucharistic elevations between subsidiary and high altars. Furthermore, this may suggest that there was an order of precedence, or spiritual hierarchy, in parish church ritual and that there was an attempt to synchronise these rituals. Orders of precedence between subsidiary and high altars in larger institutions have been

104   Dix 1945: 484.
105   Turner 1987: 235.
106   I.H.P. 1845.
107   Cole 1847; Graves 2000.
108   Green 1926.
109   Duffy 1992.
110   Chatwin 1965.

briefly discussed by Edwards and Harper-Bill,[111] particularly with reference to the cathedrals of Durham and Salisbury.[112] Graves has examined the visual connection between the More chapel and the Lane aisle at Cullompton, suggesting how such visual interplay in the church 'establishes the principal lay rivals in the parish'.[113] It may also be noted that the Fourth Lateran Council in 1215 demanded annual confession, and consequently some have interpreted squints as acting as confessional windows.[114] In such cases the squints might facilitate verbal communication between chapel and chancel. Although it is generally thought that private confession was a much later phenomenon in parish churches, references to priests hearing public confession do exist. For example, the Leigh chantry priest at St Michael's Southgate, Oxford, would receive regular confession outside the city gates.[115] At St John's, Winchester, the squint from the south chapel to the chancel is inserted through the back of the chancel sedilia and therefore facilitated, it can be suggested, private correspondence between an unseen individual in the south chapel and a priest sitting in the sedilia (Fig. 62). Providing the priest remained in this position, the laity could enter and leave the church and chapel without being recognised. It is possible that the squint at Whitestaunton also performed this function.

Ultimately, the variety of squint types, their size and location, when viewed collectively, suggest that they were used for a variety of functions dependent on their architectural or topographical context. The substantial aisle squints found at Hambledon, Hampshire, for example, clearly provided visual access to the high altar for laity in the aisle. Likewise, as noted above at Stoke Charity, the smaller double squint provided visual access from the aisle to the high altar and from the nave to the north wall tomb altar in the Hampton chapel (Fig. 67). Similarly, the squints found in the north chapels at Brympton d'Evercy and Yatton allowed visual access only for a small group of individuals situated at the back of the chapels. Nevertheless, some squints also assisted priests serving subsidiary altars (such as chapel altars) to view the high altar. In the case of the Paulet north and south chapels at Old Basing, the narrow squints inserted into the entrance jambs of each chapel clearly provided very limited visual access, probably for just a single person, in this case very probably the chapel priest. It is possible that squints were only relevant to particular occasions such as Easter or festivals. So-called passage squints, probably used in processions, found for example at Basingstoke, Portbury and Sherston, may further suggest such defined or limited usage. Certainly the lack of elaboration on many squints, particular compared to piscinas and other architectural details, such as the plain roughly cut examples at Stoke Charity, Yatton and Great Chalfield, suggests they may have not been used regularly. Although, of course, it should be borne in mind that squints were meant to be looked

---

111 Edwards 1967; Harper-Bill 1991.
112 Dobson 1996; Wordsworth 1901.
113 Graves 2000: 146.
114 I.H.P. 1845.
115 Wood-Legh 1965.

through, and not *at*, and that any decoration may have, literally, got in the way. Furthermore, as noted in the previous chapter, many squints may have also served as aumbries, as these features are rarely found together in chapels in the research area.

Visual relationships and chapel topography

The position of squints and their relation to other areas of the church are significant and can reveal much about the relationship and interactions between private foundations and communal piety as well as those between chantry chapels and the parish church itself. When we couple this with associated archaeological evidence and relevant primary sources, it is possible to reconstruct, to an extent, the complex visual relationship between church and chapel and thereby consider the potential level of communal devotion. On closer examination, there is much to suggest the extent of lay participation within chapels. Often devotional symbols and images were arranged to be seen, as with the elaborate decorated exterior of the Tocotes and Beauchamp chapel, Bromham, replete with images of the passion. At Ashton, Devon, the dominant religious image in the Chudleigh chapel is that of the image of pity, displayed high on the north wall of the chapel, where it could be seen and prayed for by all.[116]

As discussed above, among the various functions of the squint was the provision of a view, normally to the high altar, either for the laity or for priests celebrating masses at subsidiary altars. These features offer a precious insight not just into the former location of altars, but the visual relationship between them. In the north chapel at Yatton, the piscina for the chapel altar was located at the east end of the chapel. The squint, however, provided a view of the high altar, and is located towards the back of the chapel, close to the highly decorated tomb of Richard Newton and Emmota de Sherborne. It is possible that this western area represented an area reserved for a distinct group of people who have visual access to both the high altar and the chapel altar (Fig. 53).

This can be further demonstrated in the south chapels at South Wraxall and Great Chalfield, where the orientation of squints provided a view from the back of each chapel to the high altar. These squints were also positioned well below eye level, suggesting that the observants were either sitting or kneeling. At Brympton d'Evercy, the position of a low squint in the north-west corner of the late fifteenth-century chapel is again of particular interest. Here, the squint was not situated near the location of a former altar. Instead, as at Yatton, its position would have provided a view of the chancel for a small number of people situated at the back of the chapel. The squint is situated at waist level (with no evidence for significant change in floor level) and therefore suggests again that the observants were either sitting or kneeling. Furthermore, from

116 Duffy 2003: 60.

this position every other altar within the church could be viewed: at the east end of this chapel, in the north chapel and in the south transept. Entered via a separate doorway, the chapel was exclusive and provided a unique and commanding view of the major ritual areas of the church. Indeed, it is the sole point within the church commanding such a vantage point. Though physically separate, the addition of an internal window and the chancel arch to the north chapel indicate that the respective altars herein were still partially visible to the laity, whose participation was an important component for the efficacy of the intercessory mass (Fig. 54).

A unique example can be found at Bradford-on-Avon. Here, in the former Horton chantry in the north aisle, the squint cuts through a fourteenth-century recess in the north wall of the chapel. More significantly, however, inside the squint an inscribed memorial slab has been placed. It appears that this memorial was purposely placed to intrude itself on the priest's line of sight, and in his interaction with the high altar. It would certainly not be visible to anyone else in the church and would therefore appear to have been a deliberate attempt to 'presence' an individual in the eucharistic rituals taking place.

View-sheds, or lines of sight, are thus a highly significant factor in the negotiation of chapel and chantry space. The examination of chapel

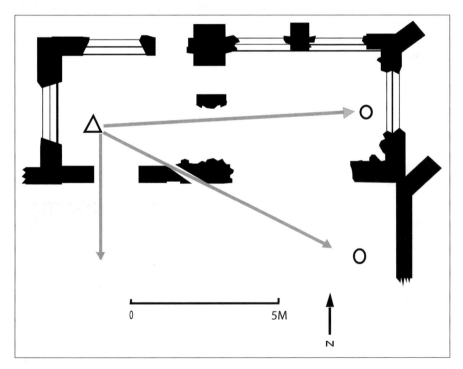

Figure 54 Plan of the north chapel, Brympton d'Evercy, showing the conjectured position of individuals either seated or kneeling at the back of the chapel and their respective views to the former altars.

topography can reveal not just their relationship to parish church space, but also how changes within the liturgical foci of chapels can be negotiated. The Hampton chapel at Stoke Charity provides a particularly good example of this approach and provides insight into the development and changing nature of ritual topography. In the fifteenth century the chapel became the Hampton family chantry, a transition which involved the reconstruction of parts of the chapel. The founder's tomb was situated in the arcade through to the chancel and obstructed visual access from the nave to the chapel altar. In the early sixteenth century, a new tomb/Easter sepulchre was placed against the chapel north wall. It seems that this new ritual focus necessitated the insertion of a double squint, which provided a view from the nave and also from the north aisle to the chancel to this new area (effectively bypassing the earlier Hampton tomb). It is also possible that an unnamed tomb in the north aisle may have originally been a focus but was also superseded, in part, by the new tomb/ Easter sepulchre in the chapel. These new alterations alert us to the changing nature of the chapel, as well as providing comparative dating evidence (for the squint and window), which enables a chronological phasing to be constructed. Significantly, it also suggests that communal visual accessibility determined a series of changes within chapel ritual geography, which in turn reaffirms that the public were meant to have a relationship with such monuments.

Similarly, at Buckland Dinham, the addition of an eastern chapel to the Dinham north chapel also involved construction of a squint to enable the laity to have visual access to this new area (Fig. 55). The construction of the north aisle and associated chantry foundation at Bridgwater also included the provision of a squint in the east wall of the porch, providing a view to both

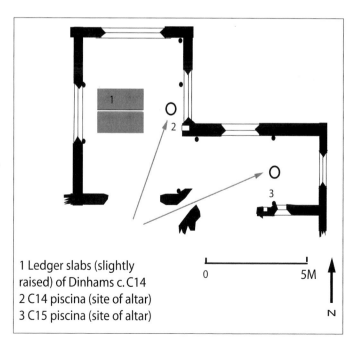

Figure 55
The north chapels at Buckland Dinham showing visual relationships between the nave and chapels. Note how the altar in the north chapel is close to the raised ledgers of the Dinhams. These formed a slight physical obstruction, probably to the serving priest, and therefore provided a physical mnemonic 'reminding' the priest of their presence.

1 Ledger slabs (slightly raised) of Dinhams c. C14
2 C14 piscina (site of altar)
3 C15 piscina (site of altar)

0   5M

N

chantries and high altar. Ultimately, it can be argued, such chapels were never really intended to be 'private' in the literal sense. Privately managed, perhaps, but they were part of common ritual topography. At Alton, two narrow squint windows in the east and west walls of the north chapel may have been inserted to allow the laity a view of the altar from *outside* the chapel. These slit windows are also relatively low, suggesting that spectators may have been kneeling to view the elevation within. It is significant that these windows are integral with the build of the chapel and therefore a conscious placement on the part of the founder, rather than an afterthought.

A 'spiritual network': chapels, chantries and the parish church

In parish churches with multiple altars it is possible to recreate the visual relationships between subsidiary altars and the high altar and to reveal the complex network of interrelationships between them. Analysis of spatial and visual relationship between the chapels and their churches indicates that they were in fact closely involved in what can be termed a spiritual network between other sacred foci within the church. As noted above, the squint may have been used to visually facilitate the staggering of celebrations between altars. As a result of the multiplication of masses within a church, including those celebrated within chapels and chantries, the high altar may have been beginning to lose precedence. Hence, a proliferation of altars in the parish church may have led to the staggering of masses so that the laity was not able to 'shirk attending longer parish masses'. Consequently it has been suggested that masses celebrated at side-altars were 'timed so that their sacrings were staggered'.[117] This may also imply an order of precedence during this time, further indicating that each respective priest needed to view the preceding elevation. It is unlikely, however, that such events occurred on a regular basis, particular in the smaller, rural churches that may have had only one or two priests celebrating once a day. Nonetheless, the presence of particular squints in some examples, as noted, suggests a visual relationship between altars.

Evidence for squints aligned upon areas of liturgical importance indicates that there was some form of visual relationship between altars. Furthermore, it suggests the importance of general visual relationships within parish church topography and religious practice. Such relationships between altars should not just be viewed as strictly hierarchical in the sense of clerical control of lay-founded or subsidiary altars. It may alternatively be argued that these relationships were wholly beneficial to the community in that the sacred areas of the church, be it chapel, chantry or high altar, were linked into a common and universal structure, which further bonded the community in its religious practices. In this sense the various altars were 'networked' into the web of public piety, as can be argued for Bradford-on-Avon (Fig. 56) and Aldbourne (Fig. 64), for example. Orders of precedence, ultimately linked to the parish

[117] Duffy 1992: 97.

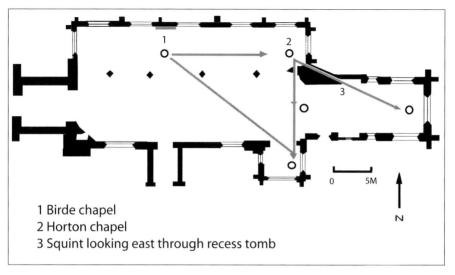

1 Birde chapel
2 Horton chapel
3 Squint looking east through recess tomb

N

Figure 56 Bradford-on-Avon, showing visual relationships between priests serving at various altars within the church.

high altar, encouraged a unified approach to the common goal of eucharistic celebration and the promise of salvation inherent within. Such an order must have been carefully worked out to ensure that timing and visual access were integrated and the dramatic continuity of the various performances ran seamlessly and with chronological precision. Orders of precedence between altars can be deduced from contemporary documents from larger institutions. For example, the chapters at St Paul's, London and York Minster 'arranged times when different masses should be celebrated' and consequently 'if one cantarist did not begin his mass immediately the preceding cantarist had finished, he would be cited before the chapter to answer for neglect'.[118] Dobson notes the drawing up of timetables at secular cathedrals for priests celebrating masses at various altars.[119] Timetabling would have also ensured that attendants at subsidiary altars did not detract from choral services in churches. At Salisbury cathedral, the chapter drew up an annual table of *missae currentes*, arranging that those chaplains who were not also vicars choral should celebrate their daily masses successively at the different cathedral altars. In the context of parish church practice, at St Mary's in Nottingham, on several occasions, priests celebrated mass as early as possible, 'without attention to their customary duty of beginning them after the offertory at the parish mass'.[120] Duffy notes that at Long Melford, Suffolk, the altar at the east end of the north aisle was provided with a double squint to enable the priest to 'see across the rear angle of the Clopton chantry and through the north wall

[118] Edwards 1967: 273–4.
[119] Dobson 1996: 80.
[120] Thompson 1947: 143.

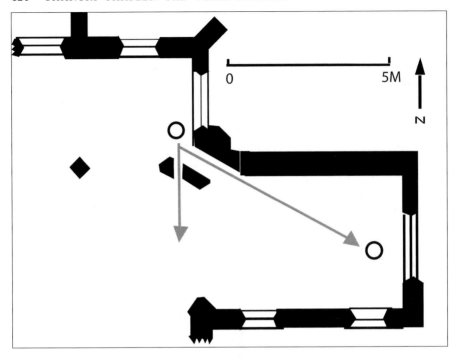

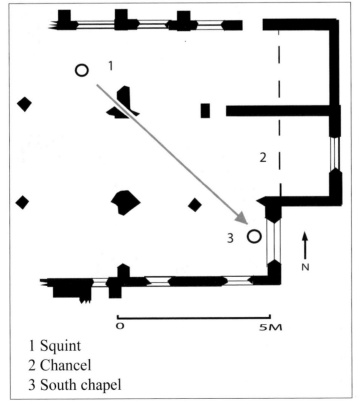

Figure 57
Churchill, showing visual relationships between the north aisle and high altar as well as to the nave or south chapel altar.

1 Squint
2 Chancel
3 South chapel

Figure 58
East end of St James's, Taunton, showing the visual relationship between altars.

of the chancel to the exact centre of the high altar'.[121] The remarkably extensive squint from the Horton north aisle to the chancel at Bradford-on-Avon highlights the effort that was made to ensure that visual relationships between altars were facilitated. However, these visual relationships were not just confined to that between subsidiary altars and the high altars. Orders of precedence also existed between subsidiary altars themselves. A particularly interesting arrangement can be seen at Churchill. Here, in the north chapel, the south-facing squint provided a view to the opposite south chapel altars, whilst the east squint gave a view to the high altar (Fig. 56). At Churchill, the squint provides a view to the south chapel only, suggesting in this case a possible order of precedence or 'spiritual hierarchy' between subsidiary altars, as well as the high altar. Here the celebrant in the north chapel could clearly see the priest serving the nave or south transept altar but could not be viewed in return due to the narrowness of the squint. This may suggest that it was

---

[121] Duffy 1992: 98.

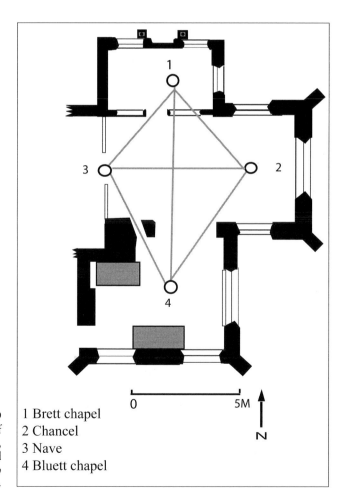

Figure 59
The east end of Whitestaunton, showing conjectured visual relationship between altars.

1 Brett chapel
2 Chancel
3 Nave
4 Bluett chapel

0   5M

N

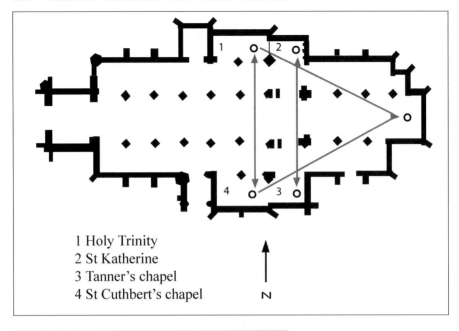

1 Holy Trinity
2 St Katherine
3 Tanner's chapel
4 St Cuthbert's chapel

N

Figure 60
Conjectured visual
relationship between altars at
St Cuthbert's, Wells.

Figure 61
The south chapel at Mere,
showing Bettisthorne brass
and the view through the
chancel to the north chapel
door. Note that this view is
also partly compromised by
the table tomb in the arcade.

not necessary for the other priests to see the elevation at the mass carried out in the north chapel (Fig. 57). Similarly, the squint at St James's, Taunton provided a view not to the high altar but to the south chapel, or alternatively a rood altar, suggesting an order of precedence between these two, with the south chapel altar taking priority (Fig. 58). At Whitestaunton, the insertion of a squint in the north-west wall of the Bluett chapel served to provide a view to a possible nave altar. Similarly, the masonry screen of the Brett chapel has two large casement windows within it to provide a line of sight to the south chapel. Examination of the jambs of the screen doorway suggests that it was likely that a half-door was inserted here to provide a view of the chapel altar from the nave (Fig. 59). A comparable network can be reconstructed at St Cuthbert's, Wells, although it can be seen here that a line of sight existed between the two westerly chapels to the high altar, and that this view was actually interrupted by St Katherine's chapel to the north-east and the Lady chapel to the south-east. It may also be significant that the two former chapels of St Cuthbert and Holy Trinity were a guild and municipal chapel respectively, and that a view of the high altar, as well as the other chapels altars may have been particularly sought after. It is perhaps in this case no coincidence that all the altars in the church would be visible from these chapels (Fig. 60). In the south chapel at Mere, views of other altars in the church could possibly be achieved by both priests and attendant laity (Fig. 61).

At St John's, Winchester, visual relationships between the north and south chapel altars and the high altar can also be reconstructed. Here, the relationship highlights another factor: the orientation of subsidiary altars with regard to the high altar. At St John's, the alignment of squints from the north and

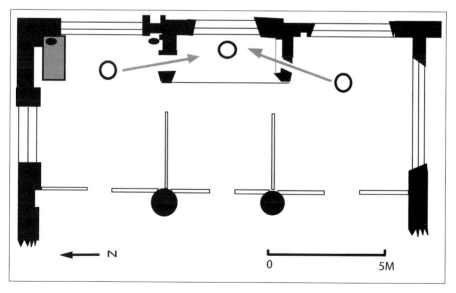

Figure 62   Visual relationship between altars in the east end of St John's, Winchester. The squint in the south chapel inserted through the chancel sedilia may also have functioned as a confessional.

particularly the south altar suggests that these altars were aligned slightly
to the west of the high altar (Fig. 62). This arrangement can be seen in
other examples referred to elsewhere, notably at Buckland Dinham (Fig. 55),
Old Basing (Fig. 63), St James's Taunton (Fig. 58), Whitestaunton (Fig. 59),
Aldbourne (Fig. 64) and Mere (Fig. 61), and may reveal the former position
of the celebrant. These particular arrangements may also indicate the former
presence of obstructions such as altar rails or steps. Alternatively, they may
imply that there was a requirement to position chantry and chapel altars
slightly westerly of the high altar. What this tells us is that, contrary to
common belief, not all altars would have necessarily been positioned at the
east end of chapels. The reconstruction of visual relationships here, in some
cases, suggests this may not always be the case. If this were not so, then
the aforementioned squints would have no logical purpose as they would be
inserted in the wrong place. The evidence overwhelmingly suggests otherwise. At Corsham, archaeological evidence suggests that the chancel itself
was extended by a half bay so that it would project more easterly from the
attached chapel to the north. The architectural similarity between chancel
extension and chapel construction is similar, suggesting that this arrangement
was contemporary. As noted previously, the position of the Bettisthorne brass

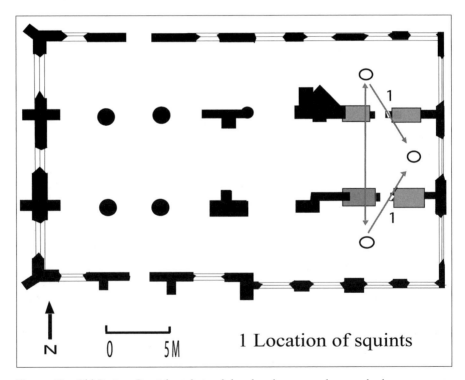

Figure 63 Old Basing. Spatial analysis of the church topography reveals the
conjectured location of the chapel celebrants as well as their relationship to the high
altar. Also note the line of sight between each chapel is 'broken' by the earliest Paulet
tombs.

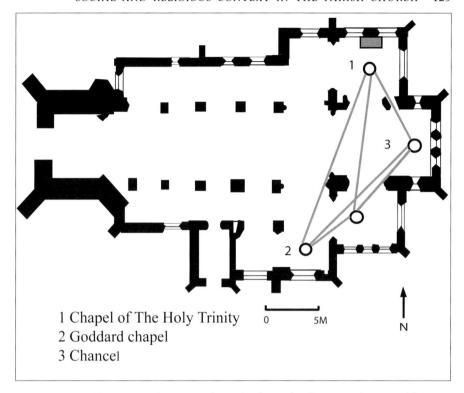

1 Chapel of The Holy Trinity

2 Goddard chapel

3 Chancel

Figure 64   Conjectured visual relationship between altars at Aldbourne.

in the south chapel at Mere may suggest a central location for the altar in this instance. Although the pattern is not shown by other examples, such as Stoke Charity and Nettlecombe, it may, nonetheless, indicate the spiritual prominence given to the high altar, further illustrating the inclusiveness of chantries and chapels in communal religious practice and the significance and value given to the parish's main ritual focus.

The analysis of chantry chapel space and fabric not only indicates how various strategies for intercession were enacted with the chapel, but also reveals the role of these chapels in communal religion. It also implies that far from being purely individualistic monuments, chantries and chapels were highly inclusive, representing part of a complex network of relationships between other ritual areas and between communal piety and intercession. The ways in which these relationships were negotiated was far from static, and further reveal the uniqueness of each chapel and chantry. Though it has to be borne in mind that many churches may have been poorly lit at particular times, visual accessibility, it can be argued, was an important element of church topography. Some chapels used squints and double squints to heighten visual accessibility. Some showed deference to the high altar by orienting their altars accordingly, while others used a series of 'presencing technologies' to make the dead present among the living. These aspects further demonstrate the versatility and all-encompassing nature of intercessory practice in the parish church and the essential contribution that such institutions made to pre-Reformation religious practice. Overall, this chapter, which has been based on detailed analysis and comparative examples, has revealed that chantries and chapels were a highly organised and integrated development, elaborating and promoting churches as centres of effective and well organised multiple celebration. By the end of the Middle Ages, chapels and chantries were core aspects of church topography and religious practice. However, this was all to change. The Reformation of the mid-sixteenth century and the consequent dissolution of the chantries ended these complex relationships, deflating, at a stroke, the parish as a centre for communal celebration. The Reformation severed both the threads between the living and the dead, and those between parish, community, chapel and church.

7

The Reformation of Chantry Chapels

Introduction

In December 1547, by act of parliament, the ancient bonds between the living and the dead were officially torn asunder and the dead exiled to eternal anonymity. The Reformation[1] was also an attack on the living, an attack that 'struck at the ordinary layfolk as no previous Reformation statute had done'.[2] The Chantry Act of 1547, for the dissolution of chantries and the abolition of prayers for the dead, not only dramatically altered the former relationship between the living and dead, but it also consigned to oblivion the elaborate rituals and practices, colours, lights, symbols and artistic representations in which this relationship had been expressed. The rituals, and in many cases the monuments, were not consigned to memory, but physically eradicated and effectively erased from history. It has been noted how few historians of the post-Reformation period have shown 'any inclination to add perspective to assessments of the laity's role in late sixteenth and seventeenth century by comparison with early practice'.[3] Likewise, archaeological examination of the effects of the Reformation on the parish church has been neglected. Only recently has this complex subject been studied via a joint conference of the Society for Medieval Archaeology and the Society for Post-Medieval Archaeology on 'The Archaeology of Reformation' held at the British Museum in 2001. The proceedings of this conference have been recently published.[4] This section considers the physical effects of the Reformation on individual chantry chapels. Physical evidence for the re-use of former chapels as a context for commemoration is assessed alongside the iconoclasm of space in the conscious reorganisation of chapel topography. A feature of particular

[1]   Again, one must be wary with words. As Clive Burgess has pointed out, the loaded nature of the word 'reform' is potentially problematic in that it suggests 'improvement'. This, of course, may not necessarily be the case in all instances (Burgess 2004: ix).
[2]   Scarisbrick 1984: 66.
[3]   Burgess 1996: 256.
[4]   Gaimster and Gilchrist 2003.

interest was the placing of dominant status-driven monuments effectively to appropriate and de-ritualise former liturgical space.

Chantries on the eve of the Reformation: A monument in decline?

Historians are divided about whether or not the desire to found chantries was in decline prior to the Reformation. Alan Kreider has suggested that in many cases the number of chantry foundations was falling off in certain areas of England in the early sixteenth century.[5] Michael Hicks on the other hand has pointed out that the dissolution of the monasteries in the 1530s may have accounted for much of this and therefore we are getting a false perception of the popularity of chantry foundation at parish level at this time.[6] This being said, there is in some areas, such as the south-east of England, documentary evidence for decline in parishes.[7] A similar pattern has been observed in York by Dobson who suggests that decline there was the result of financial, and not religious, pressure.[8] There was perhaps a growing awareness of approaching reform. Some opposition in academic circles to the doctrine of purgatory and prayers for the dead had been emerging since at least the early fifteenth century. There is no doubt that the premature dissolution of chantries in the years leading up to a perceived official dissolution was an economically motivated and not a religious act. In Wiltshire, five parish chantries were prematurely dissolved at Bromham, Chute, Market Lavington, Ogbourne St George and Ramsbury,[9] although at least eight parish chantries were founded during this period, largely in rural parish churches. In Somerset, in 1547, the chantry at Porlock was 'resigned? a yeare past and more', whilst the churchyard chantry at Yatton had been in decay for several years.[10] Certainly parish church chantries founded on the eve of the Reformation, such as the Leigh chantry at Godshill, the Paulet south chapel at Old Basing, the Horton chapel at Holy Trinity, Bradford-on-Avon, and the richly decorated Lane aisle at Cullompton, suggest that they were still regarded as important foundations and established without fear of any impending abolition. Two outer or processional aisles were added to St Mary Magdalene, Taunton, between 1480 and 1514; each was used as a site for new chantry foundations. Probably the last recorded chantry foundation, that at Welsh Newton, Hertfordshire, was founded only a few months before the act of dissolution.[11] Ritually, a mass such as that to the Five Wounds of Christ, whose symbolism adorns many chantries and churches of this period, was still growing in popularity up to the very eve of the Reformation. Indeed, there is nothing to suggest that before this period there was any 'appreciable

5   Kreider 1979.
6   Hicks 1985.
7   Kreider 1979.
8   Dobson 1996: 262.
9   Kreider 1979.
10   Green 1888: 88.
11   Cook 1947: 58.

falling off in popular belief in the efficacy of memorial masses'.[12] It could be argued that if they were unimportant, and did not provide an impediment to religious reform, then there was no real need for organised abolition, except only to appropriate their wealth. 'Lay assertiveness and participation' has been seen as being the 'more likely ancestors' of religious change.[13] The rare survival of chapels and chantries in the archaeological record, the desecration of their furnishings and adornments and the reuse of their former sacred space for secular and more mundane purposes suggests that, contrary to the wishes of a great number of people, the chapels and chantries were destroyed *primarily* for religious motives. As Woodward states, the Chantry Act was in essence a religious reform to abolish 'a remnant of papal apparatus which was both obsolete and irrelevant to the new religion'.[14] Some charitable institutions, such as Winchester College and some hospitals, were allowed to continue, though without endowments for superstitious uses. Consequently, the living were forced to subscribe to a new, less emotive religion; the dead were left to fend for themselves.

The effects of the Reformation

The Reformation of chantry chapels took place on four levels: *Prohibition:* the official dissolution of chantries, legal proscription of lights, obits, intercession and prayers for the dead; *Iconoclasm:* the destruction of paintings, sculpture and glass; *Confiscation:* the appropriation of related goods of value as well as attached land endowments, and finally, *Reorganisation:* the demolition or renegotiation of chapel and chantry space, including the obstruction and de-ritualising of former focal areas, chapel topography and communal accessibility.[15] The effects of the Reformation were cataclysmic for traditional religion. This was a period that apparently brought about the 'necessity of destroying, of cutting, hammering, scraping, or melting into a deserved oblivion the monuments of popery'.[16] In many cases such losses were almost immediate. At St John's, Glastonbury, the loss included not just silver plate, vestments, carved seats and screens, but 21 chained books. At Nunney, Wiltshire, even the iron bars of the founder's tomb were considered for appropriation. At Bridgwater, however, everything except a lone silver chalice had been spirited away by locals beforehand. A tradition exists at Porlock, Somerset, that chantry goods were hidden prior to official appropriation. The dissolution of the chantries also led to the loss of many dependent rural chapels. The dissolution of the

---

12 Platt 1981: 111.
13 Kümin 1996: 182.
14 Woodward 1982: vi.
15 Roffey 2003.
16 Duffy 1992: 480.

chantries at Mere, for example, meant that the dependent chapels at Zeals, Deverell and 'Chadenwych' could no longer function.[17]

The dissolution of the chantries not only destroyed a context for intercession, but also dramatically changed the nature of communal and individual piety at a local level. The colour, sound, light and spiritual vibrancy that chantries and chapels had brought into popular religious practice was extinguished. The emotive focus of the chantry altar, adorned with burning lights and colourful images, and the elaborate and formal eucharistic rituals were forbidden. Many chantries were destroyed, with their images desecrated, wall paintings white-washed, glass smashed and their screens torn down. Many former chapels were also put to more secular use such as vestries and, later, organ rooms, as at Devizes and Binsted. The south chapel at St Michael's, Southampton became a barber's shop before being demolished. The outline of the former arch into this chapel can still be seen, as can that to the former south chapel as at St Michael's, Oulton, Suffolk.

The 'Borbach' chapel at West Dean, Wiltshire, was eventually more fortu-nate (albeit in different circumstances): it became the parish church after the original church was demolished in the nineteenth century. Much of the loss and misappropriation of chantry furniture is attested by documentary sources such as the Chantry Certificates of 1547. Evidence for the reorganisation of former ritual space is hinted at in churchwardens' accounts of the period. For example, the accounts for Stoke Charity inform us that the largest expense for the year following the dissolution of the chantries was for the whitewashing of the church: in effect an act of iconoclasm. The sum referred to forms about a quarter of the recorded sum spent for that year. This period also witnessed the 'Takinge downe of the Aulters'.[18] At St John's, Winchester, money was provided for pulling down the screens as well as a large sale of church goods.[19] Nevertheless, this latter account may suggest that such goods were still valued by the community. Significantly, medieval screens survive at St John's, suggesting that they may have been preserved and put up again at a later date. Some screens may have been spirited away and eventually found themselves in other churches, such as the elaborate chancel screen at Compton Bassett, Wiltshire, which may have come originally from one of the chantry chapels at Salisbury cathedral.[20]

Change and continuity, 1548–1558

As argued, chantry founders consciously sought to elicit a popular response from the living as a result of having enriched parish worship: each helped the other. With the dissolution of chapels and chantries as intercessory

[17]   Godfrey 1954: 100.
[18]   Williams 1913: 78–79.
[19]   Ibid.: 166.
[20]   Reynolds 1993.

monuments, and the proscription of prayers for the dead, such a relationship was drastically altered. Many former chapels remained in private hands, but the laity was left without any reciprocal role. The abolition of the doctrine of purgatory and prayers for the dead thus changed the relationship between the living and the dead and there appears to be a degree of ambiguity in the immediate post-Reformation period concerning the location of the dead.[21] Although such ambiguities were largely doctrinally removed by the early 1550s, it appears that certain concessions had to be made for a general need for commemoration. Bainbridge asserts that at a popular level these were 'tolerated rather than countenanced by the church'.[22] Commemoration, it seems, to some extent satisfied the social and psychological needs that had been represented by rituals of intercession.

It appears that such ambiguity, at least concerning the dead, carried on into the brief period of the Marian restoration between 1553 and 1558. There is also some evidence to suggest that, at least until the 1570s, provisions, obits, months minds and prayers for the dead were still referred to in wills.[23] It is plausible that, in time, like the foundation of new monastic houses, this period might have seen the eventual re-foundation of chantries, had the Catholic restoration proved more resilient. Certainly there is evidence for the reinstallation of former chapel altars. At Ashburton in 1553, money was provided for the making of new altars,[24] and at Stoke Charity the previously noted removed altars were replaced, specifically the 'altar of St Katherine', probably in the Hampton chapel, although it was swiftly removed again after the death of Queen Mary. Also at Stoke Charity, in the year 1557–8, money was made available 'For the lyght at John Comlyn's moneth'[25] – suggesting some continuation of intercessory practice. Though rare, some evidence does survive in wills for the continuation of intercessory practice (or at least the intent). In 1555, Thomas Wichefilde, who was buried at Wedmore, requested 'ten preests to celebrate Dirige and Masseys and to praye for my soule, my father's and mother's and all christen soules'. Wichefilde went on to state that 'one of the said masses to be of the Trinitie, the secounde of the Holly Goste, the thirde of the Fyve Wondes, the fourthe of Or Lady and the fivethe to be masse of Requiem'.[26] This particular example also witnesses some attempt to provide further intercessory prayers at a later date, appealing for 'my executors in the places where they dwell to give at their discretion to a preest to pray for my soule, saving that I wolde my executors send to a Curatt where I shall happen to be buried 20d for a masse and a Dirige to be said there for my soule, at anytime within the month'.[27]

The continuation of intercessory practice in a period of uncertainty may lie behind the ambiguity present in the construction of chapels during this

21   Bainbridge 1994: 211.
22   Ibid.: 213.
23   Cressy 1997.
24   Butcher 1870: 33.
25   Williams 1913: 84.
26   Weaver 1905: 177.
27   Ibid.

period. At Old Basing, the south chapel has all the features one would expect of a pre-Reformation chantry, including intercessory symbolism and altar squints, but its tombs date from the post-Reformation period. These tombs contain the remains of John and William Paulet, who both died in the early 1570s. However, it is likely that the contemporary tombs and chapel were constructed prior to this period. The tombs, integral to the chapel, certainly date to a period later than the dissolution. The tombs mirror those constructed on the north side, probably sometime after 1519, where an inscription above the arcade leading to the north nave aisle provides the date of construction. The south chapel is constructed of different materials, namely brick, and has later windows in its south wall. Significantly, the south chapel substitutes unfinished heraldic shields for the niches found above the chancel entrance to the north chapel. The tombs themselves had heraldic motifs and Renaissance-influenced sculpture, instead of the flying angels that adorn those to the north. Intriguingly, it may not stretch the imagination too far to suggest that what we have here in the south chapel is a product of the uncertainty of the 1550s. A chapel with evidence for an altar, squint and associated tombs, suggesting an intercessory role, perhaps in the context of a newly founded private chapel, and mirroring that to the north, but with secular symbols and decoration – pertinent to the time, but displaying insecurity.

One of the more suggestive and perhaps enigmatic foundations of this period is the Brydges south chapel at St James's, Ludgershall. The former chapel, originally dating from the fifteenth century, was rebuilt as a chapel for the tomb of Richard Brydges (d.1558), knighted at the coronation of Mary and sheriff of Berkshire in 1555.[28] The chapel has no view of the chancel altar, so it is likely that it had a liturgical focus of its own, particularly in the light of the Catholicism of its patron. It is likely that the existing casement windows were inserted at this time to accentuate the space, added to which was an altar re-erected on the east wall where the fifteenth-century piscina survived. It is perhaps difficult to claim this structure as a 'chantry chapel', but any mass celebrated there surely had a connection to the deceased, whose tomb, complete with hovering angel and heraldic devices, is situated within the arch on the south side in direct visual line between the nave and possible chapel altar. Whether or not any mass was ever actually celebrated in the chapel is unknown. Brydges died in the year 1558, the same year as his queen, and the following year the Elizabethan settlement outlawed altars and ordered their replacement with communion tables; once again the Reformation continued.

Change and continuity, 1558–1650

Abolition of the doctrine of purgatory in 1547 changed the relationship between the living and the dead, since intercession, it was posited, would not benefit the dead. Consequently, changing attitudes towards death and burial

---

[28]   *VCH Hampshire* 1995: 119–133.

custom and the expression of ritual in the period of the Reformation and after have been stated to reflect an 'increasing stress on the individual'.[29] This stress, notable in differing types of funeral ritual, has been claimed to have reflected and reinforced social distinctions.[30] From this period, the state, or secular church, began to retake control of the individual. The heraldic funerals of the late sixteenth century consisted of elaborate ceremonies witnessing the legitimate transference of titles and power, in essence symbolising the ultimate power of the monarchy. At these funerals the individual, or his or her personal *persona*, was ignored. What was effectively 'celebrated' was the continuation of hereditary social control and hierarchy.[31] The decades after the Reformation, therefore, witnessed increasing emphasis on status and rank in life, as opposed to rituals concerned with the dead, coupled with an increasing emphasis on sorrow and loss.[32] Perhaps an obvious, if not traditional, context for this was the space vacated by former chantries and intercessory foundations. Consequently, many former chantries and chapels were used as memorial and fully private chapels. As a result they became exclusive and disconnected from the parish church community, such as the former chapel of Our Lady of the Bower at Bishops Cannings, which became the Ernle chapel within a few years after official dissolution.

Increasingly, practices associated with death and memorial were non-communal and focussed on the individual and his or her deeds in life. The after-life was viewed not as a 'slog through purgatory but as an immediate, if incomplete, felicity'.[33] Many tomb inscriptions celebrated the life (often embellished) of individuals and did not exhort any prayers for the soul, as at Farleigh Hungerford, Stogumber and Titchfield. Naturally, this dispensed with any communal role or importance being attached to these chapels. As a result, the former communal importance of such chapels no longer existed. Intercessory prayers, bolstered by those of the community, were not required. Equally, the role of the chantries as a context for eucharistic practice was no longer relevant. Emphasis was placed on the pulpit, with the church space now serving as an auditorium. Visual participation in the liturgy was consequently diminished. Except with regard to the written word, often covering earlier wall paintings, and gesticulating preachers, public involvement in formerly highly symbolic rituals was redundant. The limewashed walls and lack of candlelight provided for a more austere, and arguably less emotive, experience. The colour and decoration of such monuments was devalued and therefore a whole frame-work of public and private piety and social interaction was deconstructed. Furthermore, chapels were no longer required for congregational space, as the former chantries and chapels were not generally aligned to the pulpit. Those that were, such as at Stourton, Wiltshire and Ramsbury, became exclusively private pews.

29 Gittings 1984: 30.
30 Bassett et al. 1992: 6.
31 Gittings 1999: 168.
32 Ibid.: 169.
33 Loades 1994: 215.

Many chapels continued to be used as places of family burial and commemoration, with many medieval features still intact. Former chapels and chantries, such as those of the Bluetts at Whitestaunton, the Wadhams at Ilminster and the Phelips at Montacute, for example, continued as family chapels. The chapel of St Nicholas, Chew Magna, complete with viewing gallery, was still in use until it was partially dismantled in the late sixteenth century. The Tichborne chapel at Tichborne still retains its late sixteenth-century wooden altar, decorated with *IHS* and crosses, possibly used for secret masses. Altars were outlawed in the early years of Elizabeth I's reign and it is fairly likely that this altar was removed to the nearby manor house when necessary. As at Tichborne, some former chantries and private chapels, like the south chapel at Mapledurham, Oxfordshire and the Sydenham chapel at Stogumber, have consistently remained Catholic chapels to this day. Unlike pre-Reformation examples, certain former chapels and chantries became increasingly private and exclusive, often cut off both visually and physically from the rest of the church. Some had their floors raised to place them 'above' the laity and many had acquired their own private entrance. These chapels have been termed elaborate 'parlour pews'. Many were furnished and carpeted, and often equipped with a small fireplace, as at Brympton and Stourton, and even, in some instances, a dog-kennel.[34] The Hoare family pew at Stourton is visibly cut off from the nave stalls by a large plain screen, and its interior can only be viewed by the priest in the pew, and vice versa. The former Darrell chantry at Ramsbury had a doorway inserted into its north wall and stalls introduced for the local Popham family. Such changes forced the removal of a tomb from its recess and the blocking of the entrance from the north aisle to the chapel, effectively sealing off the chapel from the rest of the church. Many chantries and chapels retained their family connections. The Long chapel at South Wraxall, for example, become the Long family pew in 1566,[35] and in the same period the Coplestone chapel at Colebroke, Devon, became the family pew. The chantry of the Bretts, a family of notable recusants, at Whitestaunton survived as a family chapel with an elaborate portal entrance added in 1588, as did that of the Spencer family at Great Brington.

Deconstructing a symbolic world: the renegotiation of chapel space

The reorganisation of chapel topography, a form of iconoclasm, often resulted in the de-ritualising and appropriation of former, communally oriented, sacred space. One aspect of the re-organisation of chapels and former chantries related to light and the blocking of windows. Light and vision, as we have already seen, were integral components of ritual space within chapels and chantries, particularly significant for communal piety. Squints were a vital mechanism of this relationship. Likewise windows, often related to altars and

---

34   Scarisbrick 1984, 173.
35   *VCH Wilts* 1953.

tombs, emphasised these liturgical areas. Although there is no evidence in the research area for the blocking of squints, their relevance was undeniably diminished, if not defunct. Like much pre-Reformation church architecture, some squints may have been subject to structural change. Some, for example, were blocked, such as at Litton Cheney, Dorset, or restored, like the angled squints at Jevington, East Sussex, which were 'straightened' in the nineteenth century.[36] At South Petherton, Somerset, the squint from the north chapel was blocked during the nineteenth-century church 'restoration'.[37] At Brading, the tomb of William Oglander (1608) blocks the squint from the chapel to the high altar. Former lines of sight from chapels to the body of church became unimportant. At Rodney Stoke, for example, the arcade from the chancel to the north chapel is blocked by a wall inserted as part of the tomb of George Rodney (c.1650). The blocking of windows in former chapels suggests that light was perhaps no longer needed to emphasise former areas of liturgical importance. At Alton, Basingstoke, Godshill, Lacock and Tichborne, for example, windows inside former chapels were blocked up.

A significant factor in the reuse of former chapel and chantry space during this period is the conscious placement of monuments to invalidate space formerly used for intercession and now proscribed Catholic practice. The vacant spaces of former chapels allowed the church to accommodate large, or otherwise anti-social, monuments. This more subtle form of iconoclasm involved at its most basic level the spatial placing of monuments to block, or more importantly *appropriate*, features or former areas of prior importance. At Titchfield, the large alabaster Wriothesley monument of 1581, with its triple effigies and corner obelisks, attracted significant attention as well as appropriating former chapel space (Fig. 65), although here the former importance of the now spiritually defunct chapel east end is still recognised. More dramatically, the placing of the excessively large monument to Edward Hungerford (d.1648) and wife in the centre of the former chapel of St Anne at St Leonard, Farleigh Hungerford, effectively obstructed, in a supreme act of arrogance, physical and visual access in the chapel, prioritising the most important monument (Fig. 66). At Aldbourne, Rodney Stoke and Wellow, Somerset, tombs were constructed over former chapel altars.

As previously discussed, the north chapel at Stoke Charity became the Hampton family chantry from at least 1483. As noted earlier, in the early sixteenth century the chapel seems to have been the subject of some physical change, namely the introduction of a new ritual focus situated on the chapel's north wall: an Easter sepulchre and tomb. This redirection of ritual focus necessitated the insertion of a double squint. After the Reformation, the chapel remained as a private chapel for local Phellypes family. The addition of the tomb of Thomas Phellypes provides an interesting insight into the nature of post-Reformation reaction. The positioning of the tomb, on a raised

[36]   Roffey, 2006.
[37]   The area of the former chapel altar with canopied niche and squint has more recently been enclosed to provide a toilet compartment within the modern church vestry – not a particularly dignified example of the reuse of former sacred space.

Figure 65 The large and ostentatious Wriothsley tomb at Titchfield appropriates almost all of the former ritual space. (Roffey 2003)

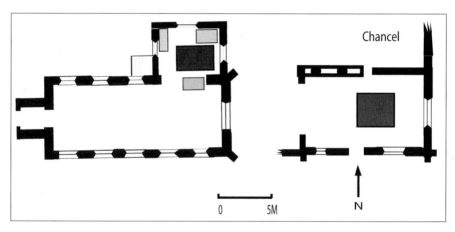

Figure 66 Farleigh Hungerford, left, and detail of the Southampton chapel, Titchfield, on the right, showing appropriation of former ritual space by post-Reformation monuments. (Roffey 2003)

plinth and at a slight angle, as well as restricting access to the chapel from the north aisle restricted visual access from this area to the chapel. In fact, the placing of the tomb at a slight angle effectively blocked out the Waller altar tomb completely and made it the dominant monument within the chapel. It appears that the placing of the memorial broached the pre-Reformation and orthodox topography of the chapel (Fig. 67).

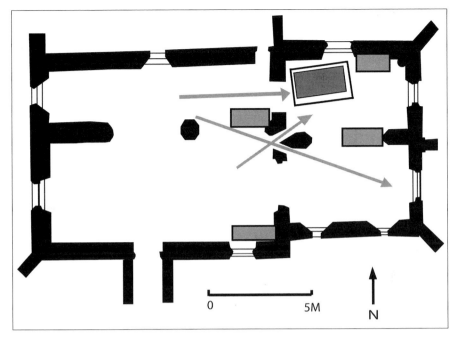

Figure 67   The Hampton chapel, Stoke Charity, showing how the addition of the Phellypes tomb obstructed former ritual space both physically and visibly.

Overall, former chapels, and tombs within them, characterised a fusion of secular and sacred elements. In some cases it is as if certain of the pre-Reformation symbols metamorphosised into more acceptable representations, such as the angel-like symbols of Hope and Charity found on the Sydenham tomb at Stogumber, for example. In fact, here their similarity to earlier overtly Catholic symbols led to their defacement in the seventeenth century.

The wider context

One of the most significant reasons why the transition was so rapid and largely unchallenged lies in the growth of rural and mercantile free enterprise, the vanguard of which were those who had formerly founded chantries within their parish churches, the English gentry.[38] Availability of land, formerly in the hands of monasteries and, to a lesser extent, chantries, enabled the redirection of energies previously spent on church building and the founding of chantries to more secular purposes. It is no coincidence that within the counties of Hampshire, Somerset and Wiltshire no significant church rebuilding was carried out after 1550 until the very end of the century. This was an age of

[38]   Richmond 1991.

social climbing and outward personal ostentation. Increasing importance was arguably placed on status and rank in *life*, as opposed to the former rituals concerned with the *dead*. Despite the grandeur of some tombs, men and women who had once built chantry chapels and founded guilds and fraternities, now increasingly directed their wealth to the building, or extensive rebuilding, of private country houses. Houses such as Bramshott Place, Basing House and the Vyne in Hampshire, Longleat and Lacock in Wiltshire, Montacute and Brympton in Somerset, were in many ways responding to social and political changes that were now shaping their lives. Many of these builders remained Catholic, and occupied privileged positions, such as Thomas Wriothesley, earl of Southampton, secretary to the king, and Cromwell, who built Titchfield House on the site of the former abbey and founded a memorial chapel in the parish church on the site of a former chantry. Liturgically sterilised, many former chantries became wholly private chapels. Shorn of intercessory paraphernalia they became an exclusive context for private religion and, in particular, family memorial and commemoration. Old mechanisms of intercession, such as altars, lights, sculpture and paintings, were removed and replaced with seating arrangements, fireplaces and, in some cases, ostentatious tombs that celebrated the deeds of the living with no reference to helping the dead, and of no relevance to the larger parish community. That many Catholic families, such as the Tichbornes and Wriothesleys of Titchfield, still chose to reconstruct their chapels can be no reflection of a change in beliefs regarding the dead, but rather an attempt to escape potential persecution and the bottom rung of the social ladder, especially as many of the *nouveau riche* Protestant families cashed in on current religious and economic changes. It is perhaps significant that both the latter families went on to achieve high honours at court.

In a sense, the dissolution was an event set in motion by earlier reformations, particularly that of the monasteries a decade earlier. England in the mid-sixteenth century was changing, the availability of land, once held by the 'dead hand' of the Catholic church, now provided the means and context for the growth of a society where status and social standing were of growing importance. This was also the period that witnessed the increasing awareness of the mercantile potential of the New World. Such an environment of economic and social enterprise gave no place to the spiritually motivated works of church rebuilding and chapel building. Chantry chapels had in many ways become superfluous to the new society, even to the remaining Catholic families, for whom overt Catholicism was becoming increasingly dangerous. For the aristocracy, this period was one of transition marked by change in religious belief, but more importantly heralded and presented by a time of limitless opportunity. The chantry would not and could not play a part in this process; it was part of the old world. In many ways the dissolution of chantries had liberated the gentry, enabling them 'legally' to 'renege on their predecessors'.[39] Former prayers for the dead were now transformed into memorial and commemoration,

---

[39]   Burgess 1987a: 205–206.

celebrating the life and (sometimes over-embellished) deeds of the living. The absence of endowments to churches and chapels was a major loss to the form and fabric of parish church life. Intercession, and its colourful rites and rituals, providing hope, existential security and an important mechanism for coping with death, loss and the insecurity of a short life, was extinguished. The real losers in this period were the common laity; they had arguably gained nothing, but lost a valuable and emotive context for public piety as well as an established system of localised social welfare and communal relationships.

8

Case Studies:
Stoke Charity, Bridgwater and Mere

Introduction

This chapter presents a series of case studies combining the archaeological analysis of individual chantry chapels with relevant documentary evidence. It shows how a survey of documentary sources can provide a useful source of background and incidental material. Such information can provide evidence for the historical presence of chantries, dedications and, in some cases, chronologies and foundation provisions. Churchwardens' accounts, where they survive, can provide useful information regarding internal fixtures, fittings and goods associated with chantry foundation. Surviving documents are thus a useful source of background information for the structural investigation of former chantries and chapels.

The three case studies, drawn from the 80 researched chapels, have been selected primarily on the basis of good surviving documentary sources and existing structural remains and show how historical and archaeological resources, where they survive, combine into a detailed biography of chantry chapel foundation.

St Michael, Stoke Charity, Hampshire

The parish church of St Michael in the Hampshire village of Stoke Charity is one of the best preserved medieval churches in the county. Nestling on the banks of the River Dever it is bordered by the earthworks of a possible former manor house to the south. The nature of the evidence from the church is diverse, and includes medieval fabric, tombs and monuments, wall painting and sculpture. There are also some documentary accounts, particularly the churchwarden's accounts which date to the mid-sixteenth century. The site was also subject to limited archaeological excavation in the early 1990s. Typically, the church consists of a chancel, nave, post-medieval tower, north aisle and north chancel chapel, the latter of which forms the basis for structural analysis as presented here.

Structural evidence

The north chancel chapel is constructed of roughly coursed flint with occasional pieces of possible Mersham greensand. It is abutted to the west by a north aisle with a twelfth-century round-headed door. In the fabric of the north wall there is also a possible fragment of a pre-Conquest window which may be comparable to one found during the excavations. The top of the chapel was raised by several courses, probably at the same time that the east window and wooden ceiling were inserted. This three-light window is late fifteenth century in style and contains some original glass with a depiction of the 'sun in splendour', a Yorkist emblem datable to 1461–83. The three-light window in the north wall is of later date: possibly early sixteenth century as its style is similar to the Waller tomb of c.1525. This window glass contains the fragments of figural depictions of St Margaret of Antioch, the Virgin and Child and the Christ child giving benediction.

Internally, the chapel is entered via the north aisle by a single arch of the early twelfth century or earlier. There is also a fifteenth-century arch from the chancel; remains of an earlier one are discernible in the south-west corner. Internally, the chapel contains re-set late fourteenth-century encaustic floor tiles, a fifteenth-century wood panel ceiling, and the remains of a medieval sculptured image of St Gregory celebrating the mass. In the south-east corner of the chapel there is a portion of wall painting depicting an unknown saint, which has been dated to the late thirteenth century.[1] A double squint is present in the south-west corner of the chapel. At the east end of the chapel is a raised plinth upon which sits a modern altar. Several Purbeck marble ledger slabs survive in the floor (many re-set). The table tomb of Thomas Hampton and wife is inserted in the arcade (c.1483). Against the north wall is the tomb and Easter sepulchre of John Waller (c.1525). This tomb has a carved reredos with an image niche. There is some evidence for vandalised painted images on the tomb including a possible St Thomas of Canterbury. To the east of the tomb is an iron wall-hook. In the west end of the chapel is the large table tomb of Thomas Phellyppes (c.1626), which sits upon a raised platform.

Interpretation

The earliest evidence for the site itself possibly dates to the early 900s when it may have been granted as part of the manor of Micheldever to Hyde abbey by Edward the Elder c. 904. There is also a reference to it in the Domesday Book.[2] Excavations in 1990 revealed some evidence for Anglo-Saxon activity outside the church, including a boundary ditch, Anglo-Saxon pottery and a

---

1   Edwards 1985.
2   *VCH Hants* 1908: 447–451.

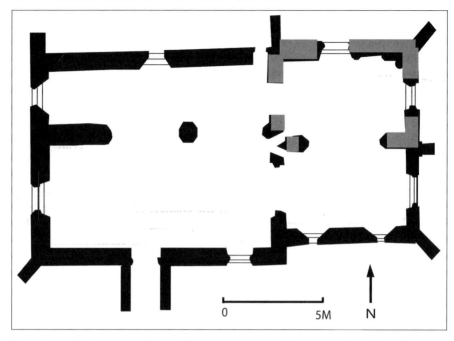

Figure 68   Plan of Stoke Charity showing surviving and conjectured evidence for eleventh-century fabric (in grey).

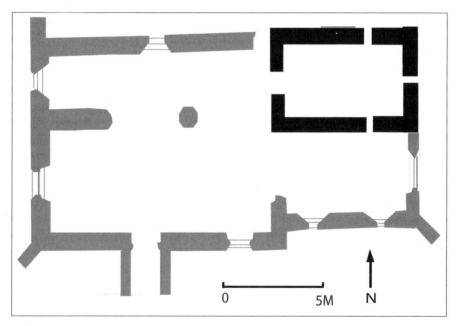

Figure 69   Conjectured reconstruction of the early proprietary chapel at Stoke Charity (later medieval church shown in grey).

fragment of the head of a narrow-headed Saxon window.[3] This form of mono-lithic window arch is similar to an example found at Muchelney, Somerset. The dimensions (c. 8 x 5 metres) and style of this chapel is comparable to the Anglo-Saxon proprietary church at Alton Barnes, Wiltshire, as well as the well-known excavated churches at Rivenhall in Essex, Raunds in Northamptonshire and the nearby site of Brighton Hill in Hampshire.[4]

Other forms of structural evidence relating to the late Anglo-Saxon period already noted include a possible eleventh or twelfth-century arch entered from the later twelfth-century north aisle. Externally there is evidence for possible Anglo-Saxon style pilaster strips and window fragment. It has also been suggested that the north wall of the Hampton chapel was re-faced or thickened sometime in the later medieval period.[5] It is possible, therefore, that the Hampton chapel was once either the chancel of an early freestanding manorial or proprietary church or more likely a single-cell chapel itself (the remains of the manor at Stoke Charity lie beneath an earthwork about 40 metres south of the church) (Fig. 68). The arch from the later twelfth-century north aisle may have once been the chancel arch or the western doorway. During the twelfth century, the nave and chancel of the parish church were reconstructed and the north aisle added. The chapel then became a chancel chapel (Fig. 69).

Late medieval period

In 1334 the site passed into the hands of de la Charité family and then to the Hampton family in 1362.[6] The chapel was probably provided with a tiled floor at this period. The fragment of arch leading from the chancel may also date to this period. In the fifteenth century the chapel became the Hampton chantry chapel, a transition which involved the significant reconstruction of parts of the chapel, including the insertion of a new east window, the construction of a wood panel ceiling, and the placing of the tomb to Thomas Hampton and wife in the reconstructed chancel arch. The east window containing glass fragments of the 'sun in splendour', a device of Edward IV (1461–83), is indicative of date and perhaps of the Yorkist sympathies of the chapel's re-founder. The location of the Hampton tomb altar between the arcade from chapel to chancel indicates a desire to make the monument visible not just from within the chapel, but also from the high altar as well as from the nave (Fig. 70). Certainly it suggests a desire for proximity to the high altar as the holier place. Interestingly, the sculpture of St Gregory celebrating mass in the north-west corner of the chapel, if positioned here or hereabouts originally, appears to 'float' just above the Hampton tomb when viewed from the chancel. It is tempting to see this as a device to remind the viewer (possibly the parish priest serving the high altar) of the tomb's occupants and an intercessory patron.

---

3   Qualmann 1991.
4   Fasham, Keevill and Coe: 1995.
5   Qualmann 1991.
6   *VCH Hants* 1908.

In the early sixteenth century the chapel seems to have been subject to changes once again, namely the redirection of the liturgical focus in the chapel from the altar at the east end to a new altar of John Waller (d.1525), situated on the chapel's north wall (Fig. 71). This tomb, with its elaborate canopy and niches, as well as evidence for a metal hook or 'riddel', may have also served as an Easter sepulchre. The riddel may have been used to hang a veil over the sepulchre during Easter week to symbolise the entombment of Christ. The redirection of ritual focus also necessitated the insertion of a new window in the north wall to accentuate this new ritual space, as well as the insertion of the double squint to permit people to see the table tomb from the nave. The squint may have also enabled people in the north aisle to see the chancel. Alternatively, the unmarked set of tombs in the north aisle may have also been the location of an altar, and the squint gave the presiding priest a view over to the high altar. If this was so, he would also be able to see both the Waller tomb and the chapel altar through the twelfth-century arch.

These alterations alert us to the changing nature of the chapel, as well as providing comparative dating evidence (for the squint and window), which enables a chronological phasing to be constructed. Significantly, it also suggests that communal visual accessibility was priority and determined a series of changes within chapel ritual geography, which in turn reaffirms that the public were meant to have a relationship with such monuments. Like many other similar chapels and churches, Stoke Charity was to be victim to the drastic changes of the Reformation. The churchwardens' accounts offer

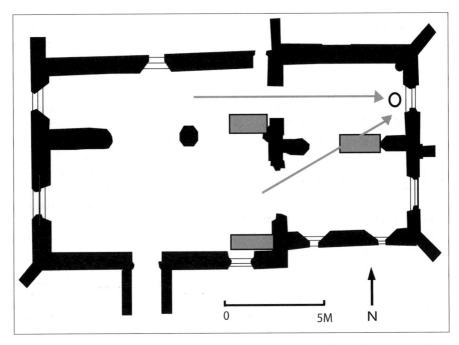

Figure 70 Stoke Charity in the fifteenth century, showing the lines of sight from the nave and north aisle into the Hampton chapel.

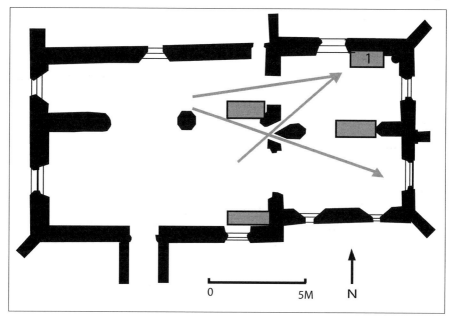

Figure 71 Stoke Charity in the early sixteenth century. Here, the Waller tomb/Easter sepulchre (1) became a new ritual focus necessitating the insertion of a double squint. Thus, the visual participation of the laity is still ensured. The squint also gives a better view of the chancel from the north aisle.

us an invaluable insight into some of the changes of this period and give a particular view on the period of uncertainty before, during and after the Catholic restoration of Queen Mary (1553–58). For example, in 1550 money was provided for the taking down of the altars. This is unlikely to refer to the high altar and may actually refer to altars in the Hampton chapel and elsewhere. Interestingly, a year later Richard Waller was buried under a memorial ledger slab in the chapel at the base of his father's tomb and Easter Sepulchre. In 1554, during the first few years of Mary's reign, the accounts inform us that money was provided for the making of St Katherine's altar and for the acquisition of images of St Mary and St John. Three years later we hear that the light for John Comlyn's anniversary light or month mind was also provided for.[7] This tells us that at least some elements of Stoke Charity society did not dispense with traditional customs that easily. However, much of this was in vain, as a few years later in 1561 the altars were once again dismantled, and this time for good.[8]

By the following century, the period of uncertainty was largely over. However, the former ritual places of the pre-Reformation were still imbued with some significance. During this period, the former Hampton chapel at Stoke Charity seems to have become a private chapel for the local Phellypes

[7]   Williams 1913: 81.
[8]   Ibid.

family. The addition of the tomb of Thomas Phellypes (1626), on a raised plinth and at a slight angle, restricted access to the chapel from the north aisle. It also restricted visual access into the chapel. Here, the placing of the tomb at a slight angle effectively blocked out the earlier Waller tomb and Easter sepulchre completely and made the Phellypes tomb the dominant monument within the chapel (Fig. 67). It appears that the placing of the memorial breached the pre-Reformation and orthodox topography of the chapel. It thus suggests that such places still had some relevance. The west end of the north aisle seems to have been the predominant place of burial for important local families at this time and until the end of the seventeenth century, when the last lord of the manor died. This suggests that the north side of the church still retained some significance with regard to mortuary practice well after the Reformation.

St Mary, Bridgwater, Somerset

The parish church of St Mary is a large, well-preserved urban parish church closely flanked on its north side by the busy town of Bridgwater. Unlike the previous example of Stoke Charity, not a great deal survives internally in the way of tombs and internal fixtures of the once documented chantries. However, the fabric 'shell' of various former chapels does survive, with significant evidence for structural features and changes. Importantly, this can be related to a wealth of documentary evidence, in particular those that are contained in the borough archives, which extend across much of the late medieval period. The archives contain material relating to chantry foundation, churchwardens' accounts, wills and related records. The church typically consists of an aisled chancel and nave, shallow north and south transepts, chancel north chapel and south chapels, west tower and spire and nineteenth-century vestry on the north side of the chancel. The south side also has a nineteenth-century two-storey porch. The area under investigation here comprises a composite structure of two-storey north porch with east short aisle and adjoining transept.

Structural evidence

The external fabric of the north transept is constructed largely of small blocks of Blue Lias stone. However, on the east side of the transept there is some earlier red sandstone, which suggests a rebuilding and refacing of the chapel (Fig. 72). The reconstructed north porch is built of Blue Lias, but there is evidence on its west side of an earlier structure, again, of red sandstone. Internally, the north porch has been greatly restored. Externally, there are two low doors in the north transept to a crypt; one in the east wall and one in the north wall surrounded by two decorated recesses of fourteenth-century style with eroded effigies. Image niches are placed either side of the two-storey porch entrance and there is an unusual round window at first-floor level. There

Figure 72
The north transept, St Mary, Bridgwater, looking west.

Figure 73
St Mary, Bridgwater, showing adjoining aisle, possibly the site of St Katherine's chapel, between the north transept and porch.

is also a continuous parapet along the porch, aisle and transept. Windows in the east wall of the transept appear to be of the fifteenth century – the northerly one offers some indication of being inserted into pre-existing fabric – whilst the single north windows of the transept and aisle contain some geometrical designs and may therefore be of the late fourteenth century. The porch is abutted by a fifteenth-century nave aisle (Fig. 73), whilst the transept appears to abut the chancel north aisle and is connected via a small structure to the aisle chapel. Internally, there is not much surviving evidence. There is much evidence for restoration inside, including the existing arcade that replaced a partition wall in the mid-nineteenth century. The former wall was probably the original west wall of the transept. On the west side of the porch there is a large internal window providing a view into the north transept. This was once part of a series of squints removed in the mid-nineteenth century. Two other squints were placed in the wall dividing the north transept from the aisle, and in the corner between the north transept and the chancel north chapel.[9]

Interpretation

During the medieval period the church of Bridgwater had several documented chantries. Three of these were dissolved in 1548: that of Holy Trinity, St George and St Mary.[10] However, the records throughout the period also refer to the chantries of St Katherine, Holy Rood (possibly two), St Anne, All Saints and St Erasmus. The most comprehensive documentary evidence survives for the chapel of the Virgin Mary, which, it is claimed, was situated behind the high altar.[11] The accounts of the chantry wardens prior to the 1390s suggest that this chantry was in decline at this period. One particular cause appears to be the failure in rents from cottages and tenants, including one where a house was literally falling down from neglect.[12] This resulted in the re-foundation of the chapel as an ecclesiastical benefice in 1393.[13] By the fifteenth century, the merchant guild chapel dedicated to the Holy Trinity was the richest chantry in the church, even holding its own court on occasions.[14] The chapel of the Holy Trinity was mentioned numerous times throughout the fifteenth century and by 1490, we are told, it was under the control of wardens.[15] The location of this chapel is, however, problematic. Dilks suggests that it may have been in the north chancel chapel, and that by the fifteenth century the chapel to St Katherine was in the north transept and that to St Anne in the west, possibly the aisle or porch area.[16] It is also possible that the chantry of St Mary was actually in the north chancel chapel. It is one of the

9   I.H.P. 1845.
10   Calendar of Chantry Grants CPR Mary 1.992; Green 1888: 56–57.
11   Dilks 1938.
12   Ibid.: 53.
13   Ovid: 220
14   Dilks 1933: xl
15   Dilks 1945, 1971.
16   Dilks 1971: 11, 13.

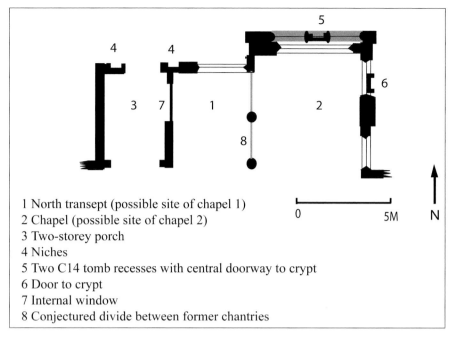

1 North transept (possible site of chapel 1)
2 Chapel (possible site of chapel 2)
3 Two-storey porch
4 Niches
5 Two C14 tomb recesses with central doorway to crypt
6 Door to crypt
7 Internal window
8 Conjectured divide between former chantries

0   5M   N

Figure 74   St Mary, Bridgwater. Plan of conjectured chapels: 1) St Katherine 2) Holy Trinity.

earliest foundations, dating to around the 1360s, and its construction clearly predates the north transept, which abuts it. Significantly, the north chancel chapel is also constructed largely of red sandstone, a building material used predominantly in the earlier phases of the church.

It is possible that the chapel of the Holy Trinity was in fact in the north transept and prior to c.1400 may have been originally the chapel of All Saints (chapel 2 in Fig. 74). The churchwardens' accounts in 1385 inform us that a roofer was hired for fifteen days work to repair the roofs of both the north porch and the chapel of All Saints. Money was also provided for the purchase of 1000 stones and lime and sand. This suggests a significant rebuilding.[17] Once again in 1394 work was conducted on the chapel at the behest of the churchwardens, suggesting that it may have been under the control of the church and the wardens. If so it may have presented a space ripe for re-founding. Significantly there is no mention of the chapel of All Saints from 1400 onwards.

In 1415, the churchwardens' accounts refer to a boatload of stones being brought from Pibsbury for repairs to the chapels of the Virgin Mary and the Holy Trinity. It also refers to the purchase of scaffolding, weatherboarding, lime and sand. This is clearly a fairly major building project. Furthermore, the accounts also refer to building of Holy Trinity chapel in the time of

[17]   Dilks 1938: 162–168.

the churchwardens Robert Daysham and John Canon and 'various labourers raising stones on to the chapel from the ground'.[18] At this time, we are told that the windows of the Holy Trinity chapel were worked on by a specialist John Glasyer from Wells. Daysham is mentioned in two documents of 1403–4.[19] It is therefore likely that significant episodes of work were carried out on the chapel from the last few years of the fourteenth century until around 1415, when we are also told, somewhat unusually, of a sum of £20 being levied on parishioners as a collection.[20]

When we look at the structural evidence, the porch, north transept and interconnecting aisle were clearly the subject of several episodes of rebuilding. It is likely that the red sandstone on the west wall of the porch represents an earlier structure – possibly a porch or shallow transept. The work, carried out in the late fourteenth and early fifteenth centuries, may reflect the change in the status of the chapel and, possibly, its refoundation as the merchant guild chapel of Holy Trinity. It is likely that the chapel of St Katherine was in the small aisle between the porch and north transept (against the now removed wall) (chapel 1 in Fig. 74). The presence of an arcade between the aisle and north transept may indicate the original dividing line between the two chapels, delineating the respective ritual spaces of both. In 1384, we hear of the reversion of tenement to churchwardens in the event of there being no chaplain for the chantry of St Katherine.[21] In 1445, the wardens and chantries of Holy Trinity, Holy Cross (Rood) and St Katherine leased a tenement to William and Alice Elver, suggesting that by this period these three chapels were amalgamated.[22]

As the chantry of the guild of the Holy Trinity was the wealthiest of all the chantries in the church, we might expect its chapel to reflect this structurally. Certainly the two-storey porch and the small north aisle and north transept are visually impressive buildings and are constructed of good-quality stone. The windows, particularly those in the porch and north wall of the transept, are impressive. The chapels are also, importantly, located close to the main entrance of the church. It is tempting to conjecture that the two niches once held the dedicated saints of the two chantry chapels. The porch itself contains an internal window which would provide a view, not just to the chantries of the Holy Trinity and St Katherine, but through these to the high altar, suggesting a significant group of people were given visual access to the chapels at certain times. And, significantly, from the chapels a view of all the major altars in the church could be achieved: that of the chantry of the Holy Cross in the rood screen, the chancel north chapel, the south chapel and the high altar. The specific location of the chapels of the Holy Trinity and St Katherine are therefore of ritual significance. It is also possible that the crypt was for the exclusive use of the guild members.

18   Dilks 1943: 46–53.
19   Ibid.: 21.
20   Dilks 1943: xiii.
21   Dilks 1938: 156.
22   Dilks 1945: 1.

In conclusion, we see how the study of contemporary documents coupled with structural analysis can provide an interpretation of the former use of church space. It is possible that the actual location of the chapel of the Holy Trinity was elsewhere – perhaps we shall never know. However, the structural evidence supports the documented episodes of rebuilding, and the nature of the building itself suggests that the north transept, porch and associated aisle were areas of some importance, befitting, perhaps, the site of the church's and town's most important and influential chapel.

St Michael, Mere, Wiltshire

The church of St Michael sits in a large churchyard in the Wiltshire town of Mere. The churchyard itself is impressive, containing evidence for a medieval charnel house to the west and several other buildings of possible medieval and post-medieval date to the north. We are also told that the former chantry priest house was to the north.[23] The church as it survives is largely of perpendicular style, consisting of an aisle and clerestoried nave with western tower and north and south porches, a narrow chancel flanked by two chancel chapels, each with central stair turrets (Fig. 75). These chapels – the 'Bettisthorne' chapel to the south and the 'Still' chapel to the north – were the subjects of detailed survey.

Structural evidence

The Bettisthorne chapel. This is a two-bay south chapel constructed mostly of Chilmark limestone ashlar. The chapel flanks a three-bay chancel. Two windows are present in the south wall, the easternmost being of fourteenth-century style. The south window in the western bay of the chapel appears to be more elaborate, with quatrefoil ogee-cells in a casement, suggesting a slightly later date. The east window of the chapel is of fifteenth-century date. All three windows differ in their particular style. There is a stair turret to the roof on the north wall and the chapel has a flat roof with a plain parapet. The alignment of the buttress on the south-west corner may suggest that the chapel pre-dates the south aisle, though it clearly abuts the chancel. There is evidence internally that suggests that an earlier aisle was widened to 'align' with the newly-constructed chapel; the earlier roof line of which is noticeable on the chapel wall.

Internally, the chapel is divided from the chancel by two fourteenth-century arches, though the arcade to the east may have been reconstructed in the fifteenth century. The south of the chapel has one arch through to the south aisle of the fourteenth century. The surviving screens to the west and north are of fifteenth-century style. The western screen (to the south aisle) has small elevation or 'peep' holes inserted. The restored roof rests on medieval corbels.

23 Godfrey 1954.

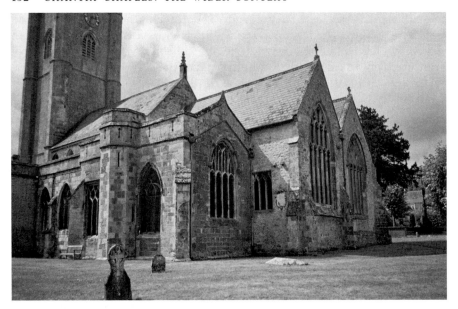

Figure 75   Mere parish church showing north and south chapels and chancel.

There are several ledger memorials with brasses on the floor, and there is a slightly raised platform at the east end of the chapel. In the north arcade there is a table tomb of Purbeck marble, which dates to the second half of the fifteenth century. In the centre of the chapel floor there is a monumental brass to John Bettisthorne (c.1398) and on the eastern altar platform, one to John Berkeley of c.1430. There is also a piscina with a shelf in the south-east corner. On the west wall of the chapel (aisle side), above the arch, is evidence for a sloping roofline of the earlier aisle. In the south wall is a fourteenth-century door to the stair.

The Still chapel. This is a three-bay north chancel chapel constructed of Zeal greensand mixed with Chilmark limestone. The north wall of the chapel is of ashlar while the east wall is roughly coursed and matches the east wall of the chancel. There are three north casement windows of similar design and an arched east window; all are secondary insertions of the fifteenth century. The windows in the north wall are similar to those found in the nave north aisle. The chapel abuts the north aisle, which like the south aisle was originally narrower. It is likely therefore that the construction of the chapel also involved the reconstruction of the north aisle. The eastern bay of the chapel is also unusual in that it is wider than the other two bays and the window is off-centre. It is possible that this bay represents an extension at some period.

Internally, there is a medieval doorway in the south wall giving access from the east end of the chancel. Above this is a late thirteenth-century window that is cut through by the door. The chapel has a wooden barrel ceiling of 1604. In the west side of the chapel is a loft for a former organ and a balcony that contained pews in the seventeenth century. Evidence from the internal fabric suggests that the north aisle to the west was widened in the fourteenth century to align with the new north chapel. In the south wall of the chapel is a triangular-headed piscina just to the east of the doorway and fairly central to the chapel.

Interpretation

Originally this was a church with narrow north and south aisles. The late thirteenth-century window in the north wall of the chancel indicates that this was an external wall at this period. In the fourteenth century two chapels were added to the chancel, necessitating the widening of the respective aisles. In the north chapel the earlier chancel north wall with its window was kept and a door was inserted underneath it, giving access from the chancel. It is likely that the north chapel was constructed slightly earlier than that to the south. In the fifteenth century the north chapel was possibly extended, perhaps to draw its altar closer to the high altar, and new windows were added. The piscina just to the east of the doorway is situated in the centre of the chapel and may suggest the original location of the altar (and therefore the chapel east end) before its extension. Before the eastern extension this chapel would have mirrored that to the south.

The south chapel was founded by John Bettisthorne who died in 1398. He was the lord of the manor of Charnage and is buried in the chapel under a monumental brass. Sometime after his death the chapel passed on to John Berkeley who had married his daughter. On November 20 1399 a licence was granted to Berkeley and his wife Elizabeth 'to augment a chantry in the chapel of St Mary in the parish church of Mere, Wiltshire, founded of old of one chaplain in honour of the annunciation of which they are patrons as in her right'.[24] The licence goes on to relate that this would therefore augment two existing chaplains to make three in all. This further suggests that now two chaplains would be serving one chapel.

The chantry certificates of the sixteenth century also refer to the Berkeley chapel at Mere,[25] to which three priests may have been attached.[26] Godfrey therefore believes that both the north chapel and the south chapel had become 'Berkeley' chantries by this period.[27] However, despite the claim that the north chapel may have operated as the Stourton chapel sometime in the fifteenth century,[28] the tomb of the first lord Stourton, John, tentatively identified by Pevsner and Cherry,[29] lies in the north arcade of the south chapel. We have previously seen the importance of sight lines and the placing or 'presencing' of tombs within them; importantly this tomb lies in a direct visual route between

24   Godfrey 1954:153.
25   E 301/58.
26   Walcott 1876: 21.
27   Godfrey 1954.
28   Ibid.: 157.
29   Pevsner and Cherry 1975: 346–347.

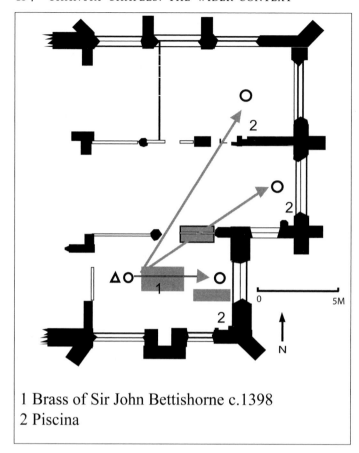

1 Brass of Sir John Bettishorne c.1398
2 Piscina

Figure 76
The east end of Mere church, showing visual relationships between the south and north chapels and high altar. Any laity present in the south chapel would have also had a view of the north chapel and high altars.

the south chapel and the high altar, suggesting its ritual significance. Indeed, the north chapel is identified as the Berkeley chapel some sixty years later at the dissolution. The north chapel itself was originally founded around 1350. In 1380 it was enlarged to the east, possibly under the influence of Berkeley, and was consequently reconstructed with the new windows added. It is likely it remained thus until the post-Reformation period when it became known as the Still chapel.

The church had at least one other chantry: that founded by John Forward in 1540 in the south aisle, where a piscina indicates the former location of the altar. The chantry priest, a Richard Chafyn, became the vicar in 1556.[30] This may be why this chapel was referred to as the Chafyn chapel in the post-medieval period and may also suggest why this chantry was located in the south aisle and not in the pre-existing chapels which were already under patronage.

30 Godfrey 1954: 154–160.

Spatial analysis of the north and south chapels reveals a complex ritual arrangement between them and the high altar (Fig. 76). In the south chapel there is no direct line of sight to the high altar unless the chapel altar was in the centre of the chapel, or that high altar was further west, which is unlikely. The inscription on the memorial brass of John Bettisthorne (c.1398), placed in the centre of the chapel floor, is oriented so as to be 'read' by people situated at the west of the of chapel, further supporting this arrangement. We have previously seen that evidence for a more centrally placed altar (or priest) exists at Old Basing, for example, so this may be a possibility. There is also from this point a line of sight to the north chapel if the doorway between the north chapel and chancel was open. This may suggest why the door was kept when the chapel was extended as it serves no real purpose otherwise. Likewise, in the north chapel a corresponding view to the south chapel can be achieved through the door.

The presence of the external stair turret in the centre of the south chapel is more perplexing. It appears to be integral with the build of the chapel and therefore of the late fourteenth century. Internally its position lines up with the central pier of the north arcade, so it may suggest a former access to a screen. However, no evidence for a former screen survives here and its location would effectively cut across the Bettisthorne memorial brass. It is possible that some form of screen was here which 'framed' the memorial, and would therefore support the claim for an altar being located here. This would effectively divide the chapel. At the eastern end of the chapel is a raised dais with the memorial brass of John Berkeley (c.1430). It is possible that this was the Berkeley chapel, before it moved to the north side, when this area came under the control of John Stourton.

As can be seen, analysis of the fabric coupled with surviving documentary sources and spatial analysis can offer some possible interpretations as to the conjectured arrangements of the Mere chantry chapels. A conjectured statement of their location and development can therefore be offered. Sometime in the middle of the fourteenth century a two-bay north chapel was constructed, possibly the Lady chapel. It is also possible that this was founded by John of Mere, a name which comes up in relation to the church in the first quarter of the fourteenth century. This was followed by a south chapel, constructed towards the end of the century as the chantry of John Bettisthorne. At some stage this chapel may have been divided into two distinct areas, perhaps marked by a central screen, the stair turret of which survives. This would have perhaps divided the chapel into a 'lay' area to the west and a 'clergy' area to the east. Within a year or two of Bettisthorne's death, a licence was granted to John Berkeley to found another chantry and augment the two existing priests by a third. This may have in fact been the north chapel and the 'refoundation' resulted in the extension of the north chapel by a bay and the addition of the new windows. At some time in the same century the south chapel (or part of it) may have become the Stourton chapel and a new table tomb was placed in the arcade between chapel and chancel. From then on the Berkeley chantry remained in the north chapel until its dissolution.

The legacy of the chantries at Mere was not to disappear completely after the Reformation. One chantry priest, the aforementioned Richard Chafyn, became the parish priest and no doubt quickly adapted himself (on the surface at least) to the new liturgies. The north chapel became a private chapel and as a result a new wooden barrel ceiling was added around 1604. To the west of the chapel, and utilising the former medieval rood stairwell, a gallery was placed with private seating. To some extent, at least, the former chantry chapel still had some place in the religious experience of the Mere parishioners. However, it was one that was less universally accessible.

9

Conclusions

Traditional perspectives on the social dimension of chantry and chapel foundation

For several years, studies of popular religion within pre-Reformation England have tended to emphasise that, as a result of the foundation of chapels and chantries, religious practice within the parish churches became increasingly privatised.[1] Others have under-emphasised or neglected the wider link between elite and common orthodoxy, or orthodoxy at a common level.[2] Significantly, the wider social role of chantries has been underestimated; some even go so far as to claim that they were 'socially useless'.[3] In reaction to traditional interpretations, more recently some historians have attempted to redress the balance.[4] Duffy has shown the widespread appeal of late medieval popular Catholicism and suggests that 'no substantial gulf existed between the religion of the clergy and the educated elite on the one hand, and that of the people at large on the other'.[5] Burgess, more specifically, has considered the wider social role of parish church chantries and concluded, convincingly, that they were an integral element of parish church life and worship, and of great benefit to all. In particular, chapels and chantries were an important and influential element within late medieval religion, at many levels of society. Despite being claimed as monuments wholly dedicated to individualism and individual intercession, as also emphasised by Wood-Legh[6] and Brooke,[7] many chapels and chantries have thus been claimed to have been 'off-limits' to the general laity. Consequently, it is claimed, many chapels were status symbols demonstrating the power and prestige of local families.[8] However, overall, chapels and chantries operated in a much wider social and religious context. They were, in a sense, a mixture of individual *and* communal motives, which

---

1   Cross 1976; Richmond 1984; Carpenter 1987.
2   Thomas 1971; Cross 1976.
3   Westlake 1919: 60–64
4   For example, Burgess 1991, 1996; Duffy 1992; Kümin 1996; French 2001; Marks 2004.
5   Duffy 1992: 2.
6   Wood-Legh 1965.
7   Brooke 1971.
8   French 2001: 155, 171.

was in fact typical of the medieval period.[9] Therefore, the issue here was not one of privatisation, as suggested by Carpenter,[10] or perhaps even 'domination', as proposed by Duffy,[11] but control, or even management. This was a management, however, that was mutually beneficial, and promoted what has been termed a 'self-interested altruism'.[12] Consequently, it is argued, chantry foundation, particularly multiple chantry foundation, fostered a 'communal self-regard producing a parish which in its own estimation mattered'.[13]

At face-value, therefore, many documentary sources emphasise the exclusive role or influence of individuals on chapel and chantry foundation. And, except for the few exceptions noted above, this may be why traditional studies of chantries and chapels have under-emphasised their wider social role. Certainly cursory examination of surviving chapels, replete with elitist memorials, may also support this. Much of the traditional discussion on chantries and chapels is therefore pitched in unhelpful terms, suggesting in particular that such monuments were wholly 'private'. However, when they are examined in more detail, and using primarily archaeological approaches, very different conclusions can be reached. The examination of the chapel form and fabric, together with spatial analysis of topography and viewsheds, indicates that such foundations clearly had a wider social dimension.

Since the early 1990s the archaeological study of the late medieval church has begun to apply a broader range of approaches to the study of late medieval religion and belief. Influenced largely by the application of social theory in principally prehistoric contexts, archaeologists have begun to focus on what the construction, organisation and embellishment of churches can tell us about social structure and the nature of religious experience enacted within their spaces. Coupled with this, recent works of some historians and art historians, such as Duffy[14] and more recently Barnwell, Cross and Rycroft,[15] have shown that the pre-Reformation parish church was an arena in which a religious drama was consciously unfolding, and that it was a drama which all drew from and all contributed to. Furthermore, such contributions, it has been shown, were often reflected within a myriad of pious gifts, religious objects and associated devotional practices which served both to inspire and unite religious practice at parish church level.[16] However, despite the insights that documentary and architectural study can provide with regard to the popularity of religion prior to the Reformation, archaeological examination of parish church fabric can illustrate aspects of religious practice which may not be evident from the restrictive scope of many historical sources. This book, based primarily on recent research in the south and west of England,[17] has shown the value of an archaeological

9   Kümin 1996: 160.
10   Carpenter 1987.
11   Duffy 1992: 122.
12   Burgess 1991b: 69.
13   Burgess 1996: 252.
14   Duffy 1992.
15   Barnwell, Cross and Rycroft 2005.
16   Goodall 2001; Marks 2004.
17   Roffey 2004b.

approach and how structural analysis of surviving chapel fabric can be used to reconstruct the spatial and visual arrangements of the pre-Reformation parish church and give an insight into a little studied medieval institution. Moreover, this work strongly suggests that chantry chapels, despite being founded by individuals, were actually influenced and guided by the participation, not exclusion, of all members of the parish community. It has also provided an insight into the early origins of intercessory practice prior to the first documented chantries of the thirteenth century and their possible physical manifestations in an emerging 'parish' church. Overall, these investigations have provided an insight into how aspects of medieval piety actually 'worked' in practice and the corporate nature of religious experience at parish level.

An archaeological perspective

Archaeological examination of chapel structure and topography provided by this book provides an insight into the form and fabric of religious practices which, in many cases, remains largely 'invisible' from the historical sources. Indeed such practices, it has also been argued here, had their seeds several centuries before the first documented chantry foundations appear and may have developed hand in hand with the early formation of what would become the parish church. The planned organisation of many late medieval chantry chapels provided a defined and often unique space that facilitated the rites of intercession. But more than this, this research indicates that the construction and spatial arrangement of chantries and chapels only really worked on a corporate basis – the parish church was being transformed into something more organic and holistic. The placing of monuments juxtaposed with altars or within public lines of sight or access routes and the placing of secular or religious symbolism and devotional images all emphasised the communal nature of chapel foundation. It informs us how individual strategies for intercession were devised and acted out within the physical environment and, significantly, were dependent on the participation of all members of the parish community. Furthermore, the archaeological reconstruction of chapel ritual topography sheds light on the religious experience of the participants and particularly how eucharistic and intercessory rituals were enacted within a sacred topography of church space and fabric.

Moreover, this work has also revealed how the location of the chapel itself was of prime importance. It has been shown that many chapels, or the location of their altars, may have been designed to place special importance on, and show deference to, the high altar. Some examples exhibit a clear tendency for close proximity to high altars. In many examples in the research area, particularly in Somerset, there is marked trend for a location in the north part of the parish church. Such trends may be suggestive of eschatological considerations behind chapel orientation. These concerns for chapel orientation may be supported by evidence for the presence of an Easter sepulchre situated in the north of the church; a monument specifically dedicated to eucharistic practice prompted by the death and resurrection of Christ. Foundation of chapels on the north side of churches may indicate the importance given to the north in rituals associated with intercession and commemoration, or indeed could be an attempt to provide a setting for an Easter sepulchre, thus forging a direct link between this most important of celebrations and intercession for one's soul. In this case, it would also provide a link between individual intercession and public piety in that it provides space and a context for Easter celebration (as well as perhaps providing a priest and relevant paraphernalia for this busiest of times in the ecclesiastical calendar).

Thus, these various strategies for intercession facilitated a bond between the individual and the church community. As has been seen, one of the most important media for the relationship between chapels, chantries and the community and parish church, was vision. The visual senses were integral to interaction between the complex symbols of the chapels and chantries, their tombs and decorations. More importantly, vision enabled communion with that most important aspect of the mass: the elevation of the host. Viewshed analysis of church topography reveals how visual accessibility both to and from chapels to other ritual areas of the church was of prime importance. In particular, it seems to have been a prerequisite in the majority of cases to make chapels visible from public areas of the church. Furthermore, there appears to be archaeological evidence to suggest an effort was made to 'tie' the intercessory rituals enacted in such chapels into the general 'network' of rituals within the parish church itself, such as those celebrated within other chapels and especially the high altar. This research therefore strongly suggests that there was a visual relationship between subsidiary altars in many instances, while others can be inferred and conjectured. Consequently, the evidence presented suggests the extent to which chantries and chapels were very much part of the parish community and religious practice.

Chapel foundation could also have a more practical role and benefit for the parish community. The foundation of certain chapels provided for the construction of a porch, thereby providing an extra-liturgical area for important public rites such as marriage and funerals. In certain instances, chapel construction also led to the embellishment or rebuilding of the parish church, and the addition of vestries serving the parish church may have been an integral component of chapel foundation. At Devizes, for instance, the provision for an anchorite cell appears to have been integral with the construction of the Lamb chapel.

Reconstruction of the relationships between these features and their role in chapel ritual topography indicates the active role of the community in chantry-centred practice. What can be seen in these instances is that the role of the general laity is implicit and that there is evidence that this role was not one of mere passive observation or sub-conscious assimilation and reaction to the complex rituals and symbolism. It was a role that involved active participation. Thus, individual founders were really thinking about planning in a wider, holistic perspective. Though chantries and chapels were founded and managed by individuals, or by specific collectives, they were very much public monuments and an important feature in communal piety. The spatial capacity of many chapels, evidence for seating arrangements, and the provision of squints to provide visual accessibility, suggests that in many cases chantries and chapels were public monuments. Analysis of topographical arrangements proves this. Accessibility was often from public areas of the church, such as the nave or aisles, and even when they were screened, provision was still made for visual accessibility, at the very least. Chapels and chantries founded with the body of the church brought the setting of eucharistic practice out of the confines of the chancel and into the public domain. The foundation of chantries and chapels actively promoted inclusivity and communal participation and greatly embellished, enhanced and encouraged parish church religious practice.

Chantries and chapels and the parish church: a wider perspective

One of the essential conclusions of this research is that it reveals that there were substantial changes to the parish churches of the later medieval period as a direct consequence of chantry and chapel foundation. During the fourteenth and fifteenth centuries these changes point in one direction. At a period of demographic change, parish churches were still expanding. It has been shown that there was a concerted attempt to provide more church space specifically for the increase in divine services. As a result, we see that there arises a complex network of interactions and visual relationships within parish church topography. Such arrangements, this research shows, were facilitated by the use of squints, the location of tombs and altars, and devotional architecture. These relationships were wholly beneficial to the community in that the sacred areas of the church were linked into a common and universal structure, which further bonded the community in its religious practices. However, the implication of these conclusions is significant. It raises the question as to whether such developments occurred by accident, as a result of 'fashion', or were a direct consequence of a co-ordinated, or more likely emulated, policy. The answer may lie in examining such phenomena in the light of wider, national developments, particularly those occurring in cathedrals and secular colleges. Burgess has recently suggested that liturgical developments taking place in such institutions became 'increasingly identified with national interest and benefit'.[18] Such a concept, it is further claimed, may be seen in the context of prolonged war with France and the newly found status of the English nation, ever-more investing and engaging in corporate liturgy and 'outstripping the French by leading the nation into the paths of righteousness'.[19] Such motives, whether influenced by nationalism or by a desire for religious innovation, may have filtered down to parish level under the influence of the gentry and mercantile classes. Significantly, as this research shows, such influences were not just confined to the wealthy urban churches, but are found in rural examples also. It seems, therefore, that what we are seeing may be a co-ordinated

[18]   Burgess 2005.
[19]   Ibid.: 8.

policy. This was a policy that was taking its lead from secular colleges and cathedrals. Here we see the ruling classes using their parish churches in a way for national good. The heart of the policy was the increase in divine service and an associated corporate response; its context was the foundation, layout and ordering of the parish church chantry and chapel. The complex visual relationships between the growing number of altars constructed within the spaces of the later medieval parish churches may have been directly influenced by developments in monasteries and cathedrals, particularly with regard to the timetabling of masses and orders of precedence between altars. Importantly, however, such arrangements within the parish churches were inclusive: the visual relationships were structured so as to involve all members of the parish in shared religious experience.

Conclusion

This book has presented an archaeology of medieval chantry chapels. It has illustrated how the application of archaeological techniques, coupled with relevant documentary sources, can shed light on an important medieval institution. It has also shown how a detailed survey of a sample of individual chapels can provide an extensive database from which to examine aspects of chapel form and fabric and fixtures and fittings. The value of such a database is that it can then provide a detailed framework for wider comparative discussion as seen in this research. Furthermore, this study has indicated potential directions for future research in many related and more specific areas, for example the reconstruction of visual relationships in the parish church as a whole. Other related studies could include the study of church burial customs over time, specifically with regard to the use of wall burials, recesses, ledgers and effigies. Some of the patterns, such as strategies for intercession and orders of precedence, discussed here in the context of individual studies, could be related to general practices within the whole of the parish church itself. The implications of a co-ordinated policy for the increase in divine service operating at parish level also warrant further investigation. In particular, the contribution of the mercantile and gentry classes to a popular and 'national' religion requires wider examination. In relation to this, documentary evidence for how this policy was actually enshrined in church directives could be further investigated. Other avenues of research might include a comparison of chantry chapels founded in traditional areas, such as Lancashire and the West Country, and in Lollard-influenced areas such as Kent and the Chilterns, for example. An examination of the social and religious context of chantries founded in monasteries and those in parish churches would also provide a useful comparative study.[20]

The present research has demonstrated how elements of ritual topography can be reconstructed by the application of archaeological techniques to a

[20] Roffey (in preparation).

particular form of standing building. This particular emphasis has revealed the relationships between space, vision and religious practice within chantry chapels and the rest of the church. It has also shown how mechanisms and strategies for intercession were constructed, and has allowed for the wider investigation of the social dimension of chantry foundation, thus providing an insight into the level of public participation within associated religious practice. Despite the destructive effects of the Reformation and ensuing centuries, much survives from the late medieval period to enable the reconstruction of the social context of chantry and chapel foundation as reflected in their form, function and fabric. Consequently, this research has been seen to contribute to recent, largely document-based, research into the wider social dimension and communal involvement of chapels and chantries in medieval society. In particular, this work supports, substantiates and develops the work of related historical research and provides an archaeological perspective to a key feature of medieval piety. It demonstrates, archaeologically, how the relationships between individual and communal piety were negotiated, and, in certain cases, constantly renegotiated in the parish church. This relationship, it is argued, was one of mutual benefit to all parties, and represented the inter-relatedness of individual concerns for intercession, and an accessible context for communal piety. Ultimately, it achieves this in ways that would be difficult, if not impossible, if one were to rely solely on written evidence.

Glossary

Aisle	Lateral chambers often flanking the north or south side of the nave or chancel and separated by an arcade of columns or piers usually divided into bays.
Altar	A table or slab consecrated for celebration of *mass*. In addition to the *high altar*, other subsidiary altars dedicated to particular saints were located in chapels around the church.
Ashlar	Dressed masonry blocks.
Aumbry	A small wall recess used as a cupboard.
Buttress	A masonry support projecting from, or built against, a wall to give additional strength.
Capital	The head of a column.
Chancel	The east end of the church and the setting for the high altar. Usually reserved for the clergy.
Crypt	A burial chamber or vault beneath the main floor.
Easter Sepulchre	An architectural feature used to display a symbol of Christ during Easter.
Eucharist	One of the seven sacraments and the principal ritual of the church in which bread and wine would be transformed into the body and blood of Christ. The Eucharist could only be celebrated by a priest.
High Altar	The church's main altar, located in the *chancel*.
The Host	A wafer of bread which is believed to be miraculously transformed into the flesh of Christ through the process of transubstantiation during the ritual of the *Eucharist*.
In-situ	'In its original position'.
Lady Chapel	A chapel dedicated to the Virgin Mary.
Mass	Eucharistic celebration. The central rite of the medieval Christian church and performed at an *altar*.
Nave	The western part of the church and often the area reserved for the laity.
Niche	A small recess for an image, often decorated.
Parclose screen	A wooden or stone screen enclosing a chapel.
Perpendicular	The final phase of Gothic architecture in England and prevalent throughout the fifteenth and early sixteenth centuries. It is characterised largely by vertical tracery and flattened arches.
Pier	An upright support between openings such as arcades. The pier is generally more substantial than a column.

Piscina	A water drain often placed in a wall near an *altar*.
Prie-Dieu	A prayer desk.
Purgatory	A place or state where those who have died in the grace of God must spend time expiating their venial sins before being assured Salvation.
Reformation	A series of religious changes and reforms occurring largely between the sixteenth and seventeenth centuries.
Reredos	A carved or painted wall or panel behind an *altar*.
Rood	A cross often depicting Christ crucified and normally placed above the *chancel* arch in the parish church. Roods often had figures of the Virgin Mary on one side and St John on the other.
Rood Loft	The gallery upon which the *rood* is supported.
Rood Screen	A screen built beneath the *rood loft*.
Sedilia	Seating, often in the *chancel* of a church, reserved for the clergy at *mass*.
Squint	A hole through a pier or wall providing a view to an *altar*.
Stratigraphy	In the case of buildings: the structural sequence between elements of construction.
Transept	Transverse portion of a cruciform church.
Vestry	A room for the storage of sacred vessels, liturgical books and priestly vestments.
View-shed	Line of sight between specific areas.

Selected National Gazetteer of Chantry Chapels

The majority of former parish chantry chapels are now lost to us. During the periods of reformation many where dismantled or destroyed, or converted to other uses. More recently, many surviving chapels have been neglected, or converted to drab functional spaces, shorn of any former decoration or furnishing. However, some still remain in part to offer a unique insight into the former nature of these foundations. These structures, although much altered with time, are still a noticeable feature of many parish churches. This gazetteer presents examples of some of these former chantry chapels. It is by no means a comprehensive survey, but nonetheless offers a selection of some of the best surviving, and most impressive, examples in the country.

Bedfordshire

Barnard chapel, St Mary's, Luton. This chapel is arguably one of the smallest in the country and therefore warrants inclusion for its uniqueness. It comprises a small sunken recess in the south wall of the chancel, the floor being about 35 cm below the chancel floor. The chapel was founded by Richard Bedford, vicar of Luton in 1477–92. The small structure has a lierne vault and a separate entrance with lobby. The fourteenth-century Wenlock Chapel, off the north transept, has a double-arched screen of 1461. Beneath the screen are the tombs of William Wenlock (d.1392) and Lady Alice Rotherham.

Berkshire

St Michael's, Bray. The parish church contained two chantry chapels. The Foxley Chapel (or Chapel of All Saints) was in the south aisle. Here can be found the impressive brass of Sir John Foxley (1378) and his two wives. The chapel once had its own door, removed in 1840. In the north aisle is the Norreys Chapel (or Chapel of St Nicholas). The chantry chapel of Our Lady that stands in the churchyard was probably built around the same time as the church. The carving of a dog/horse (?) encased in its walls may be from an earlier Norman building.

Buckinghamshire

Buckingham Chantry Chapel, Market Hill, Buckingham. This building was originally a twelfth-century hospital. In 1268, the Archdeacon of Buckingham, Matthew de Stratton, founded a chantry here. The building was partially rebuilt in 1471 and 1481 by archdeacon Ruding. The chantry priests are believed to have been the first schoolmasters of what became known as The Royal Latin School. After the Reformation the chantry chapel was converted to a school with a schoolmaster's house added to the north. Today it is under the protection of the National Trust.

Cheshire

The Savage chapel, St Michael's, Cheshire. This is a large chapel flanking the south aisle built by Thomas Savage, archbishop of York (1501–1507). The chapel consists of two bays and has a highly decorated three-storey porch to the west with canopied niches and an oriel window. The three-storey porch is adorned with the shields of Rochester, London and York; the places where Thomas Savage was bishop before becoming the archbishop of York. On the south wall of the chapel are two large decorated recesses, the easternmost one opening into a small lit chamber containing alabaster effigy tombs of John and Elizabeth Savage c.1528. Other tombs in the chapel include the alabaster tomb of Sir John Savage c.1492.

Cumbria

Holy Trinity, Kendal. This church once contained several chantries including the Parr chapel at the east end of the chancel south aisle. The chapel dates to the fourteenth century and was probably founded by the Parr family, who inhabited Kendal Castle in the early part of that century. Later, Katherine Parr became one of the wives of Henry VIII. The family coat of arms can be seen carved in the ceiling. To the west of the Parr chapel was St Mary's chantry founded in 1321. Two other chapels were located in the chancel aisles: the Strickland Chapel to the south, and the Beckett or Chambre chapel to the north. Perhaps the most impressive chapel is the Bellingham chapel in the north outer aisle of the chancel. This chapel dates to the late fifteenth or early sixteenth century and contains a clerestory with eastern rose window and restored lierne- vault ceiling.

Derbyshire

All Saints, Chesterfield. Famous for it fourteenth-century twisted spire, the church contains many former chapels due to the numerous guilds which once existed in the town. The two-bay chancel is flanked by a chapel dedicated to St Katherine to the north and by the Lady chapel to the south. The Lady chapel was once enclosed by a parclose, since removed to the south transept. To the south of this was the Calton chapel (fourteenth century) which, unusually, terminates in a three-sided apse. Two chapels in the north of the church dedicated to St Mary Magdalene and St Michael, and Jesus Christ and the Holy Cross were also founded, the latter possibly by the parishioners and the vicar in 1393. In the south wall of the Jesus Christ and Holy Cross chapel is a large squint with five openings. Other chapels included those dedicated to the Holy Cross and St Peter.

The Bateman Mausoleum, St Matthew's Church, Morley. The mausoleum was actually constructed in 1897 and designed as a medieval chantry chapel. It is therefore a unique anachronism. The structure is independent but was built into part of the medieval church wall. The chapel is suitably furnished with sculpture and stained glass. At its centre is the tomb of Hugh Alleyn Sacheverell Bateman, The cross on the tomb chest is set with small crystal inserts through which the coffin may be seen.

Devon

The Lane aisle, St Andrew's, Cullompton. This foundation comprises an outer south aisle which was built by John Lane, a local wool merchant, in 1525–6 (he died 1528). The porch is in place of the west bay of the inner south aisle and an inscription commemorating Lane runs at low-level along the west wall of the aisle so that it could be viewed by all those entering the church. The large windows are separated by buttresses carved with symbols including sheep shears, astrological symbols for tin, and monograms. Externally there are decorated battlements and below this runs a frieze depicting the life of Christ. Inside the piers have small buttresses decorated with saints on the east, west and north sides. The aisle is vaulted with pendants depicting symbols of the passion, shears and tin. On the floor is Lane's tombstone.

Kirkham chantry, St John the Baptist, Paignton. This is a south transept chapel divided by a screen with two wide-arched openings within which sit large tomb chests and a central opening. Two effigies sit upon each tomb-chest. All three openings are fan vaulted with pendants and crowning pinnacles with angels. There are carved images of various saints on the tombs and door surrounds.

Greenway Chapel, St Peter's, Tiverton. The south porch and chapel was built by John Greenway in 1517. Greenway was a merchant and ship-owner who became a member of the Drapers' Company of London in 1497. The chapel and porch are highly decorated with image niches and friezes of ships that possibly refer to Greenway's piously named vessels the *Trinity Greenway* and *Charity Greenway* which operated out of Dartmouth. The inner doorway of the porch has a depiction of the assumption of the virgin flanked by an image of the donor with the initials I.G. Here there is also a stone vault with depictions of eagles and fishes. Inside, the chantry chapel is separated from the south aisle by a low stone screen. The chapel is decorated with Greenway's monograms and merchant marks and has a shallow stone vault with decorated pendants and a preserved Greenway brass of c.1519. A second chantry chapel, in memory of the famous Courtenay family, the Earls of Devon, apparently once stood in the churchyard.

Essex

All Saints, East Horndon. Unusual brick built two-storey shallow south transept of the late fifteenth century possibly associated with the Tyrell family. The chapel has a small lobby/porch to the south with an image niche above the door. There is a large casement in the south wall of the chapel and a smaller, possibly rebuilt, window above. Inside there is a south gallery leading to a priest's room with a fireplace.

Gloucestershire

The Berkeley chapel, St Mary's, Berkeley. This is a chancel south chapel of the Berkeley family built around 1450 by James, 11th Lord Berkeley (d.1463). Inside the chapel are two monuments. One monument is situated below a high level chancel window under a canopy within the chancel wall. This contains the recumbent alabaster effigies of James 11th Lord Berkeley and his son, James, resting on an alabaster tomb chest. At the east end of the chapel is the second monument, of Henry, 17th Lord Berkeley (d. 1615) and his wife. The chapel has a lierne-vault with carved bosses depicting the annunciation and assumption of the Blessed Virgin, the Holy Trinity and Christ in glory. There are also symbols of the four evangelists and badges of the Berkeley family. Externally, the chapel's parapet has carved enrichments of strawberry leaves and figures of angels holding shields. At the same time of the construction of the chapel an upper floor was added to the porch. This may have been a priest's room. Early monuments to Lord Thomas of Berkeley (d.1362) and his wife Lady Katherine (d.1385) are situated in the north arcade of the south aisle. The burial chapel is the property of the Berkeley family and is not open to the public.

St John the Baptist, Cirencester. Dominating the market place of Cirencester is the medieval church of St John the Baptist, built when the town was one of the most important wool markets in England. Cirencester has a remarkable arrangement of chapels which cluster around the church. These include the north chancel chapel of St Catherine, the south chancel chapel of St John the Baptist, and the north Lady Chapel, extended in the mid-fifteenth century. There is also the large four-bay chapel of the Holy Trinity on the north side of the nave and the smaller oak-screen parclosed Garstang chapel of c.1440 in the south-east corner of the nave. Of particular interest is the wall painting of St Christopher in St Catherine's chapel and also the fan vault here of c.1500. The chapel of the Holy Trinity has an original timber roof and squints.

Hampshire

De La Bere chapel, Holy Cross, Binsted. In 1332 Richard de la Bere obtained a licence for the foundation of a chantry. This licence was granted for alienation in mortmain of certain lands in Kingsley and Binsted for a chaplain to celebrate daily in the newly built chapel at Binsted. The chapel, comprising the north transept, is constructed of redstone and Binsted stone, though very roughly-coursed and patchy. The external fabric of the east wall indicates several phases of rebuilding from the twelfth century until the fourteenth, including the possible extension of the chapel to the north. Internally, the two-bay arcade through to the chancel is of mid-thirteenth-century style. Two piscinas in the east wall (N and S) suggest the former presence of two altars here. There is also an image corbel by the site of the southernmost piscina, and a raised area at the north end of the chapel is possibly associated with a crypt underneath. There is a monument to Richard de la Bere in the northwest side of the chapel.

Leigh Chantry, All Saints, Godshill. A chantry was founded in the south transept by John Leigh and dedicated to St Stephen in 1520. The chantry certificate of 1547 states that the chantry priest also taught grammar to the local children. The chapel itself is of rough rubble construction with diagonal buttresses. Above the south window is a large bellcote/niche alcove on the apex of the roof gable. The church is unusual in that it has a double chancel. On the north side of the southernmost chancel is the tomb of Sir John Leigh c.1529. His chantry, however, was in the south transept. On the east wall of the south transept there is a painting of 'Christ on the Lily Cross' and traces of *IHS* motifs on the walls.

Paulet chapels, St Mary's, Old Basing. To the north is a fifteenth-century chancel chapel constructed primarily of roughly-coursed flint with some later brick rebuilding. The chapel is large and spacious and is dominated by the two composite canopy tomb altars of John Paulet (c.1488), and his son (c.1519). A central doorway leads through to the chancel. There are several large corbels just below the present ceiling decorated with symbols and heraldic shields, and a rood stair in north-west corner of the chapel. There is an inscription above the archway to the north aisle with the name of John Paulet (c.1519) and the date of construction. Interestingly the will of John Paulet senior, dated 1470, bequeaths 40s to the Holy Trinity chapel in the church. This suggests that this structure may have earlier origins. If this is the case, then his son may have rebuilt part of it and that the evidence for the partial rebuilding in brick and the insertion of the east window may reflect this.

The south chapel is of the mid-sixteenth century and is constructed wholly of brick. This chapel is similar to the north in design; it has a similar tomb arrangement on the north wall pierced by a central doorway containing a narrow squint. The chapel was constructed by William Paulet before 1543, though his will indicates that it may have been unfinished at his death in the early 1570s. However, evidence from the heraldic shields above his tomb suggests that it must have been finished before 1566 at least, as they do not show the arms of his second wife. Furthermore, architectural evidence indicates the presence of an altar with a squint to the chancel. This may therefore suggest a date before the Elizabethan proscription of altars. Consequently a tentative date for the chapel can be conjectured to be between 1543 and the late 1550s.

Leicestershire

St Luke's, Gaddesby. This impressive three-bay south aisle chapel stands out from the rest of the church by the superior quality of its stonework and the elaborately decorated exterior. The chapel is of the mid-fourteenth century and has a highly decorated western façade with a motif of a large window in the form of a spherical triangle which encloses three cusped spherical quadrangles. There is also a row of narrow blank gables accompanying three niches, a central doorway and decorated battlements. The carved stone cornice contains a variety of interesting and imaginative subjects, such as human and animal heads, chickens and hens and mermaids.

Middlesex

Frowyk chantry, St Giles, South Mimms. Between 1439 and 1447 Thomas Frowyk founded a chantry chapel for his own and his parents' souls. This may have been re-founded later in 1527 by Henry Frowyk. The chapel is on the north side of the chancel and is divided by a fifteenth-century wooden screen from the chancel and north aisle. Inside, there are some medieval glass fragments, dated to 1526, showing groups of kneeling figures and the canopied effigy tomb of Henry Frowyk the younger in the chapel. There are surviving wall paintings in the chapel depicting floral *IHS* motifs.

Northamptonshire

Spencer chapel, St Mary's, Great Brington. This consists of a large north chancel chapel built by Sir John Spencer, who died in 1522. The chapel, which is larger than the church chancel itself, is of three bays with an unusual polygonal-recessed bay window with fan vault, built into the north wall. The chapel also contains the original iron railings and some window glass. The exterior was restored in the nineteenth century. The chapel is lined by many Spencer tombs. The tomb of John Spencer and wife is in the south eastern arch through to the chancel. This elaborate monument is decorated with the figures of angels and was probably partly based on the contemporary tomb of Henry VII at Westminster.

Norfolk

Rose chapel, SS Peter and Paul, Salle. North chapel founded by Thomas Rose (d.1441). There was once a window in the transept with a dated inscription.

There are roof bosses on the beam intersections of the ceiling carved with 'T's and roses. Apparently there was once a monograph 'M' on the walls prior to their re-plastering. The wooden screen and piscina also survive. The chapel of Thomas Boleyn is in the south transept (c.1411).

North Yorkshire

St Mary's, Scarborough. The church contained four chapels which, unusually, were built side by side at right angles to the south aisle, extending from the transept to the porch. In 1380 the chapel of St James was constructed to the east of the church next to the south transept. It was licensed to pray for the soul of Robert Galon – a wealthy burgher of Scarborough who endowed it with the sum of six pounds per annum. The chapel of St Nicholas, to the west of this, was licensed and probably completed in 1390 as a chantry for Agnes Burn. A third chapel was dedicated to St Stephen and founded by William de Rillington and was licensed in 1381. The fourth and westernmost chapel was dedicated to Our Lord Jesus Christ, the Blessed Virgin Mary and All Saints. Its license dates from 1390, but its foundation did not take place until 1397. The foundation declared its establishment for the souls of Emily, Edwin and Reginald Mylner. The chapel is now used as a baptistery. The chantry chapels have pointed barrel vaults with closely spaced shallow ribs. There was also a chapel of St Mary Magdalene in the churchyard.

Nottinghamshire

Babington memorial, St Winifred's, Kingston-on-Soar. The Babington memorial is on the north side of the chancel. The memorial is either a sort of setting for a chantry and/or a now lost tomb. It consists of an ornate canopy probably constructed by Thomas Babington (c.1540–47). The canopy, possibly not in its original location, is constructed of columns with a network of hexagonal panels which contain figures and tracery. One row has a depiction of the dance of death and others have saints and figures. The capitals are decorated with carvings of babes and tuns (a play on words for 'Babington'). Inside the east wall of the monument is a relief of the Last Judgment.

Markham and Meyring chapels, St Mary Magdalene's, Newark. These two chapels are unique in that they are both cage chantries of the type normally found in greater churches. Here they both occupy an important position in the chancel of the church. The earlier Meyring chapel is to the north and the Markham chapel is to the south. The Meyring chapel was founded by Thomas Meyring in 1500. It is a largely enclosed stone-cage chapel with stepped eastern entrance. It is decorated with shields, image niches and panels inside and out. By comparison, the Markham chapel founded by Robert Markham, in or around 1505, is more open having no vault and large windows. Inside, there is a large north arch opening up to the chancel. The chapel is decorated with shields and panels, two of which contain depictions of the 'dance of death'.

Oxfordshire

St John the Baptist, Burford. This once wealthy parish church contained a series of chapels. The small parclosed chapel of St Peter, placed against the east respond of the north aisle, is made up largely of wooden screens dismantled at the Reformation. However, at its east end is a fourteenth-century stone canopy which formed part of a chantry chapel that adjoined the rood-screen. On either side of the south porch are the chapels of St Thomas (eastern) and St Mary and St Anne (western). This latter chapel must have originally stood in the churchyard and was originally founded by the local merchants' guild around 1200. By the late medieval period this chapel, now adjoined to the church, became the Lady Chapel. The thirteenth-century chapel of St Thomas was in the south transept. The floor of the chapel is raised and sits above a crypt. The large opening toward the east would have given a good view of the chancel and the later south chancel chapel. The south and north chapels are of the fifteenth century. The eastern exterior of the south chapel is highly decorated with niches and panels and inside. Under the east window (former location of the medieval altar) there is sixteenth-century inscription from Tyndale's Bible translation.

St Mary's, Chipping Norton. This church once had several chapels. These included the chapel of St Mary, founded before 1290 by Richard Wale, probably to the north of the chancel. The chapel of St James was possibly at the east end of the south aisle. All that survives of the former chantry are the partial remains of a carved reredos and an adjoining piscina. The chapel of St John Baptist may have been in the outer north aisle. The Trinity guild chapel was founded about 1450 at the altar of St Katherine, by the vicar and four wool merchants, who installed two chaplains. This chapel may have been located in front of the north pillar of the chancel arch, where the carved reredos exists. This reredos has three canopied niches. The chapel probably extended westwards as far as the next pier and there would have been timber screens around three sides, perhaps with a decorated canopy above, in a similar arrangement to that at Burford (see above).

North aisle, St Bartholomew's, Ducklington. The north aisle was possibly the chapel of the Dyve family, lords of the manor in the thirteenth and fourteenth centuries, or alternatively the de Dockelhunton chapel, a wealthy Oxfordshire family. The aisle dates to around c.1340 and contains elaborate flowing tracery on the windows with a continuous string course of ballflowers and motifs of the coronation of the virgin in the tracery of the east window (this would have linked with the stained glass). There are also some disfigured sculptures of the visitation, annunciation and nativity plus one unknown. The aisle contains two ogee-recesses decorated with vines and grapes; these emerge from a crouched figure in the point where the canopies meet, and probably represented Jesse and his descendants. There are three niches on the east wall. On the two round pillars that separate the north aisle from the nave are two exquisitely carved heads of King Edward III and his Queen Phillipa.

Chapel of St John the Baptist, St Mary's, Ewelme. The chapel of St John the Baptist on the south side of the chancel is a beautiful example of rich perpendicular work. Much of the original decorative scheme survives here. The roof is panelled and embossed with angels bearing shields ornamented with the *IHS* emblem, and the walls are decorated with the *IHS* monogram in alternate groups of black and red and with texts in Gothic lettering bordering the ceiling. The altar is flanked by two canopied niches. The impressive alabaster canopied tomb of Alice, duchess of Suffolk (d.1475), founder of the chapel, is on the north side of the chapel. The altar is flanked by canopied niches. A school and almshouses were also founded in 1437 by the earl and countess of Suffolk for thirteen poor men under the care of two chaplains. The impressive domestic dwellings within their collegiate quad-plan still survive.

Wilcote chantry, St Mary's, Northleigh. This chantry was founded around the middle of the fifteenth century and is located to the north of the chancel being an extension of the nave north aisle. The chapel has an impressive fan vault (unique to the churches of the county) and alabaster tomb effigies of Lady Elizabeth Wilcote and husband, William. The arcade through to the chancel consists of an elaborate ogee arch decorated with carved angels with shields.

Shropshire

Vernon chapel, St Bartholomew's, Tong. St Bartholomew's was originally a chantry college founded by Sir Fulke de Pembruge. The Vernon chapel was founded by Sir Henry Vernon to the south of the chancel and was probably completed around 1519. Like the Spencer chapel at Great Brington, elements of its decoration were influenced by the Henry VII chapel at Westminster Abbey. Internally, the chapel is highly decorated and the fan vault with pendants is particularly impressive. The chapel also contains various monuments including the large tomb of Henry Vernon and wife replete with effigies and table tomb decorated with mourners.

Somerset

North chapel, St Andrew's, Brympton d'Evercy. An impressive north chapel constructed of small blocks of honey-coloured local Ham Hill stone. To the north of the church are the Elizabethan manor house, and the former priest's house (this may, in fact, have been the earlier manor house as it is a very substantial building). Inside the chapel there are a range of recess tombs and ledger slabs and a central north-south wall pierced by both a large 'window' and doorway leading to an eastern adjunct. In the western part of the chapel is a squint, positioned toward the centre of the chapel. The arrangement of east and west rooms may further suggest that the chapel consisted of two components; a private chapel at the western end, and a chantry chapel at the east, similar, perhaps, to the Clopton chapel at Long Melford, Suffolk.

De Wyke and Newton Chapels, St Mary's, Yatton. This is a north transept with adjoining north chancel chapel. Documentary evidence states that there was a chantry founded here by Isobel de Cheddar for her husband, Sir John Newton, around 1488. Their canopied tomb is situated on the north wall of the north chancel chapel. The east, or 'Newton', chapel was possibly dedicated to St Katherine as churchwardens' accounts for 1502 refer to money paid for an altar stone of St Katherine and for table stones (parapet) and money for a 'carved corbel upon which sits St Katherine'. This latter could be the elaborate canopied niche, with piscina underneath, situated on the east wall of the chapel. The transept chapel may have been dedicated to St James as there is a rood stair in the west wall of the transept that may be associated with a payment in 1505 for the timber to make the 'quere at St James chapel'. This chapel was probably enlarged to form the north chancel chapel of St Katherine in 1451 by the churchwarden Lady Isabel Newton in 1451–2. Churchwardens' accounts also mention the painting of the chapel roof and payment for a carved corbel in 1501. In 1516 and 1542 there are references to the payment of the chapel priest. The alabaster effigy tomb of Richard Newton (d.1449) and Emmota de Sherborne (d.1475) lies at the east end of the north transept. A small squint in the south east pier of the transept would have provided a view to the high altar, possibly for a small group of lay people. A passage squint is situated at the south-east corner of the chancel chapel and would have provided a view, and access, to the high altar for the chapel priest.

Suffolk

Spring and Spourne chapels, Ss Peter and Paul, Lavenham. The former chapel of Thomas Spring, a wealthy Suffolk merchant, is situated on the north side of the church. The chapel (c.1525) is enclosed by a unique wooden canopied parclose which also has small elevation squints inserted into it. The chapel also has an impressive fan vault. The Spring chapel was probably one of several chantries in the church, including the Branch chapel on the north side of the church with a date of c.1500, and possibly the Spourne chantry, another parclosed chapel, in the south aisle. The will of Thomas Spring also provided money for the upper stage of the elaborately decorated west tower.

Clopton chantry and chapel, Holy Trinity, Long Melford. The Clopton chapel (c.1490s) is a large chamber east of the north aisle with an external entrance in the north wall. In the chapel there are a series of brass memorials. The chantry proper of c.1490 is to the east of the chapel and approached by a tiny vestibule or priest's room with paneled ceiling. The chantry contains a sedilia, piscina and squint. Within the arcade that opens to the chancel is the tomb/Easter sepulchre of John Clopton and wife (1490), and above this are image niches. The chantry has a remarkable painted wooden ceiling below which are inscribed panels with verses written by John Lydgate (c.1450). One such verse reads: 'O Jesus Mercy, with support of Thy grace … Remember our complaint. During our life with many great trespass, by many wrong path where we have miswent.' There is also a fragment of original glass depicting 'Christ on the Lily Cross' in the east window of the chantry. The chapels and chantry are one component of a liturgically elaborate east end, with south chapels, choir vestry, priest's passage and, unusually for a parish church, a Lady chapel at the east end.

Warwickshire

Holy Trinity, Coventry. This large urban church had several chantry chapels. The Marler Chapel (or Mercers' Chapel), north of the chancel was founded in 1526–7 and was built by Richard Marler, a Coventry merchant. The ceiling is finely carved, the west bay in particular, which has a vine scroll pattern and Marler's merchant's mark. There is also an elaborate piscina in the chapel. In the south transept was the 'Jesus chapel' dating from around 1478. There was originally a public passageway under the transept. A priests' house was also built next to the south wall and referred to as 'Jesus Hall'. North of the nave, and east of the porch, was the chapel of St Thomas the Martyr, originally founded in 1296. Other chapels included the Tanners' chapel at the west end of the south aisle, the Butchers' chapel in the chancel south aisle and the Lady and Trinity chapels toward the north and south of the sanctuary respectively.

Chantry of Holywell, St Alphege's, Solihull. In 1277 William de Odingsells founded the chantry of Haliwell (or Holy Well). In 1438 an endowment by Thomas Greswold was added. The chapel is on the north-east side of the chancel. Unusually, there is a chantry chapel above and an undercroft below with a stone rib-vault which springs from finely carved corbels similar to those in the chancel. The chapel's two-storey arrangement is unique. Little has changed since 1277 when this was possibly the chantry priest's chamber with his chapel above. Shutter hinges still exist in the jambs of the windows and in the west wall is a fireplace. The most remarkable survival is the original altar. In the north side of the altar is an aumbry. The windows portray St Alphege, St Francis and St Clare, both of Assisi, and St. Thomas à Becket.

Beauchamp chapel, St Mary's, Warwick. This foundation was begun in 1443 under the will of Richard Beauchamp, earl of Warwick. It was completed in 1464 and consecrated in 1475. It is of three-bays with a low eastern vestry. The chapel was originally detached from the chancel. Inside, the chapel is magnificently decorated with niches and panels and large traceried windows. The wooden ceiling is decorated with roof bosses with symbols of the assumption and other religious symbols. On the west wall there is a frieze of monsters and leaves and carved images within. Inside the chapel there are stalls. There is a small lobby north of the chapel with original benches. In the centre of the chapel is the impressive brass effigy tomb of Richard Beauchamp (d.1439) decorated with angels and mourners.

West Yorkshire

Bridge chapel of St Mary the Virgin, Wakefield. The chantry chapel of St Mary the Virgin is situated south of the city on the bridge over the River Calder and was built between 1342 and 1356, the date when the chapel was licensed. The west front of the chapel is divided into five panels containing depictions of the annunciation, the nativity, the resurrection, ascension and the coronation of the virgin. Beneath the depictions are five arches, three containing doorways and the other two with tracery. In the north east corner of the building is a winding staircase leading to the roof and bell tower. This staircase also descends to a small crypt.

Wiltshire

Tocotes and Beauchamp chapel, St Nicholas, Bromham. South chancel chantry chapel founded and constructed in the 1480s by Sir Richard Beauchamp and Sir Roger Tocotes and possibly dedicated to Blessed Virgin Mary. Beauchamp also founded chapels at Devizes and All Cannings in the same county. The chapel itself is highly decorated. Externally, the south and east wall parapets are decorated with floriate designs and coats of arms and the walls have slim decorated buttresses. Angels carrying shields depicting symbols of the passion adorn the apex of the windows, and the east wall carries a large canopied niche at the roof apex. Internally the chapel contains several tombs; that of Roger Tocotes (d.1492), a large alabaster effigy tomb, lies in the centre of the chapel. The canopy tomb of Elizabeth Tocotes (d.1491) is placed in the north-east arcade through to the chancel. There are also several sixteenth-century brasses on the floor. The chapel also has a wooden screen in the north and west arcades and a wood-panel ceiling with carved shields and several image corbels and niches adorn the walls. There is an interesting lobby-like structure situated on the west side of the chapel, and continuous stone seating along the south wall of the chapel.

Beauchamp chapel, St John's, Devizes. Like Bromham, this south chancel chapel was also founded by Richard Beauchamp in or around 1483, and is similar in design. This chapel probably contained at least one of three documented altars dedications to the Virgin Mary, St Catherine and St Leonard. The exterior of the chapel is highly decorated with slim embellished buttresses and parapet with angels on the window apexes. There is also a canopied niche on the eastern gable. Internally, the north arcade is decorated with trefoil cells and floriate designs with image niches in the north-east and south-east corners as well as on the south wall and central pier of the north arcade through to the chancel. There is also a clergy bench along the south wall and an aumbry in the north-east corner. The chapel has a wood-panel ceiling supported by angel corbels. There is a small squint in the central pier of the north arcade and evidence for a former screen here and to the east.

Bibliography

Addyman, P. and Morris, R. (eds) (1976) *The Archaeological Study of Churches*, CBA Research Report 13.

Aston, M. and Lewis, C. (eds) (1994) *The Medieval Landscape of Wessex*, Oxford: Oxbow Monograph 46.

Bainbridge, V.R. (1994) 'The Medieval Way of Death: Commemoration and the After-life in Pre-Reformation Cambridgeshire', in Wilks, 183–204.

Barnwell, P.S., Cross, C. and Rycroft, A. (eds) (2005) *Mass and the Parish in Late Medieval England: the Use of York*, Reading: Spire.

Barron, C. and Harper-Bill, C. (eds) (1985) *The Pre-Reformation Church in England 1400–1530*, London: Longmans.

Bassett, S. (ed.) (1992) *Death in Towns: Urban Responses to the Dying and the Dead 1000–1600*, Leicester: Leicester University Press.

Bassett, S., Dyer, C. and Holt, R (1992) 'Introduction', in Bassett, 1–7.

Beresford, M. and Hurst, J. (1990) *Wharram Percy*, London: English Heritage.

Binski, P. (1996) *Medieval Death: Ritual and Representation*, London: British Museum Press.

Bird, J. and Bird, D.G., (eds) (1987) *The Archaeology of Surrey to 1540*, Guildford: Surrey Archaeological Society, 223–61.

Biver, F. and Howard, F.G. (1909) 'Chantry Chapels in England', *Arch. Journ.*, 66, 1–32.

Blair, J. (ed.) (1988) *Minsters and Parish Churches: the Local Church in Transition 950–1200*, Oxford: Oxford University Committee for Archaeology 17.

Blair, J. (1991) *Early Medieval Surrey: Landholding, Church and Settlement before 1300*, Gloucester: Alan Sutton.

Blair, J. and Golding, B. (eds) (1996) *The Cloister and the World: Essays in Medieval History in Honour of Barbara Harvey*, Oxford: Clarendon Press.

Blair, J. and Sharpe, R. (1992) (eds) *Pastoral Care before the Parish*, Leicester: Leicester University Press.

Boddington, A., Cadman, G. and Cramp, R. (1996) *Raunds Furnells: The Anglo-Saxon Church and Churchyard*, English Heritage Research Report 7.

Boldrick, S. (1997) 'The Rise of Chantry Space in England from Ca. 1260–Ca. 1400', unpublished PhD thesis for University of Manchester.

Bond, C.J. (1988) 'Church and Parish in Norman Worcestershire', in Blair, J., 119–35.

Bond, F. (1913) *An Introduction to English Church Architecture from the Eleventh to the Sixteenth Centuries* (2 vols), London: Oxford University Press.

Bossy, J. (1983) 'The Mass as a Social Institution 1200–1700', *Past and Present* 100, 29–61.

Bossy, J. (1991) 'Christian Life in the Later Middle Ages: Prayers', *Transactions of the Royal Historical Society*, sixth series, 1, 137–48.

Bourdieu, P. (1977) *Outline of a Theory of Practice*, Cambridge: Cambridge University Press.

Brooke, C.N.L. (1971) *Medieval Church and Society*, London: Sidgwick and Jackson.

Brooke, C.N.L. and Brooke, R. (1984) *Popular Religion in the Middle Ages*, London: Thames and Hudson.

Burgess. C.R. (1985) 'For the Increase of Divine Service: Chantries in the Parish of Late Medieval Bristol', *Journal of Ecclesiastical History* 36, 46–65.

Burgess, C. R. (1987a) 'A Service for the Dead: the Form and Function of the Anniversary in Late Medieval Bristol', *Transactions of the Bristol and Gloucestershire Archaeological Society* 105, 183–211.

Burgess, C.R. (1987b) 'By Quick and by Dead: Wills and Provision in Late Medieval Bristol', *English Historical Review* CLL, 837–58.

Burgess, C.R. (1988) 'A Fond Thing Vainly Invented: An Essay on Purgatory and Pious Motive in Later Medieval England', in Wright, 56–85.

Burgess, C.R. (1991a) 'Strategies for Eternity: Perpetual Chantry Foundation in Late Medieval Bristol', in Harper- Bill, 1–33.

Burgess, C.R. (1991b) 'The Benefactions of Mortality: the Lay Response in the Urban Parish Church', in Smith, 65–87.

Burgess, C.R. (1995) *The Pre-Reformation Records of All Saints', Bristol, Part 1*, Bristol: Bristol Record Society Publication, vol. 46.

Burgess, C.R. (1996) 'St Mary-at-Hill, London', in Blair and Golding, 247–72.

Burgess, C.R. (2000a) '"Longing to be Prayed For": Death and Commemoration in an English Parish in the Later Middle Ages', in Gordon and Marshall, 44–65.

Burgess, C.R. (2000b) *The Pre-Reformation Records of All Saints', Bristol, Part 1*, Bristol: Bristol Record Society Publication, vol. 53.

Burgess, C.R. (2004) *The Pre-Reformation Records of All Saints', Bristol, Part 2*, Bristol: Bristol Record Society Publication, vol. 56.

Burgess, C.R. (2005) 'St George's College, Windsor: Context and Consequence', in Saul, 63–97.

Butcher, J.J. (1870) *The Parish of Ashburton in the 15th and 16th Centuries as it Appears from Extracts from the Churchwardens' Accs. A.D. 1479–1580*, London: Yates and Alexander.

Carpenter, C. (1987) 'The Religion of the Gentry in Fifteenth-Century England', in Williams, D., 53–74.

Chantry Certificates for the County of Hampshire, PRO E 301/51.

Chantry Certificates for the County of Somerset, PRO E 302/ 42.

Chantry Certificates for the County of Wiltshire, PRO E 301/56; E3 01/ 58.

Chatwin, P.B. (1965) 'Squints in Warwickshire Churches', *Transactions and Proceedings of the Birmingham Archaeological Society for the Year 1962*, 80, 10–6.

Cherry, B. (1984) 'An Early Sixteenth-Century London Tomb Design', in Newman, 34–45.

Cobb, P.G. (1978) 'The Architectural Setting of the Liturgy', in Jones, Wainwright and Yarnold, 37–51.

Coffin, R.S.P. (trans.) (1961) *Confessions*, London: Harmondsworth.

Cole, J.J. (1847) 'Notes on Low-Side Windows and Squints', *Arch. Journ.* 5, 70–2.

Colgrave, B. and Mynors, R.A.B. (1969) *Bede's Ecclesiastical History*, Oxford: Clarendon Press.

Colvin, H.M. (1991) *Architecture and Afterlife*, London: Yale University Press.

Colvin, H.M. (2000) 'The Origin of Chantries', *Journal of Medieval History* 26, 163–73.

Cook, G.H. (1947) *Medieval Chantries and Chantry Chapels*, London: Phoenix.

Cressy, D. (1997) *Birth, Marriage, and Death, Ritual; Religion and the Life-cycle in Tudor and Stuart England*, Oxford: Oxford University Press.

Cross, C. (1976) *Church and People 1450–1660*, London: Collins.

Crouch, D. (2001) 'The Origin of Chantries: Some Further Anglo-Norman Evidence', in *Journal of Medieval History* 27, 159–80.

Dilks, T.B. (1933) *Bridgwater Borough Archives 1200–1377*, Somerset Record Society 48.

Dilks, T.B. (1938) *Bridgwater Borough Archives 1377–1400*, Somerset Record Society 53.

Dilks, T.B. (1943) *Bridgwater Borough Archives 1400–1445*, Somerset Record Society 58.

Dilks, T.B. (1945) *Bridgwater Borough Archives 1445–1468*, Somerset Record Society 60.

Dilks, T.B. (1971) *The Story of Bridgwater Parish Church*, Gloucester: British Publishing Company.

Dix, G. (1945) *The Shape of the Liturgy*, London: A. and C. Black.

Dobson, R.B. (ed.) (1984) *The Church, Patronage and Politics in the Fifteenth Century*, Gloucester: Alan Sutton.

Dobson, R.B. (1996) *Church and Society in the Medieval North of England*, London: Hambledon Press.

Doree, S.G. (1994) *The Churchwardens' Accounts of Bishop Stortford 1431–1558*, Herefordshire Record Society Publications 10.

Du Boulay, F.R.H and Barron, C. (1971) *The Reign of Richard II*, University of London: Athlone Press.

Duffy, E. (1992) *The Stripping of the Altars. Traditional Religion in England c.1400–c.1580*, London: Yale University Press.

Duffy, E. (2001) *The Voices of Morebath: Reformation and Rebellion in an English Village*, New Haven and London: Yale University Press.

Duffy, E. (2003) 'Late Medieval Religion', in Marks and Williamson, 56–67.

Echard, S. (ed.) (2004) *A Gower Companion*, London: Boydell Press.

Edwards, J. (1985) 'A Medieval Wall Painting at St Mary and St Michael's Church, Stoke Charity', *HFCAS* 41, 139–48.

Edwards, K. (1967) *The English Secular Cathedrals in the Middle Ages*, Manchester: Manchester University Press.

Fasham, P.J., Keevill, G. and Coe, D. (1995) *Brighton Hill South (Hatch Warren): An Iron Age Farmstead and Deserted Medieval Village in Hampshire*, Salisbury: Wessex Archaeology Report 17.

Fawcett, R. (2002) *Scottish Medieval Churches: Architecture and Furnishings*, Stroud Tempus.

Ferguson, T.J. (1996) *Historic Zuni: Architecture and Society*, Tucson: University of Arizona Press.

Ferrey, B. (1851) 'St Cuthbert's Wells', *SAS* 2, 93–7.

Finch, J. (2000) *Church Monuments in Norfolk before 1850*, Oxford: BAR British Series 317.

Fisher, P., Farelly, C., Maddocks, A. and Ruggles, C. (1997) 'Spatial Analysis of Visible Areas from the Bronze Age Cairns of Mull', *Journal of Archaeological Science* 24:5, 81–92.

Foster, A. (1997) 'Churchwardens' Accounts of Early Modern England and Wales: Some Problems to Note, but Much to be Gained', in French, Gibbs and Kümin, 74–94.

French, K.L. (2001) *The People of the Parish: Community Life in a Late Medieval English Diocese*, Philadelphia: University of Pennsylvania.

French, K.L., Gibbs, G. G. and Kümin, B. (eds) (1997) *The Parish in English Life 1400–1600*, Manchester: Manchester University Press.

Fry, V. (1905) 'Dorset Chantries', *Dorset Natural History and Archaeological Society Proceedings*, vol. 27, 214.

Fry, V. (1906) 'Dorset Chantries', *Dorset Natural History and Archaeological Society Proceedings*, vol. 28, 12–13.

Fry, V. (1907) 'Dorset Chantries', *Dorset Natural History and Archaeological Society Proceedings*, vol. 29, 30.

Fry, V. (1908) 'Dorset Chantries', *Dorset Natural History and Archaeological Society Proceedings*, vol. 30, 13.

Fry, V. (1909) 'Dorset Chantries', *Dorset Natural History and Archaeological Society Proceedings*, vol. 31, 81 and 85.

Gaimster, D. and Gilchrist, R. (eds) (2003) *The Archaeology of Reformation*, Society for Post-Medieval Archaeology Monograph 1, London: Maney.

Geary, P.J. (1994) *Living with the Dead in the Middle Ages*, Ithaca and London: Cornell University Press.

Gee, E. (1984) 'The Topography of Altars, Chantries and Shrines in York Minster', *Antiq. Journ.* 64, 337–51.

Gilchrist, R. (1989) 'Community and Self: Perceptions and Use of Space in Medieval Monasteries', *Scottish Archaeological Review* 6, 55–64.

Gilchrist, R. (1994) *Gender and Material Culture. The Archaeology of Religious Women*, London: Routledge.

Gilchrist, R. (1995) *Contemplation and Action: the Other Monasticism*, Leicester: Leicester University Press.

Gilchrist, R. (2005) *Norwich Cathedral: The Evolution of the English Cathedral Landscape*, Woodbridge: Boydell Press.

Gilchrist, R. and Sloane, B. (2005) *Requiem: The Medieval Monastic Cemetery in Britain*, London: Museum of London Archaeology Service.

Giles, K. (2000) *An Archaeology of Social Identity: Guildhalls in York, c.1350–1630*, Oxford: BAR British Series 315.

Gittings, C. (1984) *Death, Burial and the Individual in Early Modern England*, London: Croom Helm.

Gittings, C. (1999) 'Sacred and Secular', in Jupp and Gittings, 147–74.

Gittos, H. (2001) 'Sacred Space in Anglo-Saxon England: Liturgy, Architecture and Place', unpublished PhD thesis for University of Oxford.

Godfrey, C.J. (1954) 'The Chantries of Mere and their Priests', WAM 55, 153–60.

Golding, P. (1986) 'Anglo-Norman Knightly Burials', in Harper-Bill and Harvey, 35–49.

Goodall, J.A.A. (2001) *God's House at Ewelme. Life, Devotion and Architecture in a Fifteenth Century Almshouse*, London: Ashgate Press.

Gordon, B. and Marshall, P. (eds) (2000) *The Place of the Dead: Death and Remembrance in Late Medieval and Early Modern Europe*, Cambridge: Cambridge University Press.

Gowring, J.G. (1866) 'Ilminster Church and Grammar school', SAS 13, 35–41.

Graves, C.P. (1989) 'Social Space in the English Medieval Parish Church', *Economy and Society* 18, 297–322.

Graves, C.P. (2000) *Form and Fabric of Belief: The Archaeology of Lay Experience in Medieval Norfolk and Devon*, Oxford: BAR British Series 311.

Green, A.R. (1926) ' The Low-Side Windows of Hampshire Churches', HFCAS 10, 127–48.

Green, E. (1888) *Survey and Rental of the Chantries, Colleges, and Parish Churches, Guilds Fraternities, Lamps, Lights and Obits in the County of Somerset AD 1548*, Somerset Record Society 2.

Grenville, J. (2001) 'Out of the Shunting Yards–One Academic's Approach to Recording Small Buildings', in Pearson and Meeson, 11–27.

Hadley, D.M. (2001) *Death in Medieval England*, Stroud: Tempus.

Hanham, H.J. (1967) 'The Suppression of the Chantries in Ashburton', *Transactions of the Devonshire Association* 99, 111–37.

Hardison, O.B. (1965) *Christian Rite and Christian Drama in the Middle Age*, Baltimore: John Hopkins Press.

Harper-Bill, C. (ed.) (1991) *Religious Belief and Ecclesiastical Careers in Late Medieval England*, Woodbridge: Boydell.

Harper-Bill, C. and Harvey, R. (eds) (1986) *The Ideals and Practice of Medieval Knighthood, Papers from the First and Second Strawberry Hill Conference*, Woodbridge: Boydell.

Hase, P.H. (1994) 'The Church in the Wessex Heartlands', in Aston and Lewis, 47–81.

Hicks, M.A. (1985) 'Chantries, Obits and Almshouses in the Hungerford Foundations 1325–1478', in Barron and Harper-Bill, 123–42.

Hill, R. (1971) 'A Chaunterie for Soules: London Chantries in the Reign of Richard II', in Du Boulay and Barron, 242–56.

Hillier, B. and Hanson, J. (1984) *The Social Logic of Space*, Cambridge: Cambridge University Press.

Hines, J., Cohen, N. and Roffey, S. (2004) 'Iohannes Gower, Armiger, Poeta: Records and Memorials of his Life and Death', in Echard, 1–41.

Hobhouse, E. (1890) *Churchwardens' Accounts of Croscombe, Pilton, Yatton, Tintinhull, Morebath and St Michael's Bath*, Somerset Record Society 3.

Horrox, R. (ed.) (1994) *Fifteenth Century Attitudes and Perceptions of Society in Late Medieval England*, Cambridge: Cambridge University Press.

Hutton, R. (1994) *The Rise and Fall of Merry England: The Ritual Year 1400–1700*, Oxford: Oxford University Press.

I.H.P. (1845) 'On Some Perforations in the Wall of Churches', *Arch. Journ.* 3, 299–308.

Jackson, J.E. (1885) 'Wiltshire Chantry Furniture', *WAM* 22, 318–29.

Jones, C., Wainwright, E. and Yarnold, E. (eds) (1978) *The Study of the Liturgy*, London: SPCK.

Jones, W.A. (1857) 'An Inventory of the Vestments and Belongings of "St Katherine's Ile" in the Church of Bridgwater', *SAS* 7, 100–5.

Jupp, P. and Gittings, C. (eds) (1999) *Death in England: An Illustrated History*, Manchester: Manchester University Press.

Kisby, F. (ed.) (2001) *Music and Musicians in Renaissance Cities and Towns*, Cambridge: Cambridge University Press.

Kreider, A. (1979) *English Chantries: The Road to Dissolution*, London: Harvard University Press.

Kümin, B. (1996) *The Shaping of a Community: The Rise and Reformation of the English Parish, c.1400–1560*, Aldershot: Scholar Press.

Kümin, B. (2001) 'Mass, Morris and Metrical Psalms: Music in the English Parish Church, 1400–1600', in Kisby, 70–82.

Lake, M.W., Woodman, P.E., and Mithins, S.J. (1998) 'Tailoring GIS Software for Archaeological Applications: an Example Concerning View-Shed Analysis', *Journal of Archaeological Science* 25, 27:38.

Le Goff, J. (1984) *The Birth of Purgatory*, trans. A. Goldhammer, London: Scholar Press.

Livett, G.M. (1909) 'Nettleshead Church', *Archaeologia Cantiana* 28, 251–77.

Loades, D. (1994) 'Rites of Passage and the Prayer Books of 1549 and 1552', in Wilks, 205–16.

Lucy, S. and Reynolds, A. (2002) *Burial in Early Medieval England and Wales*, Society for Medieval Archaeology Monograph 17.

Maclean, J. (1884) 'Chantry Certificates for Gloucester', *Bristol and Gloucestershire Archaeological Society Transactions* 8, 229–308.

Marks, R. (2004) *Image and Devotion in Late Medieval England*, Stroud: Sutton.

Marks, R. and Williamson, P., (eds) (2003) *Gothic Art for England 1400–1547*, London: V&A Publications.

Markus, T. (1993) *Buildings and Power: Freedom and Control in the Origins of Modern Building Types*, London: Routledge.

Morris, R. (1989) *Churches in the Landscape*, London: Phoenix.

Morriss, R.K. (2000) *The Archaeology of Buildings*, Stroud: Tempus.

Newman, J. (ed.) (1984) *Design and Practice in British Architecture: Studies in Architectural History Presented to Howard Colvin*, Architectural History 27.

Orme, N. (1976) *Education in the West of England, 1066–1548*, Exeter: University of Exeter Press.

Orme, N. (1979) 'The Dissolution of the Chantries in Devon, 1546–8', *Devonshire Association Report and Transactions* 3, 75–93.

Orme, N. (1996) 'Church and Chapel in Medieval England', *Transactions of the Royal Historical Society* 6, 75–103.

Parsons, D. (2000) *Lost Chantries and Chapels of Medieval Northamptonshire*, Brixworth: Brixworth Lecture Series 3.

Peacock, E. (1902) *Instructions for Parish Priests, by John Myrc*, Early English Text Society Original Series 31.

Pearson, S. and Meeson, B. (2001) *Vernacular Buildings in a Changing World: Understanding, Recording and Conservation*, CBA Research Report 126.

Pevsner, N. (1958a) *Buildings of England Series: North Somerset and Bristol*, London: Penguin.

Pevsner, N. (1958b) *Buildings of England Series: South and West Somerset*, London: Penguin.

Pevsner, N. (1966) *Buildings of England Series: Berkshire*, London: Penguin.

Pevsner, N. and Cherry, B. (1975) *Buildings of England Series: Wiltshire*, London: Penguin.

Pevsner, N. and Lloyd, D. (1967) *Buildings of England Series: Hampshire and the Isle of Wight*, London: Penguin.

Platt, C. (1981) *The Parish Churches of Medieval England*, London: Secker and Warburg.

Pollard, J. and Reynolds, A. (2002) *Avebury: The Biography of a Landscape*, Stroud: Tempus.

Pounds, N. (2000) *History of the Parish*, Cambridge: Cambridge University Press.

Qualmann, K. (1992) *Excavations at St Mary and St Michael's Stoke Charity 1991*, Winchester: Winchester Museums Service.

Reynolds, A. (1993) 'A Survey of the Parish Church of St Swithin at Compton Bassett, Wiltshire', *WAM* 86, 102–12.

Richmond, C. (1984) 'Religion and the Fifteenth-Century English Gentleman', in Dobson, 195–205.

Richmond, C. (1991) 'The English Gentry and Religion c.1500', in Harper-Bill, 121–51.

Richmond, C. (1994) 'Religion', in Horrox, 183–202.

Rodwell, W. (1997) 'Landmarks in Church Archaeology: a Review of the Last Thirty Years', *Church Archaeology* 1, 1–16.

Rodwell, W. and Rodwell, K. (1985) *Rivenhall: Investigations of a Roman Villa, Church and Village 1950–1977*, CBA Research Report 55.

Roffey, S. (1998) 'The Early History and Development of St. Marie Overie Priory, Southwark: the 12th Century Chapel of St. John', *The London Archaeologist* 8:10, 255–62.

Roffey, S. (2003) 'Deconstructing a Symbolic World: The Reformation and the English Medieval Parish Chantry', in Gaimster and Gilchrist, 342–55.

Roffey, S. (2004a) Reconstructing English Medieval Parish Church Chantries and Chapels: an Archaeological Approach', *Church Archaeology* 5–6, 62–8.

Roffey, S. (2004b) 'A Social Archaeology of Parish Church Chantries and Chapels: a Perspective from the South and West of England', unpublished PhD thesis for University of Southampton.

Roffey, S. (2006) 'Constructing a Vision of Salvation: Chantries and the Social Dimension of Religious Experience in the Medieval Parish Church', *Arch. Journ.* 163, 122–46.

Roffey, S. (in preparation) *Medieval Strategies for the Afterlife*, Stroud: Tempus.

Rosenthal, J. (1972) *The Purchase of Paradise. Gift Giving and the Aristocracy*, London: Routledge and Kegan Paul.

Rosser, G. (1992) 'The Cure of Souls in English Towns before 1100', in Blair and Sharpe, 266–84.

Rubin, M. (1991) *Corpus Christi: The Eucharist in Late Medieval Culture*, Cambridge: Cambridge University Press.

Saul, N. (ed.) (1992) *The Age of Chivalry: Art and Society in Late Medieval England*, London: Collins.

Saul, N. (1992) '"Forget-me-nots": Patronage in Gothic England', in Saul, 36–48.

Saul, N. (2005) *St Georges Chapel, Windsor, in the Fourteenth Century*, Woodbridge: Boydell.

Scarisbrick, J. (1984) *The Reformation and the English People*, Oxford: Clarendon Press.

Schofield, J. (1994) 'Saxon and Medieval Parish Churches in the City of London', *Transactions of the London and Middlesex Archaeological Society* 45, 23–145.

Smith, D.M., (1991) *Studies in Clergy and Ministry in Medieval England*, Borthwick Studies in History 1, University of York: Borthwick Institute of Historical Research.

Snell, L. (1960) (ed.) *The Chantry Certificates for Devon and the City*, London: J. Townshend and Sons.

Southern, R.W. (1970) *Western Society and the Church*, London: Harmondsworth.

Southern, R.W. (1982) 'Between Heaven and Hell', in *Times Literary Supplement*, 18 June, 651–652.

Swayne, H.J.F. (1896) *The Churchwardens' Accounts of St Edmund and St Thomas, Sarum, 1443–1702*, Wiltshire Record Society.

Symons, T. (1953) *Regularis Concordia*, London: Nelson.

Tatton-Brown, T. (1980) 'The Roper Chantry in St Dunstan's Canterbury', *Antiq. Journ.* 60, 227–47.

Tatton-Brown T. (1997) 'The Church of St Thomas of Canterbury, Salisbury', *WAM.* 90, 101–9.

Taylor, H.M. (1976) 'The Foundations of Architectural History', in Addyman and Morris, 1–7.

Thomas, K. (1971) *Religion and the Decline of Magic*, London: Weidenfeld and Nicolson.

Thompson, A.H. (1947) *The English Clergy and their Organization in the Later Middle Ages*, Oxford: Clarendon Press.

Thompson, V. (2002) 'Constructing Salvation: A Homiletic and Penitential Context for Late Anglo-Saxon Burial Practice', in Lucy and Reynolds, 229–40.

Thomson, J.A.F. (1983) *The Transformation of Medieval England 1370–1529*, London: Longmans.

Turner, D.J. (1987) 'The Archaeology of Surrey, 1066–1540', in Bird and Bird, 223–61.

Vallance, A. (1936) *English Church Screens*, London: Batsford.

Victoria History for the County of Hampshire (1900–).

Victoria County History for the County of Somerset (1906–).

Victoria History for the County of Wiltshire (1953–).

Walcott, M.E.C. (1876) *Inventory of Church Goods and Chantries of Wiltshire*, London.

Warren, F.E. (1913) *The Sarum Missal in English* I and II, Alcuin Club Collection 11.

Watkins, C.S. (2002) 'Sin, Penance and Purgatory in the Anglo-Norman Realm: The Evidence of Visions and Ghost Stories', *Past and Present* 175, 3–33.

Weaver, F.W. (1901) *Somerset Medieval Wills, 1383–1500*, Somerset Record Society 16.

Weaver, F.W. (1903) *Somerset Medieval Wills, 1501–1530*, Somerset Record Society 19.

Weaver, F.W. (1905) *Somerset Medieval Wills, 1531–1558*, Somerset Record Society 21.

Westlake, H.F. (1919) *The Parish Gilds of Medieval England*, London and New York: SPCK.

Wilkinson, L. (1895) 'The Chantries of Westbury-on-Severn', *Transactions of the Bristol and Gloucester Archaeological Society* 19, 374–93.

Wilks, M. (ed.) (1994) *Prophecy and Eschatology, Studies in Church History Subsidia* 10.

Williams, D. (ed.) (1987) *England in the Fifteenth Century*, Woodbridge: Boydell.

Williams, E.E. (1950) *The Chantries of William Canynges in St Mary Redcliffe, Bristol, with a Survey of Chantries in General*, Oxford: Blackwell.

Williams, H. (ed.) (2003) *Archaeologies of Remembrance: Death and Memory in Past Societies*, London: Kluwer Academic/Plenum Publishing.

Williams, H. (2003) 'Remembering and Forgetting the Dead', in Williams, H., 227–55.

Wood-Legh, K.L. (1965) *Perpetual Chantries in Britain*, Cambridge: Cambridge University Press.

Williams, J.F. (1913) *The Early Churchwardens' Accounts of Hampshire*, London: Warren and Sons.

Woodward, G.H. (ed.) (1982) *Calendar of Somerset Chantry Grants 1548–1603*, Somerset Record Society 77.

Woodward, G.H. (1983) 'The Dispersal of Chantry Lands in Somerset 1548–1603, *Southern History* 5, 95–114.

Wordsworth, C. (1901) *Ceremonies and Processions of the Cathedral Church of Salisbury*, Cambridge: Cambridge University Press.

Wright, S.J. (1988) *Parish Church and People: Local Studies in Lay Religion 1350–1750*, London: Hutchinson.

Index

Note: **Bold** entries refer to churches mentioned in the text

Other volumes in
Studies in the History of Medieval Religion